The Nordic, Baltic and Visegrád Small Powers in Europe

This volume addresses and seeks to answer a number of questions on the current issues facing small states/powers in Europe. How can small European states survive and prosper within a multipolar world of great powers? What part should small states take in European integration? Are EU fiscal and monetary policies allowing for Keynesian economic stimulus when needed and are euro area convergence criteria viable as the world recovers from the COVID-19 crisis? Are small state alliances within the EU useful to counterbalance the influence of the larger EU member states? How far should EU and NATO expansion go? Should it include countries such as Ukraine? Can the EU rely on US leadership of NATO for its security? How should small states relate to great powers seeking to influence Europe, most notably the US, the People's Republic of China and the Russian Federation? Do smaller states need to choose a single ally among the major powers?

Using an interdisciplinary approach, the author discusses issues of economic policy, international relations and politics, economic and political integration, as well as the effects of global and regional institutions, and priorities in bilateral development cooperation, demonstrating how policies are shaped by the interaction between small states (small powers) and large states (great powers).

Hilmar Þór Hilmarsson is a Professor at the University of Akureyri, Faculty of Business Administration, Iceland. He served as a specialist and coordinator with the World Bank Group in Washington, DC, US, from 1990 to 1995, at the World Bank office in Rīga, Latvia, from 1999 to 2003, and at the World Bank office in Hanoi, Viet Nam, from 2003 to 2006. From 1995 to 1999 he served as a Special Adviser to the Icelandic Minister for Foreign Affairs. Dr Hilmarsson has published over 80 scholarly articles and book chapters, and three books.

Europa Regional Perspectives

Providing in-depth analysis with a global reach, this series from Europa examines a wide range of contemporary political, economic, developmental and social issues in regional perspective. Intended to complement the Europa Regional Surveys of the World series, Europa Regional Perspectives will be a valuable resource for academics, students, researchers, policymakers, business people and anyone with an interest in current world affairs with an emphasis on regional issues.

While the Europa World Year Book and its associated Regional Surveys inform on and analyse contemporary economic, political and social developments, the Editors considered the need for more in-depth volumes written and/or edited by specialists in their field, in order to delve into particular regional situations. Volumes in the series are not constrained by any particular template, but may explore recent political, economic, international relations, social, defence, or other issues in order to increase knowledge. Regions are thus not specifically defined, and volumes may focus on small or large group of countries, regions or blocs.

Catalonia, Scotland and the EU
Visions of Independence and Integration
Niklas Bremberg and Richard Gillespie

Social Welfare Issues in Southern Europe
Edited by Maria Brown and Michael Briguglio

Constructive Competition in the Caspian Sea Region?
An Alternative Image
Agha Bayramov

Central Asia's Economic Rebirth in the Shadow of the New Great Game
Djoomart Otorbaev

The Nordic, Baltic and Visegrád Small Powers in Europe
A Dance with Giants for Survival and Prosperity
Hilmar Þór Hilmarsson

For more information about this series, please visit: www.routledge.com/Europa-Regional-Perspectives/book-series/ERP.

The Nordic, Baltic and Visegrád Small Powers in Europe

A Dance with Giants for Survival and Prosperity

Hilmar Þór Hilmarsson

Routledge
Taylor & Francis Group
LONDON AND NEW YORK

Designed cover image: © Shutterstock

First published 2023
by Routledge
4 Park Square, Milton Park, Abingdon, Oxon OX14 4RN

and by Routledge
605 Third Avenue, New York, NY 10158

Routledge is an imprint of the Taylor & Francis Group, an informa business

British Library Cataloguing in Publication Data
A catalogue record for this book is available from the British Library

ISBN: 978-1-032-08015-4 (hbk)
ISBN: 978-1-032-08018-5 (pbk)
ISBN: 978-1-003-21253-9 (ebk)

DOI: 10.4324/9781003212539

Typeset in Times New Roman
by Taylor & Francis Books

Contents

Figures

Tables

Boxes

The author

Hilmar Þór Hilmarsson is a Professor at the University of Akureyri, Faculty of Business Administration, Iceland, where he teaches courses on international business and macroeconomics. He received his cand.oecon. degree in Economics from the University of Iceland in 1987, an MA in Economics from New York University, US, in 1989, and a PhD in public administration and economic development from the American University in Washington, DC, in 1992. He served as a specialist and coordinator with the World Bank Group in Washington, DC, from 1990 to 1995, at the World Bank office in Rīga, Latvia, from 1999 to 2003, and at the World Bank office in Hanoi, Viet Nam, from 2003 to 2006. From 1995 to 1999 he served as a Special Adviser to the Icelandic Minister for Foreign Affairs. Dr Hilmarsson has published over 80 scholarly articles and book chapters, and three books. He has lectured and made presentations at more than 30 universities in Europe and the USA, including the American University in Washington, DC, Aalborg University (Denmark), Cornell University (US), Georgetown University (US), the Stockholm School of Economics (Sweden), the University of California, Berkeley (US), the University of California, Los Angeles (US), the University of Latvia, the University of Mauritius, the University of Porto (Portugal), the University of Tartu (Estonia), the University of Washington, Vytautas Magnus University (Lithuania), the University of York (UK) and Yale University (US). He has travelled to about 60 countries.

Professor Hilmarsson has held visiting appointments at several top universities in the US and Europe. He was a Visiting Professor at the Stockholm School of Economics during the fall semester 2013, a Visiting Scholar at the University of Washington in Seattle in the spring semester 2014, a Visiting Professor at Cornell University during the fall semester 2015, a Visiting Scholar at the University of California, Berkeley during the fall semester 2016 and a Visiting Scholar at the University of Cambridge, UK, during the fall semester 2017 and 2018.

Acknowledgements

I started thinking about this book in 2020 and submitted my book proposal to Routledge in January 2021. I have been interested in challenges facing small states/powers for a while, but this time I also wanted to focus on how small states form alliances and are affected by their interactions with great powers. This is a topic of growing importance as we shift from a unipolar world with one great power to a multipolar world. I selected the Baltic states, the Nordic countries and the Visegrád group for comparative analysis. The Baltics states were Soviet republics for decades, the Visegrád counties are former Soviet satellite states, while the Nordic welfare states were part of the West during the Soviet era. The countries discussed in the book have sought to form alliances among themselves and have also joined larger alliances. I have carried out research on the Nordic countries and the Baltic states before but needed to study the Visegrád group in greater depth. This was done during the visits listed below when I met with government officials and academics from those countries. In the Visegrád group there is one large country, Poland, and the book contains a chapter which makes a comparative analysis of Poland and Ukraine. Since 2019 I have been in contact with the Warsaw School of Economics in Poland and have benefited from discussions with academic colleagues there including Professor Ewa Latoszek, Professor and the Director of the Jean Monnet Chair of European Union and Eliza Przeździecka, Professor and Director of the Institute of International Economics.

Travel was not easy during the COVID-19 pandemic, but I visited Latvia in September 2021 and benefited from discussions with Agnija Antanoviča, Secretary-General, Secretariat of the Baltic Assembly; Professor Ērika Šumilo, head of the Department of International Economics and Business, University of Latvia; Ladislav Babčan, Ambassador to Latvia and Lithuania, embassy of Slovakia in Rīga and Stefan Eriksson, Director, Nordic Council of Ministers' Office in Latvia.

In September 2021 I visited the embassy of the Republic of Poland in Reykjavík, Iceland, and meet with Gerard Pokruszyński, Ambassador, and Maria Krasnodębska, head of the Political and Economic Department, I Secretary. At the Icelandic Ministry for Foreign Affairs, I benefited from discussions with Gunnar Snorri Gunnarsson, Ambassador and Þórður Bjarni Guðjónsson, Minister Counsellor at the Directorate for Bilateral and Regional Affairs.

In November 2021 I visited the Island and Small States Institute in Malta and at the University of Malta I benefited from discussions with Lino Briguglio, Professor; Stefano Moncada, Director, Islands and Small States Institute; Roderick Pace, Professor, Jean Monnet Chair, Institute for European Studies and Mark Harwood, Director, Institute for European Studies. In November 2021 I also met with diplomats in Brussels, Belgium. I benefited from discussions with Gábor Baranyai, Deputy Permanent Representative and Ambassador Extraordinary and Plenipotentiary at the Permanent Representation of Hungary to the European Union; Balázs Géczy, Deputy Permanent Representative, Permanent Delegation of Hungary to NATO; Peter Kormuth, Ambassador of the Slovak Republic to the Kingdom of Belgium and the Grand Duchy of Luxembourg; Eva Kordová, Minister-Counsellor, Deputy Head of Mission, embassy of the Czech Republic to Belgium; Deividas Matulionis, Ambassador, Permanent Representative of Lithuania to NATO; Andris Razans, Ambassador of Latvia in the Kingdom of Belgium and the Grand Duchy of Luxembourg and Dr Zsolt Darvas, Senior Fellow, Brussels European and Global Economic Laboratory (Bruegel).

In June 2022 I visited Hungary which at the time held the presidency of the Visegrád group. Prior to my visit I was in contact with Eszter Sándorfi, Ambassador, and Beatrix Kosztyi, Commercial Attaché at the embassy of Hungary in Oslo, both of whom were extremely helpful in arranging meetings for me before my visit. In Budapest I benefited from discussions with András Lázár, National Visegrád Coordinator. At the Hungarian Ministry of Foreign Affairs and Trade I met with Edit Szilágyiné Bátorfi, head of Department for Northern Europe and Barnabás Nagy-Vécsei, Desk Officer. At the National University of Public Service, I met with Balázs Mártonffy, Director of the Institute for American Studies and Péter Stepper, Adjunct Professor. At the of the Institute for Foreign Affairs and Trade I met and benefited from discussions with Márton Ugrósdy, Director. At the Mathias Corvinus Collegium Foundation, I had detailed discussions with Máté György Vigóczki, an expert on Russia, Centre for Geopolitics, Csaba Bóta, International Relations Coordinator, International Directorate, and Attila Demkó, head of the Centre for Geopolitics.

Since joining the University of Akureyri in 2006 I have greatly benefited from visiting and interacting with many students and faculty members at the following universities while teaching, giving seminars or speaking at conferences: Aalborg University (Denmark), the American University Washington, DC (US), Bifröst University (Iceland), Bucharest Academy of Economic Studies (Romania), Copenhagen Business Academy (Denmark), Cornell University (US), Georgetown University (US), Haaga-Helia University of Applied Sciences (Finland), International Humanitarian University

(Ukraine), Kaunas University of Applied Sciences (Lithuania), Klaipeda University (Lithuania), Pacific Lutheran University (US), Odessa National Academy of Food Technologies (Ukraine), Riga Stradiņš University (Latvia), Stockholm School of Economics (Latvia and Sweden), Södertörn University (Sweden), Tallinn University of Technology (Estonia), the University of Akureyri (Iceland), the University of the Basque Country (Spain), the University of Iceland (Iceland), the University of Illinois at Chicago (US), the University of Latvia (Latvia), the University of Malta (Malta), the University of Mauritius (Mauritius), the University of Porto (Portugal), the University of Tartu (Estonia), the University of Washington (US), the University of California, Berkeley (US), the University of California, Los Angeles (US), the University of York (UK), Vytautas Magnus University (Lithuania) and Yale University (US). The Erasmus programme funded many of my visits to the Baltic states and I also received grants from Eko-TekNord and the Nord Plus programme to visit both the Nordic countries and the Baltic states.

I have also benefited from countless conversations with academic colleagues as Visiting Professor at the Stockholm School of Economics in Rīga during the fall semester 2013, as Visiting Scholar at the University of Washington in Seattle in the spring semester 2014, as Visiting Professor at Cornell University during the fall semester 2015, as Visiting Scholar at the University of California, Berkeley during the fall semester 2016 and as Visiting Scholar at the University of Cambridge, UK, during the fall semester 2017 and 2018.

I would like to thank some of my Icelandic colleagues whom I talked to during my research. These include especially Guðmundur Kristján Óskarsson, Associate Professor at the University of Akureyri, who in addition to his comments and advice, provided invaluable help with all the graphs and tables contained in this book, as well as with its overall formatting. I also want to thank Trung Quang Dinh, Assistant Professor at the University of Akureyri, once my student and now my colleague, and Þorvaldur Gylfason, Professor at the University of Iceland. Special thanks to Þráinn Eggertsson, Professor at the University of Iceland and at the Hertie School of Governance, Berlin, for constructive discussions and good advice over the last three decades. I would also like to thank the University of Akureyri Science Fund for providing generous financial support for this book.

I want to thank the staff at Routledge, especially Cathy Hartley, Regional Editor and Europa Commissioning Editor. It was not easy to do this research during the COVID-19 pandemic when travel to conduct interviews was complicated. Then the Russian Federation invaded Ukraine and the world of international affairs was constantly changing while I was writing the book. Cathy's encouragement, support and understanding were all critical for me to be able to finish this book.

Finally, I want to thank Alison Phillips, copyeditor of this book, and Dominic Corti, Senior Digital Content Editor, for their excellent work.

Abbreviations and acronyms

AfDB	African Development Bank
ADB	Asian Development Bank
AIIB	Asia Infrastructure Investment Bank
AUKUS	Australia – United Kingdom – United States partnership
Baltics	The Baltic states (Estonia, Latvia, Lithuania)
BRI	Belt and Road Initiative
BRICS	Brazil, Russia, India, China, South Africa
CEE	Central and Eastern Europe
D-10	Democracies 10
EBRD	European Bank for Reconstruction and Development
ECB	European Central Bank
EEA	European Economic Area
EEC	European Economic Community
EFTA	European Free Trade Association
EIB	European Investment Bank
EMU	Economic and Monetary Union
EU	European Union
FDI	Foreign Direct Investment
G20	Group of Twenty
G7	Group of Seven
GATT	General Agreement on Tariffs and Trade
GDP	gross domestic product
GNI	gross national income
IBRD	International Bank for Reconstruction and Development
IDB	Inter-American Development Bank
IMF	International Monetary Fund
NATO	North Atlantic Treaty Organisation
NB8	Nordic-Baltic Eight
NB6	Nordic-Baltic Six
NDB	New Development Bank
NIB	Nordic Investment Bank
Nordics	The Nordic countries (Iceland, Norway, Denmark, Sweden, Finland)

ODA	Overseas Development Assistance
OECD	Organisation for Economic Co-operation and Development
QUAD	Quadrilateral Security Dialogue
PPP	Purchasing power parity
SGP	Stability and Growth Pact
UK	United Kingdom
UN	United Nations
US	United States of America
USSR	Union of Soviet Socialist Republics
Visegrád	The Visegrád group (Czech Republic, Hungary, Poland, Slovakia)
V4	the Visegrád group
WTO	World Trade Organization

Introduction

As suggested by the title of this book – *The Nordic, Baltic and Visegrád Small Powers: A Dance with Giants for Survival and Prosperity* – it is a challenge for small states to maintain their sovereignty and wellbeing in a global world with rival and competing great powers, such as the US, the People's Republic of China and the Russian Federation, that represent interests that small states may support, but can also conflict with those of small states. In addition to their interaction with great powers the countries discussed in the book also participate in regional integration that has both costs and benefits to which small states are liable. All 12 countries discussed in the book participate in European integration. All of them are in the European economic area with access to the EU internal market (also known as the single market) allowing for the free movement of goods, services, capital and people. All the countries discussed are in the Schengen area which facilitates the free movement of people whereby countries in effect abolish their internal borders. Ten out of 12 of the countries discussed are European Union (EU) and North Atlantic Treaty Organization (NATO) member states and five out of 12 countries are also euro area member states with a common currency, the euro, as their legal tender. At the time of writing both Finland and Sweden had applied for membership of NATO.

The book seeks to explain why these countries have taken such different approaches to European integration, economic and social policy, as well as security policy. Part of the European integration project has to do with economic and political issues as well as a common culture, but security also comes into play, and in Europe it is supported by a distant great power – the US – mainly via NATO. In fact, all 12 countries in the Baltic, Nordic and Visegrád groups fall, formally or informally, under the US security umbrella.

Europe's security was for decades threatened by the Soviet Union and now by instability in Russia, mostly felt by countries that are located close to Russia such as the Baltic states. Some of the countries discussed in the book feel threatened by Russia's military activities in Georgia and the ongoing conflict in Ukraine, and the Ukrainian case will be discussed in some detail in Chapter 8 in this volume. Recently there have been tensions on the Belarus–Poland border. Three of the Visegrád countries, Hungary, Poland and Slovakia, have a border with Ukraine.

DOI: 10.4324/9781003212539-1

Many countries also have concerns about the rising power of China economically and militarily and Chinese intentions. China could eventually have even greater influence in Europe than Russia, not only economically but also in terms of security. Some of the countries discussed in the book expect growing Chinese investment that they perhaps hope can fill the gap left by limited EU investment funds. While they can benefit from increased trade and investments some are concerned about their sovereignty in their dealings with a great distant power. A too close relationship with China can also create tensions with the US.

Why focus on the Nordic countries, the Baltic states and the Visegrád group?

The country groups that form the focus of the book are the Baltic states (Estonia, Latvia and Lithuania), the Nordic countries (Denmark, Finland, Iceland, Norway and Sweden) and the Visegrád group, also known as the Visegrád Four, or V4 (the Czech Republic (Czechia), Hungary, Poland and Slovakia).

The countries chosen for analysis in the book can all be classified as small states except for Poland, which has a large population (see Table I.1). Economically, measured by gross domestic product (GDP),[1] Poland's economy is only marginally larger than that of Sweden. Poland has a special status within the Visegrád group. Geographically it is larger than all the other Visegrád countries combined, and it also has a larger GDP and a larger population than the other V4 countries combined. However, Poland does not yet have the wealth that the richer Western EU member states enjoy.

The countries discussed have formed alliances and work together to further their interests economically and politically, for example, via participation in European integration and on security, most notably through membership of NATO. Alliances allow these countries to cooperate owing to their shared interests, culture and history, as well their proximity to one another. This is not unusual for small states/powers. Some differences exist among these groups, but in many ways they are like-minded. The country alliances are as follows:

- The Nordic group (comprising the Western welfare states). Their cooperation has been institutionalized via the Nordic Council and the Nordic Council of Ministers.
- The Baltic states (known as the comprising former Soviet[2] republics) cooperate via the Baltic Assembly and the Baltic Council of Ministers.
- The Nordic-Baltic states also cooperate in a regional framework known as the Nordic-Baltic Eight (NB8), and as Nordic and Baltic EU member states via the Nordic-Baltic Six (NB6).
- The Visegrád group, or the V4, comprises former Soviet satellite states, and after the fall of the Soviet Union they cooperated in their common

efforts to join the EU and NATO. Unlike the Baltic states and the Nordic countries, the Visegrád group has not formalized its cooperation with institutions, with the exception of the Visegrád Fund.[3]
- All these groups, Nordic, Baltic and Visegrád, also cooperate among themselves and organize joint meetings to discuss issues of common interest, e.g. Nordic-Baltic meetings, Visegrád group+ meetings, etc. Together they represent an important part of Northern, Eastern and Central Europe and can have a considerable influence in Europe overall.

The countries and country groups share similarities in the sense that they are all participants in European integration and cooperate with NATO and the US, albeit that their chosen paths are somewhat different. They are thus interesting subjects for case studies and comparative analysis. The Baltics states were all Soviet republics for decades, and the Visegrád counties are former Soviet satellite states, but the Nordic welfare states were linked to the West via institutions, most notably NATO,[4] the European Free Trade Association (EFTA), the EU, etc., and have formally or informally been allied with the US directly or indirectly since the Second World War.

Denmark, Iceland and Norway are NATO member states. Meanwhile, Sweden and Finland have maintained their neutrality, but cooperate with NATO, have participated in NATO military exercises, and at the time of writing have applied for NATO membership. Denmark, Finland and Sweden are EU member states, while Norway and Iceland are not but do cooperate with the EU via the EFTA and are part of the European Economic Area. Finland and Sweden applied for EU membership after the fall of the Soviet Union when Russia was weak but were until recently reluctant to seek NATO membership that surely would not be welcomed in Russia given that it opposes further NATO expansion. Finland and Sweden may see the conflict in Ukraine as an opportunity to join NATO since Russia appears weaker in the war with Ukraine than many expected. The Nordic countries were never part of the Soviet Union, although Finland has, due to its eastern border with Russia, long lived under the shadow of either Russia or the Soviet Union.

The Baltic states, Estonia, Latvia and Lithuania, are all EU, euro area and NATO member states. The Visegrád group, the Czech Republic, Hungary, Poland and Slovakia, are all EU and NATO member states, but only Slovakia has adopted the euro.

The Nordic countries are the wealthiest group as measured by GDP per capita and are known for their generous welfare states and social policies. The Baltic states and the Visegrád countries enjoy similar income levels measured by GDP per capita, yet their social performance appears to very different, according to Eurostat data, with the Visegrád group reporting less poverty and inequality in terms of income compared to that in the Baltic states (see Table I.1). According to the World Bank, the Baltic states perform better than the Visegrád group when one considers the ease of doing business

Table I.1 Nordic, Baltic and Visegrád countries: some key indicators, 2019

Country	*GDP,[5] current prices (US$, billions)*	*World ranking, size of economy[6]*	*GDP[7] per capita (US$)*	*The Gini index[8]*	*At-risk-of-poverty rate, %[9]*	*Ease of doing business ranking[10]*	*Population, thousands[11]*	*Land area[12] (sq km)*
Baltics								
Estonia	31,475	100	23,757	30.5	21.7	18	1.325	43,470
Latvia	34,121	99	17,771	35.2	22.9	19	1.920	62,180
Lithuania	54,225	83	19,482	35.4	20.6	11	2.783	62,642
Nordics								
Denmark	347,031	38	59,770	27.5	12.5	4	5.806	41,990
Finland	269,327	44	48,809	26.2	11.6	20	5.518	303,910
Iceland	24,224	108	67,857	23.2[13]	8.8[14]	26	0.357	100,250
Norway	403,336	30	75,294	25.4	12.7	9	5.357	365,123
Sweden	530,884	23	51,404	27.5	17.1	10	10.328	407,310
Visegrád								
Czech Republic	250,681	47	23,538	24.0	10.1	41	10.650	77,220
Hungary	160,957	56	16,469	28.0	12.3	52	9.773	90,530
Poland	592,401	21	15,600	28.5	15.4	40	37.973	306,190
Slovakia	105,434	61	19,344	22.8	11.9	45	5.450	48,080

Source: Eurostat (2021); IMF (2020); World Bank (2019a, 2019b, 2019c).

there (see Table I.1). In fact, the post-Soviet Baltic reform model was based on low tax regimes and minimal government to attract foreign investment that was to promote economic growth.

From bipolar to unipolar to multipolar world

The book will analyse small state/power politics, small state alliances and great state/power politics simultaneously. Great powers are the most important players in shaping international relations and in forming the world order. From 1945 to 1991 we lived in a bipolar system dominated by two great powers, the US and the USSR. However, the USSR never enjoyed the same level of wealth as the US, but it had the population and sufficient military capabilities to be considered a great power. Following the collapse of the Soviet Union, one can speak of a unipolar moment that lasted from 1991 to about 2017, with the US dominating as the only remaining superpower on the global stage. During the past few years, we have arguably lived in a multipolar world with the economic and military rise of China and Russia that has to some extent recovered from the fall of the Soviet Union economically and remains a nuclear power. The ongoing war in Ukraine appears to have weakened Russia as great power, but Russia is still very important for Europe's energy market, particularly gas.

The US remains the greatest power, followed by China, with Russia a distant third great power. The world is likely to change dramatically in the coming decades especially if China continues to grow economically and if its growing economic might turns into a military might not hitherto seen. How should small powers in Europe behave in this new multipolar world? What strategy is best for their survival and prosperity? Do the countries discussed in the book need to choose between the US and China? How should they relate to Russia?

European integration

Europe has been on an integration track since the end of Second World War. The continental political climate after the war favoured unity in democratic European countries and was seen by many as an escape from the extreme forms of nationalism which devastated the continent. This process, which is still ongoing, involves costs and benefits and can be challenging especially for small states wishing to benefit from such integration, but whose sovereignty may be challenged. European integration is a give and take process, and small states are especially sensitive when transferring part of their sovereignty to supranational institutions.

Within Europe there are great powers that are more influential than the small states and they play a larger role in the EU decision-making process than small states can hope to do individually. Of particular importance is Germany, Europe's most powerful country with the largest economy, and the location of the European Central Bank, arguably the EU's most powerful institution. Germany is wealthy, but hardly has the population to dominate Europe. It is a strong force that is feared by many smaller states owing to its history, but Germany seems unlikely to become a regional hegemon in Europe in the same way as the US in the Americas. The EU also has other large member states/powers such as France and to a lesser extent Italy, albeit that it remains weak economically.

Recently the EU has also faced disintegration following the departure of one of its largest member states, the United Kingdom, from the Union (known as Brexit). The UK was for a long time a reluctant partner in the European integration process and has historically led the British Commonwealth of Nations. Two world wars have taken their toll on Europe with huge population losses most notably in Germany and Russia. These population losses make the two countries weaker on the world stage when competing not just with the US but also China.

Linking with the West and the rising power in the East

There are great and competing powers outside Europe that influence European policies especially the US via its leadership of NATO. The new EU member states (those that have joined since 2004) have tended to view the US as their main security guarantor and have taken advice from the US and US-based institutions on various issues, including economic policy, during their transition from a centrally planned economy to a market economy. For Eastern and Central European countries and the Baltic states, stronger links with the West were considered important after the fall of the Soviet Union and the West was symbolized by the US more than by any other country. The stronger the links the better. But US economic policies tend to be more neoliberal than European social policies resulting in some new EU member states departing from European values of equality. Following the fall of the Soviet Union, the Baltic states tended to favour flat taxes and minimal states, while countries such as the Nordic states have long had progressive tax systems allowing for relatively larger government budgets as a percentage of GDP with which to fund their welfare states. The Visegrád countries appear to have achieved better social outcomes than the Baltic states; remarkably these successes resemble the achievements of the richer Nordic countries, according to Eurostat data (see also Table I.1).

Currently Europe is influenced by a great and rising power, namely China, and this is putting competitive pressure on Europe which can influence its economic structure and its social profile. Fierce competition with China may limit the opportunities of European countries to maintain their social programmes and welfare states. Growing Chinese power in Asia may result in greater Chinese interest in other regions, not least Europe. Recently China has shown growing interest in investing in Europe e.g. via its Belt and Road and 17+1 (now 16+1) Initiatives.

If China can eventually dominate Asia in the same way that the US dominates the Americas, Chinese interest in influencing other regions, including Europe, is likely to grow. The irony for the US is that for a long time `its foreign policy was to engage with China, integrating China into the international institutional infrastructure that it created in the wake of the Second World War, most notably the Bretton Woods institutions and the World Trade Organization (WTO) (formerly the General Agreement on Tariffs and Trade – GATT). This helped China to make the transition to a market economy that than became the foundation for rapid economic growth that was to a large extent export-led. China could not have become the power that it is today without having access to the markets of the Western world. The US thus unintentionally created a rival more powerful that it has ever seen before, more powerful than the Soviet Union ever was, more powerful than imperial Japan or imperial Germany or later Nazi Germany ever were. The rise of China will create tensions with the US that were already visible during the Trump administration and can now be seen in the Biden administration. China is also creating its own international institutional infrastructure in the shape of the the Asian Infrastructure Investment Bank (AIIB) and the New Development Bank, formerly referred to as the BRICS Development Bank, which was established by the emerging BRICS economies (Brazil, Russia, India, China and South Africa) to challenge the US-led Bretton Woods institutions. China is a rival to the US and there are military tensions in Asia, but at the same time because of its export-led growth model, China needs access to markets in the high-income countries in Europe and the US. This situation is different from the erstwhile Cold War tensions between the US and the USSR in the sense that there was hardly any trade between those two powers. In contrast, there is huge trade between the US and China and thus economic interdependence. The burning question that must be asked is can China rise peacefully? Some leading international relations scholars would answer that question with an emphatic 'no' (see, for example, Mearsheimer 2014).

Russia is not as great an economic power as the US and China, and its economy measured by GDP is currently about the same size as that of Italy. It has a declining population and is highly dependent on its oil and gas resources. Russia has neither the population nor the wealth to become as powerful as the US or China. Nevertheless, Russia remains a great nuclear power and puts pressure on European states especially those that are located close to Russia and primarily those that share borders with Russia. Finland and the Baltics, as well as countries that share borders with countries under Russian influence, feel the heat. Russia opposes NATO expansion and is willing to take hostile action as demonstrated by its invasion of Georgia and the war in Ukraine. Russia seems to have drawn a red line warning against greater Western influence in those countries through further military alliances with the West. Recent tensions at the Belarus–Poland border also raise questions about Russia's involvement and intentions. The ongoing conflict in Ukraine appears to have weakened Russia as great power, but because of its dependence on Russian gas supplies Europe is vulnerable.

The global and regional integration of the different country groups

The countries and country groups analysed in the book have all sought benefits and perhaps shelter via European integration, but in different ways. As discussed above, the former Soviet republics, the Baltics, have chosen the closest level of integration through membership of both the EU and the euro area. The former Soviet satellite states the Visegrád countries have all chosen to become members of the EU, but only one country in the V4 group, Slovakia, is a euro area member state. The Nordic countries are as a group the least integrated into the EU; Denmark, Finland and Sweden are members of the EU members, while non-EU members Iceland and Norway are EFTA member states. Finland is the only euro area member state. Historic association with the former Soviet Union and proximity to Russia appear to partially explain the preferences of these countries to integrate with the EU and its systems. Indeed, membership of the euro area has bolstered Finland's security.

Unstable Russia encourages small states to pursue European integration, especially those sharing borders with Russia. The closer a small state is to

Russia, the more European integration it tends to seek in addition to NATO membership and alliance with the US.

The EU and the euro area faced challenges during the 2008/09 financial crisis with slow economic growth, austerity, relatively high unemployment, and issues related to outward migration from poorer member states, such as the Baltics to richer member states. During the COVID-19 crisis high fiscal deficits and rising public debt as a percentage of GDP will be a challenge for the EU and the euro area. Another crisis has emerged following the outbreak of the Ukraine war including broken supply chains and high inflation. The small states need to assess their best level of integration with the EU and the feasibility of a common currency. Joining a currency union during a crisis can have severe consequences.

At the same time, the small states discussed in the book need to decide how to relate to other powers in the future, especially the US and China. Does the rise of China and its tensions with the US mean that small states need to choose between the US and China? Relations with Russia are also important. Russia is a weaker power in terms of wealth and population than the other two and it may need to choose whether it leans towards US or China? Russian instability remains a key concern to the EU and NATO.

In addition to European integration, all the countries discussed in the book have sought global integration. They are all members of the Organization for Economic Co-operation and Development, the WTO, the World Bank, the International Monetary Fund and the United Nations. They all see the benefits of global integration and the Baltic states and Visegrád group have cooperated with those institutions while making the transition from a centrally planned to a market economy. The countries have joined these global institutions at different times depending on their circumstances. For example, the collapse of the Soviet Union was necessary for the Baltics to enable them to seek membership of international organizations since the Baltic states were in effect provinces in the USSR labelled as Soviet republics.

The countries discussed in the book have different levels of engagement with regional development and reconstruction banks. The Baltic states are only members of the European Bank for Reconstruction and Development (EBRD) where they can benefit directly via their membership, as the EBRD helps countries to make the transition to a market economy. The Visegrád countries take a similar approach, with the exception of Hungary and Poland, which are also members of the China-led AIIB. All the Nordic countries, apart from Iceland, are members of the African Development Bank, the Asian Development Bank and the Inter-American Development Bank. All the Nordics are members of the EBRD and the AIIB. These countries are richer than the other two groups, are known to be welfare states and appear to have global ambitions. Iceland is different from the other Nordic countries. It is much smaller, but it is a member of the EBRD, as well as of the AIIB. By becoming members of the AIIB one could argue that these countries are preparing themselves for the increased involvement and influence of China in the world economy. All the EU member states discussed in the book became members of the European Investment Bank when they joined the Union.

All the countries discussed in the book have their own bilateral development programmes through which they channel their overseas development assistance. They have chosen different regions and priority countries that reflect their foreign policy and their development priorities.

This book differs from other previous publications since it employs a more interdisciplinary approach and covers issues relating to economic policy, international relations and politics, economic and political integration, as well as the effect of global and regional institutions, and priorities in bilateral development cooperation. It is also different in that it emphasizes the way in which policies are shaped by the interaction between small states (small powers) and large states (great powers).

Methodology

The methodology used in the book is the case study method (multiple case studies or comparative analysis). Unlike other research methods, a case study enables the researcher to examine the issues involved in greater depth (Yin 2009). Comparative analysis allows the researcher to assess and explain the political phenomena among cases (Lancaster and Montinola 1997). It helps to capture the effects of complex and interrelated causal influences and facilitates our understanding of political issues at national, regional and international level (Ragin 2014). Additionally, the literature on the use of comparative analysis is rich with suggestions on how such an inquiry should proceed (Lijphart 1975). The comparative country and country group case studies will involve analysis and synthesis of the similarities, differences and patterns across different countries and country groups that can produce knowledge about how and why particular economic policies work or fail to work. The book will also discuss and evaluate the empirical literature relevant to the countries analysed. The different countries and country groups under study allow for such analysis to take place.

Questions to be addressed in the book

When preparing a proposal for this book the following questions came to mind:

- How can small European states survive and prosper within a multipolar world of great powers?
- What part should small states take in European integration? Does one size fit all?
- Do EU fiscal and monetary policies allow for Keynesian economic stimulus when needed and are the euro area convergence criteria viable as the world recovers from the COVID-19 crisis?

- Are small state alliances within the EU useful to counterbalance the influence of the larger EU member states?
- How far should EU and NATO expansion go? Should it include countries such as Ukraine?
- Can the EU rely on a US-led NATO for its security?
- How should small states/powers relate to major powers influencing Europe, particularly the US, China and Russia?
- Do smaller states need to choose a single ally among all the great powers?

When proceeding with the research, other questions and issues came to mind. Some of these are addressed in this book, while others are subjects for future research.

Book chapters

Although this book is not intended to be a list of questions and answers, the chapters have been framed in the following way to respond to the issues raised above.

Chapter 1 looks at European integration, its costs and benefits, and the challenge of economic and political sovereignty for small powers (small states) and NATO membership. Chapter 2 discusses participation in global and regional institutions and international relations theories.

Chapter 3 outlines some small power alliances in Europe. Chapter 4 examines the economic and social performance of the different countries and country groups following the 2008/09 global financial crisis and during the COVID-19 crisis. Chapter 5 shows that great powers are influencing Europe in a world that shifted from a bipolar world (the US versus the USSR), to a unipolar world (the US) and then to a multipolar world (the US, China and Russia). Chapter 6 looks at the US, its security role in Europe, and its influence on the economic policy of the new EU member states (since 2004) following the collapse of the Soviet Union. Is the transatlantic alliance between Europe and the US viable and feasible? Chapter 7 covers the rise of China, its ambitions for Asian dominance, and its growing economic and political interest in Europe. Chapter 8 looks at countries sharing a border with Russia, particularly Ukraine, and the challenge of further EU and NATO expansion. Chapter 9 asks how can Europe move forward? Should EU and euro area policies be modified as the world recovers from the COVID-19 crisis? Could Brexit result in further disintegration? Chapter 10 asks what can small powers do to maintain their economic and political sovereignty and prosper in a multipolar world? Chapter 11 concludes the book and offers some policy implications.

Finally, when reading the book from cover to cover the reader will notice a certain amount of repetition. This is because each chapter is meant to some extent to be independent for those who prefer to dip into the book to study specific issues instead of reading the whole book in traditional 'start-to-finish' style.

Notes

1 GDP at current prices in US dollars.
2 The Union of Soviet Socialist Republics (USSR), also called the Soviet Union in this book, is the former northern Eurasian empire (1917/22–1991) stretching from the Baltic and Black Seas to the Pacific Ocean and, in its final years, consisting of 15 Soviet republics, namely Armenia, Azerbaijan, Belarus, Estonia, Georgia, Kazakhstan, Kyrgyzstan, Latvia, Lithuania, Moldova, Russia, Tajikistan, Turkmenistan, Ukraine and Uzbekistan. The capital was Moscow; it is now the capital of Russia.
3 www.visegradfund.org/.
4 The North Atlantic Treaty Organization (NATO), also called the North Atlantic Alliance, is an intergovernmental military alliance based on the North Atlantic Treaty signed on 4 April 1949. At present, NATO has 30 members. In 1949, there were 12 founding members of the Alliance, namely Belgium, Canada, Denmark, France, Iceland, Italy, Luxembourg, the Netherlands, Norway, Portugal, the United Kingdom and the US. The other member countries are Greece and Turkey (1952), Germany (1955), Spain (1982), the Czech Republic, Hungary and Poland (1999), Bulgaria, Estonia, Latvia, Lithuania, Romania, Slovakia and Slovenia (2004), Albania and Croatia (2009), Montenegro (2017) and North Macedonia (2020). See www.nato.int/cps/en/natohq/topics_52044.htm.
5 IMF (2020).
6 https://databankfiles.worldbank.org/data/download/GDP.pdf.
7 Ibid.
8 The Gini coefficient/index is a measurement of the income distribution of a country's residents. This number, which ranges between 0 and 1 and is based on residents' net income, helps to define the gap between rich and poor, with 0 representing perfect equality and 1 representing perfect inequality. It is typically expressed as a percentage, referred to as the Gini coefficient. See www.investopedia.com/terms/g/gini-index.asp http://appsso.eurostat.ec.europa.eu/nui/show.do?lang=en&dataset=ilc_di12.
9 The at-risk-of-poverty rate is the share of people with an equivalized disposable income (after social transfer) below the at-risk-of-poverty threshold, which is set at 60% of the national median equivalized disposable income after social transfers. This indicator does not measure wealth or poverty, but low income in comparison to other residents in that country, which does not necessarily imply a low standard of living. See https://ec.europa.eu/eurostat/databrowser/view/tespm010/default/table?lang=en.
10 www.doingbusiness.org/en/doingbusiness; and https://openknowledge.worldbank.org/bitstream/handle/10986/32436/9781464814402.pdf.
11 IMF (2020).
12 http://data.worldbank.org/indicator/AG.LND.TOTL.K2.
13 Gini coefficient for 2018.
14 At-risk-of-poverty rate for 2018.

References

Eurostat (2021). *Eurostat Database*. Available at: https://ec.europa.eu/eurostat/databrowser/view/tespm010/default/table?lang=en (accessed 19 February 2021).

International Monetary Fund (IMF) (2020). *World Economic Outlook Database*, October. Available at: www.imf.org/en/Publications/WEO/weo-database/2020/October (accessed 19 February 2021).

Lancaster, T. D., and Montinola G. R. (1997). Toward a Methodology for the Comparative Study of Political Corruption. *Crime, Law and Social Change*, 27, 185–206.

Lijphart, A. (1975). 'The Comparable-Cases Strategy in Comparative Research', *Comparative Political Studies*, 8, 158–177.

Mearsheimer, J. J. (2014). Can China Rise Peacefully? *The National Interest*, 25(1), 1–40.

Ragin, C. C. (2014). *The Comparative Method: Moving beyond Qualitative and Quantitative Strategies*. Berkeley: University of California Press.

World Bank (2019a). *Doing Business 2020*. Available at: www.doingbusiness.org/en/doingbusiness (accessed 7 February 2021).

World Bank (2019b). *Gross Domestic Product 2019*. Available at: http://databank.worldbank.org/data/download/GDP.pdf (accessed 7 January 2021).

World Bank (2019c). *Land Area (sq km)*. Available at: http://data.worldbank.org/indicator/AG.LND.TOTL.K2 (accessed 7 January 2021).

Yin, R. K. (2009). *Case Study Research: Design and Methods*, 4th edn, Vol. 5. Thousand Oaks, CA: SAGE.

1 The costs and benefits of European integration, and the challenges of NATO membership for small powers

European integration and NATO membership

All the Baltic, Nordic and Visegrád countries are members of the European Economic Area (EEA) and the Schengen area, most of them are European Union (EU) member states and European North Atlantic Treaty Organization (NATO) member states. It is notable that only five out of the 12 countries are euro area member states. Among the three groups only the Baltic states have a common approach. They are the most integrated group being members of the EU, the Schengen area and the euro area as well as NATO. The Visegrád group is less integrated. While they are all EU member states and participate in the Schengen Agreement, only one country, Slovakia, is a member of the euro area. All the Visegrád countries are members of NATO. The Nordic countries are less integrated than the Baltic and the Visegrád countries. Three of them are EU member states and two are non-EU European Free Trade Association (EFTA)/EEA member states (see Box 1.1) Among the Nordic countries only one, Finland, is in the euro area (see Tables 1.1 and 1.4 and Figure 1.1). Denmark, Iceland and Norway were among the founding NATO member states in 1949, but not Finland and Sweden. All the Nordic countries participate in the Schengen Agreement. The chapter seeks to explain why the countries and country groups have taken such different approaches to European integration and why two of the Nordic countries originally opted to stay out of NATO before applying to join NATO in 2022.

Different levels of European integration

For all the countries and country groups (Baltic, Nordic and Visegrád) discussed in the book free trade among themselves and within the EU internal market (also known as the single market), comprising a total of 30 EEA member states, is critical for their economic prosperity. Free trade has not always been the rule of the game in these countries. The Baltic states were part of the Soviet central planning model until 1991 and the Soviet Union did not engage extensively in trade with Western European countries. The

DOI: 10.4324/9781003212539-2

Table 1.1 European integration and NATO membership of the Baltic, Nordic and Visegrád countries

	Countries and country groups	*European Economic Area (EEA)*[1]	*Schengen*[2]	*European Union (EU)*[3]	*European Free Trade Association (EFTA)*[4]	*Euro area*[5]	*North Atlantic Treaty Organization (NATO)*[6]
Baltics							
	Estonia	Yes	Yes	Yes	No	Yes	Yes
	Latvia	Yes	Yes	Yes	No	Yes	Yes
	Lithuania	Yes	Yes	Yes	No	Yes	Yes
Visegrád							
	Czech Republic	Yes	Yes	Yes	No	No	Yes
	Hungary	Yes	Yes	Yes	No	No	Yes
	Poland	Yes	Yes	Yes	No	No	Yes
	Slovakia	Yes	Yes	Yes	No	Yes	Yes
Nordics							
	Denmark	Yes	Yes	Yes	No	No	Yes
	Finland	Yes	Yes	Yes	No	Yes	No
	Iceland	Yes	Yes	No	Yes	No	Yes
	Norway	Yes	Yes	No	Yes	No	Yes
	Sweden	Yes	Yes	yes	No	No	No

Source: European Commission (2021a, 2021b); European Union (2021); EFTA (2021a, 2021b); NATO (2021a).

Nordic countries, on the other hand, had long enjoyed free trade among themselves and with other countries within and outside Europe and they all became EFTA member states before three of them joined the EU. The Visegrád countries were Soviet satellite states that became independent from the Soviet bloc in 1989. From an economic point of view, it was beneficial for all these countries in the three country groups to become part of the EEA. Most of them joined the EU, while two of the Nordics (Iceland and Norway) remain EFTA/EEA member states (see Tables 1.2 and 1.3).

Some benefits and costs resulting from European integration

The benefits of the common market (i.e. the EU internal market) are largely undisputed, and can be labelled as the EU's greatest asset. Classical economic theory documents the gains from international trade, demonstrating that nations can improve the welfare of their populations by engaging in cross-border trade with other nations. Trade between nations can, at least in

Table 1.2 The EU and the Baltic, Nordic and Visegrád countries, 1962–2013

1962	*Norway*, the United Kingdom, *Denmark* and Ireland apply for membership of the European Economic Community (EEC).
1973	*Denmark*, Ireland and the UK become members of the EEC. *Norway* rejects EEC membership in a popular referendum.
1994	*Norway* rejects accession to the EU in a popular referendum.
1995	Austria, *Finland* and *Sweden* become members of the EU.
2004	The Baltic states (*Estonia, Latvia and Lithuania*) join the EU. The Visegrád countries (*the Czech Republic, Hungary, Poland* and *Slovakia*) join the EU.
2009	*Iceland* applies to join the EU.
2013	The *Icelandic* government requests that 'Iceland should not be regarded as a candidate country for EU membership'.

Source: compiled by the author based on EFTA (2014).

Note: The names of the Baltic, Nordic and Visegrád countries are italicized.

theory, result in a positive-sum game, meaning that the trading countries are all better off, and benefit from their gains from trade. To this day, this is one of the fundamental principles underlying arguments for all countries to strive to expand and to promote free world trade (e.g. Czinkota et al. 2009). How the gains from trade are divided among nations is another question, so are there questions regarding fairness in international trade.

The efficiencies derived from economies of scale are also among the key arguments for economic integration: the creation of a common market facilitates larger production and trading volumes that can benefit all the participating countries through lower unit costs. The EU pursues regional integration, whereby those who have access to its common market can benefit as described above. According to regional integration theory, the level of integration varies. From the least to most integrative, they are a free trade area, a customs union, a common market and, finally, an economic and a political union. All the countries in the Nordic, Baltic and the Visegrád groups are in the EEA and therefore enjoy the benefits of a common market which include the free movement of goods, services, capital and people (see Figure 1.1). They are also all members of the Schengen area. They are also all EU member states, except for Iceland and Norway which are EFTA/EEA member states.

The EU member states are required to surrender numerous elements of their national sovereignty to supranational authorities in union-wide institutions such as the European Parliament, the European Commission and the European Council. EU member states are also required to participate in the EU common agricultural and fisheries policies.

New EU member states are also expected to adopt the EU common currency, the euro. Some of these arrangements are seen as costs that limit national sovereignty, and there has also been talk about a democratic deficit within the EU, for example, with the European Commission that is not democratically elected by voters in member states, but nevertheless initiates EU legislation. This is disputed and is one of the reasons why the UK decided to leave the EU (referred to as Brexit). The current arrangements within Europe have also been criticized by other countries for being overly complex. According to the former US Secretary of State, Madeleine Albright, 'To understand Europe, you have to be a genius – or French'.[7]

Iceland and Norway are the only non-EU member states in the country groups under study, but are members of EFTA and have access to the common market via the EEA Agreement (see Figure 1.1 and Box 1.1). Both countries are small and rely heavily on exports, so this arrangement is critically important for them. One can speculate why neither of these countries has yet joined the EU.

Iceland is an island far away from continental Europe located in the Atlantic Ocean between Europe and America. It does not lie in close proximity to any great threatening power and has rarely engaged in any serious disputes with great powers. During the Soviet era, for example, Iceland engaged in trade with the Soviet Union and also enjoyed good relations with the People's Republic of China. Exceptions to this rule are the disputes with the UK over Iceland's fishing grounds that lasted until 1976 and the cross-border banking disputes that broke out mainly with the UK and the Netherlands during the 2008/09 economic and financial crisis; however, these disputes did not directly threaten Icelandic sovereignty and Iceland has

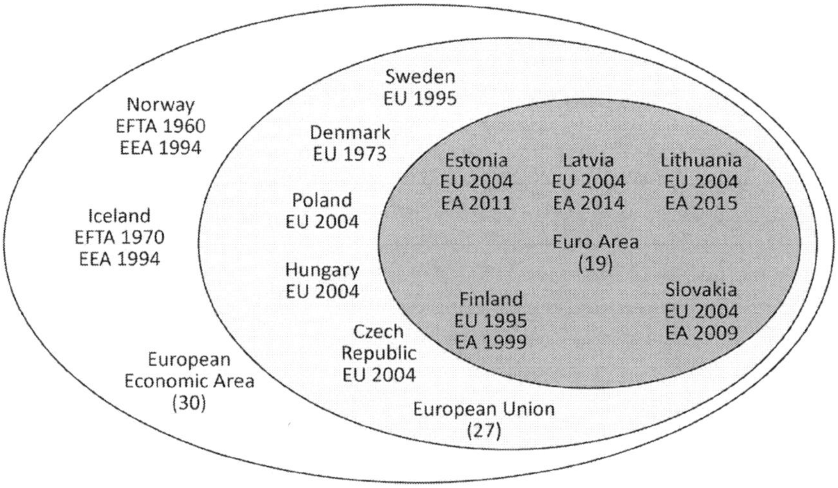

Figure 1.1 Different levels of European integration among the Baltic, Nordic and Visegrád countries

Source: compiled by the author based on European Commission (2021b) and European Union (2021).

generally had good relations with both countries. During the fisheries dispute Iceland had the indirect support of the US owing to the Bilateral Defence Agreement signed between the two countries in 1951, as well as NATO membership from 1949. During the 2008/09 crisis it was able to develop constructive cooperation with the International Monetary Fund and received temporary international assistance until its economy recovered (see Hilmarsson 2016). The EU common agriculture policy and the common fisheries policy in particular would be hard for many in Iceland to accept. Rural areas are still powerful in Icelandic politics and strong business interest in the fisheries sector would oppose EU management of Icelandic fisheries resources.

Unlike Iceland, Norway is part of continental Europe, but it is far away from any great power except Russia. It has a border with Russia in the far north of the country. This northern border has not been viewed as a major security threat for Norway, and Norway can afford to have a military including a strong and modern air force. Iceland has vast geothermal and hydropower resources and Norway is an oil-rich economy. Both countries have vibrant fisheries sectors. The fact that these countries are not immediately threatened by great powers and have strong economies with per capita gross domestic product (GDP) well above the EU average may at least partially explain why they have chosen to stay out of the EU. By staying out of the EU they can be more independent in their actions, especially with regard to economic policy, and they are not parties to the EU common fisheries or agricultural policies.

The other Nordic countries, Denmark, Finland and Sweden, have on the other hand decided to become EU member states. All the Baltic states and the Visegrád countries have recognized the benefits of full EU membership. These former Soviet republics and satellite states needed to make the transition to a democratic market economy, and created new institutions through which they received EU support. The EU has also provided financial support towards the economic modernization and development in those transition countries, including investment in the infrastructure that is vital to linking these countries more closely with the EU common market. Furthermore, the Nordic countries have sought close and irreversible integration with the West. Some have gone further than others, including membership of a currency union, as will be discussed below.

Box 1.1 Norway and Iceland in EFTA and the EEA

EFTA is a free trade area and represents the loosest form of economic integration, whereby all barriers to trade among member countries are removed. This is the route that Iceland and Norway have chosen and currently maintain in addition to access to the EU internal market via the EEA Agreement that came into force in 1994. Both countries have been reluctant participants in European integration and have so far opted to stay out of the

EU. The current arrangement pursued by Iceland and Norway does not require a common trade policy, such as a common external tariff imposed on non-members, as do customs unions such as those in the EU. Nor does it require the surrender of numerous elements of their national sovereignty to supranational authorities in union-wide institutions such as the European Parliament, the European Commission and the European Council. Nor, too, does it require participation in common agricultural or fisheries policies. Furthermore, Iceland and Norway do not take part in European Central Bank (ECB) activities, as they are not part of the monetary union and have their own currencies.

Initially, the Nordic countries, Denmark, Norway and Sweden, were among the founding members of EFTA in 1960. Other founding members were Austria, Portugal, Switzerland and the UK. Given the size of its economy, as well as its regional and global importance, the UK held a leadership role in EFTA from the beginning until it left and joined the EEC in 1973. By joining the EEC, the UK sought greater influence in shaping the EEC, a difficult or perhaps impossible task had the UK remained an EFTA member state. Nevertheless, in 2020 the UK left the EU.

Iceland became a member of EFTA in 1970 and was followed by Finland in 1986. All the Nordic countries thus decided to take part in this early regional integration effort led by EFTA. The Baltic states could not have participated in EFTA since they were occupied by the Soviet Union until their independence was re-established in 1991. To date, the only Nordic countries that remain members of EFTA are Iceland and Norway. Denmark left in 1973 to join the EEC, while Finland and Sweden left in 1995 to join the EU (see Table 1.3). These Nordic countries were willing to surrender some elements of their national sovereignty to supranational authorities in Union-wide institutions. Possibly they hoped that, as a like-minded group on many issues, they would be able to influence the EU by being *systems-affecting* in the sense suggested by Keohane (1969), namely as states that cannot affect the international system if acting alone but that can exert significant impact on the system if working through small groups or alliances or through universal or regional international organizations.

Currently, EFTA has four member states; Iceland, Liechtenstein, Norway and Switzerland. EFTA has three core tasks. The first is the liberalization of intra-EFTA trade. Second, the EFTA states have built networks of preferential trade relations throughout the world. Third, three of the four EFTA states, Iceland, Liechtenstein and Norway, are parties to the EEA Agreement, which ensures their participation in the EU internal market (EFTA, 2014). Switzerland, also an EFTA member state, does not participate in the EEA Agreement, but has signed a bilateral agreement with the EU.

As EFTA/EEA member states, Norway and Iceland have no formal influence on the decision-making process on the EU side. They cannot directly affect EU laws and regulations governing the EU internal market that they are part of. EFTA/EEA member states can, though, participate in what is known as 'decision-shaping'. This means that during the phase of preparatory work undertaken by the European Commission in drawing up new legislative proposals, the EEA Agreement contains provisions for input from the EEA/EFTA at various stages before new legislation is adopted (see Figure 1.2).

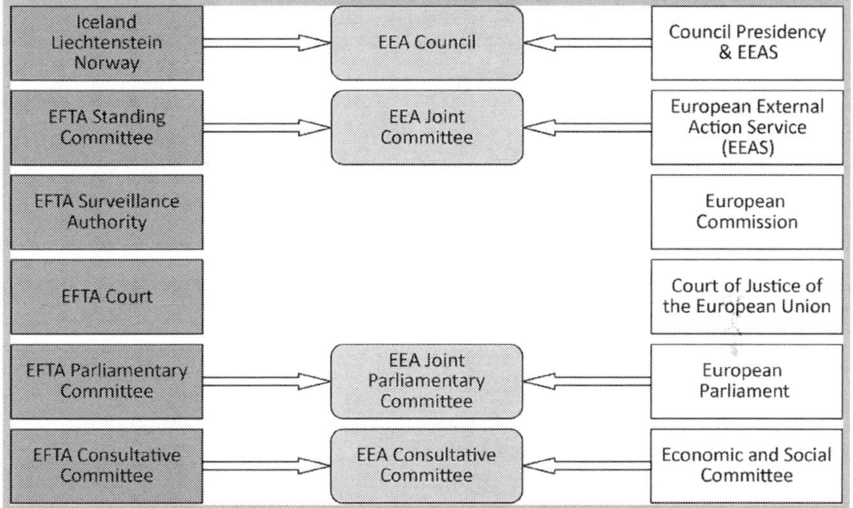

Figure 1.2 Decision-shaping: EEA/EFTA participation in the preparation of new EU laws

Source: EFTA (2014) and Hilmarsson (2016).

Given how small the EFTA/EEA member states are compared to the EU overall, it is highly questionable if they can be classified as *systems-affecting* in the EU context. The reality is that Iceland, Liechtenstein and Norway are notified of the rules and laws governing the EU internal market via email without being able to directly influence the process of making them. In this regard, we can speak of sovereignty infringement. Since Iceland and Norway can only comment on such laws and regulations at an early stage of preparation at an expert level, they are not part of the final decision-making process and must adopt whatever decisions are eventually made by EU member states. This is the cost of enjoying access to the internal market. So far the benefits have been assessed as being higher than the costs.

As Table 1.3 shows, EFTA has lost most of its members, who chose closer economic integration by joining the EEC and later the EU, including the Nordic countries, Denmark, Finland and Sweden. The Baltic states and the Visegrád countries never joined EFTA and immediately sought full EU membership.

Table 1.3 EFTA membership, 1960–1995

1960	Austria, *Denmark*, *Norway*, Portugal, *Sweden*, Switzerland and the UK establish EFTA.
1970	*Iceland* becomes a member of EFTA.
1973	*Denmark* and the UK leave EFTA to join the EEC.
1985	Portugal leaves EFTA to become a member of the EEC.
1986	*Finland* becomes a full member of EFTA.
1991	Liechtenstein becomes a member of EFTA.
1995	Austria, *Finland* and *Sweden* leave EFTA to join the EU.

Source: compiled by the author based on EFTA (2014).

Note: The names of the Nordic countries are italicized.

The euro area: costs and benefits of membership

A common currency area[8] is a geographical area throughout which a single currency circulates as the common medium of exchange (Mankiw and Taylor 2020, p. 755). The European Economic and Monetary Union (EMU) is the European currency union that has adopted the euro as its common currency. Of the 12 countries discussed in this book five have adopted the euro as a common currency and their legal tender (see Table 1.4 and Figure 1.1).[9]

Among the benefits of a common currency is the elimination of transaction costs, i.e. the cost involved in converting currencies, which is a deadweight loss. Eliminating those costs by adopting a common currency, in this case the euro, provides a gain to the members of the common currency area. Having adopted a common currency, the euro, Latvian nationals, for example, do not need to change lats into Finnish markka when visiting Finland or into Slovak koruna when visiting Slovakia.

Another benefit of a common currency is the reduction in price discrimination. It is less likely that there will be price discrimination between countries such as the Baltics, Finland and Slovakia because a single currency makes it more difficult to disguise price differences across participating countries. Having a common currency makes it easier to see whether goods and services are more expensive in either Rīga, Helsinki or Bratislava. Furthermore, the adoption of a common currency eliminates exchange rate fluctuations that create uncertainty for businesses engaging in trade between euro area countries. The Latvian lats, the Finnish markka and the Slovak koruna do not fluctuate because they do not exist anymore. For countries with a national currency, such as Sweden with its krona and Poland with is zloty, businesses can deal with this uncertainty by engaging in forward foreign exchange contracts with their banks, but banks charge for this service and a single currency eliminates these costs. The absence of exchange rate fluctuations with a common currency such as the euro makes business planning easier and can boost investment and thus economic growth.

However, there are also costs associated with a common currency. A country joining a currency union gives up its freedom to set its own monetary policy as well as macroeconomic adjustment through movements in the external value of its currency, i.e. via devaluation.

Without this adjustment mechanism, which is made possible via a national currency, Slovak policymakers might wish to see a cut in interest rates to boost aggregate demand, whereas Finnish policymakers might favour a rise in interest rates with which to contain inflation. The ECB would be unable to satisfy the needs of both countries. The ECB pursues a strategy which targets inflation. If the Slovak inflation rate is below the euro area average, then monetary policy will be too tight for them. If Finland's inflation rate is above the euro area average, then the ECB's monetary policy will be too loose for the economic conditions in Finland.

Table 1.4 shows how euro area membership has developed and Box 1.2 shows how economic growth rates have fluctuated in the Baltic, Nordic and Visegrád countries in comparison to those in the euro area. If the economic cycles of each of the countries in the currency union could be synchronized in the sense that the various economies would tend to go into recession at the same time and would enter the recovery phase of the cycle at the same time then that disagreement about best interest rate policy would be less likely to occur. Figures 1.3–1.5 show that growth rates sometimes vary greatly in the euro area in comparison to those in some of the Baltic, Nordic and Visegrád countries during specific time periods. This could cause conflict when the ECB determines its interest rates if they were all in the euro area. (see Box 1.2).

Table 1.4 The euro area and the Baltic, Nordic and Visegrád countries, 1992–2015

1992	Denmark granted opt-outs from participating in the euro.
1999	Finland becomes a member of the euro area and adopts the euro.
2003	Sweden decides not to adopt the euro for the time being in a referendum.
2009	Slovakia becomes a member of the euro area and adopts the euro.
2011	Estonia becomes a member of the euro area and adopts the euro.
2014	Latvia becomes a member of the euro area and adopts the euro.
2015	Lithuania becomes a member of the euro area and adopts the euro.

Source: compiled by the author based on European Commission (2021b).

Box 1.2 GDP in constant prices (% change) in the Baltic, Nordic and Visegrád countries

Figures 1.3–1.5 show the different GDP growth rates from 2004 to 2021 in the Baltic, Nordic and Visegrád countries compared to those of the euro area member states. When the GDP growth rate is very different in individual countries compared to those in the euro area, monetary policy at the ECB can be suitable for one country but not the others.

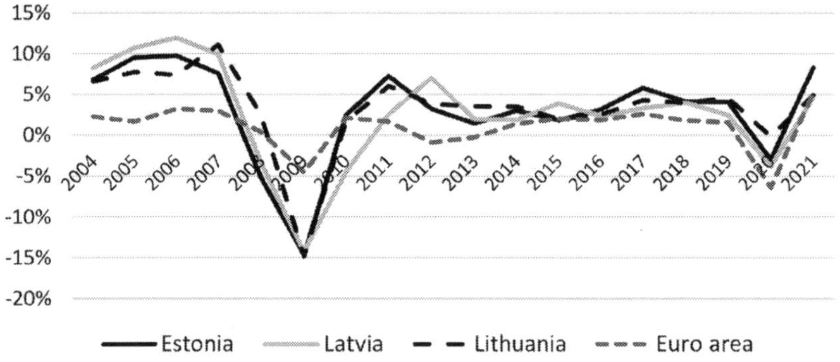

Figure 1.3 GDP in constant prices (% change) from 2004 to 2021 in the Baltic states compared to the euro area member states

Source: IMF (2022).

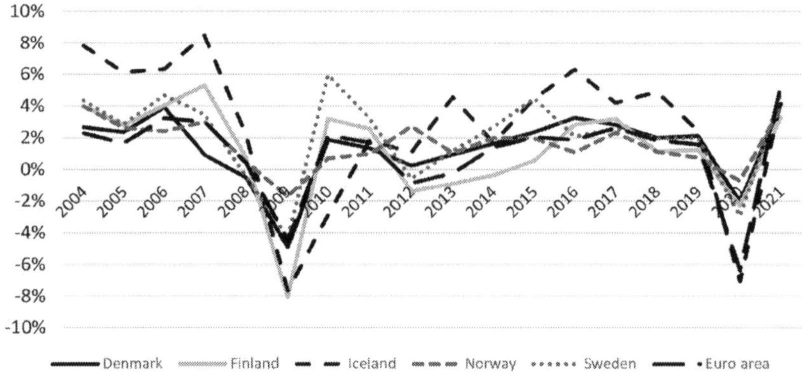

Figure 1.4 GDP in constant prices (% change) from 2004–21 in the Nordic countries compared to the euro area member states

Source: IMF (2022).

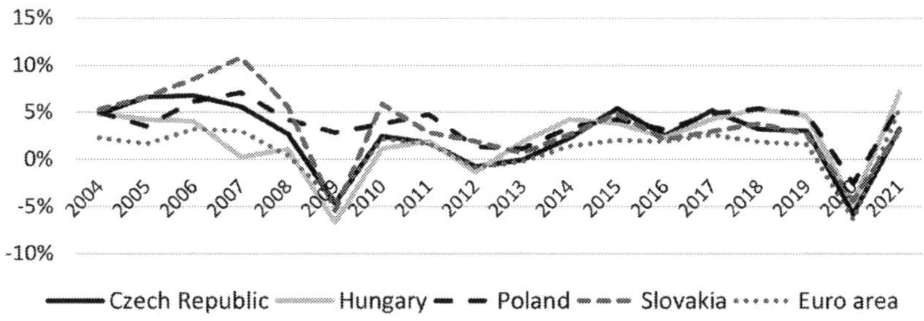

Figure 1.5 GDP in constant prices (% change) in the Visegrád countries from 2004–21 compared to the euro area member states
Source: IMF (2022).

Proximity with Russia and European integration

As Figure 1.1 shows, the closer a small power is to a large power the higher level of integration the small power tends to choose. All the Baltic, Nordic and Visegrád countries that are both EU and euro area member states either border Russia (as is the case with Estonia, Finland, Latvia and Lithuania), or like Slovakia they have a border with an unstable country under Russian influence, in this case Ukraine, now under attack from Russia. Unlike Slovakia, the Czech Republic, which is surrounded by EU member states, has not adopted the euro.

US-backed NATO security: the US security umbrella

All the Baltic, Nordic and Visegrád countries are NATO member states, except Finland and Sweden. They thus fall under the so-called US security umbrella. Russia has for years warned that it would respond to any move by Finland or Sweden to join NATO (see, for example, Borger 2016). Instead of formally joining NATO, both Finland and Sweden have worked in partnership with NATO and with the US in particular. Both countries have participated in NATO military exercises. EU membership provides these countries an added sense of security and Finland's euro area membership also further links the country with the West. Formal NATO membership is a move that these two Nordic countries have hesitated to take due to Russian opposition. However, in 2022 both countries applied for full membership of NATO. Their applications are linked to the Russian invasion of Ukraine.

It was no coincidence that both Finland and Sweden became members of the EU in 1995. When the Soviet Union collapsed in 1991 Russia was weak, and this encouraged them to apply to join the EU. During the Ukraine crisis that was ongoing in 2022 Russia appeared weaker militarily than many had expected, and both Finland and Sweden seized the opportunity to apply for membership of NATO.

Initially NATO had 12 founding member states but currently they are 30 (see Table 1.5). The most recent newcomer is North Macedonia, which became a member in 2020.

Table 1.5 NATO membership,[10] 1949–2020

1949	Belgium, Canada, *Denmark*, France, *Iceland*, Italy, Luxembourg, the Netherlands, *Norway*, Portugal, the UK, the US.
1952	Greece, Turkey
1955	West Germany
1982	Spain
1999	*The Czech Republic, Hungary, Poland*
2004	Bulgaria, *Estonia, Latvia, Lithuania*, Romania, *Slovakia*, Slovenia
2009	Albania, Croatia
2017	Montenegro
2020	North Macedonia

Source: compiled by the author based on NATO (2021a).

Note: The names of the Baltic, Nordic and Visegrád countries are italicized.

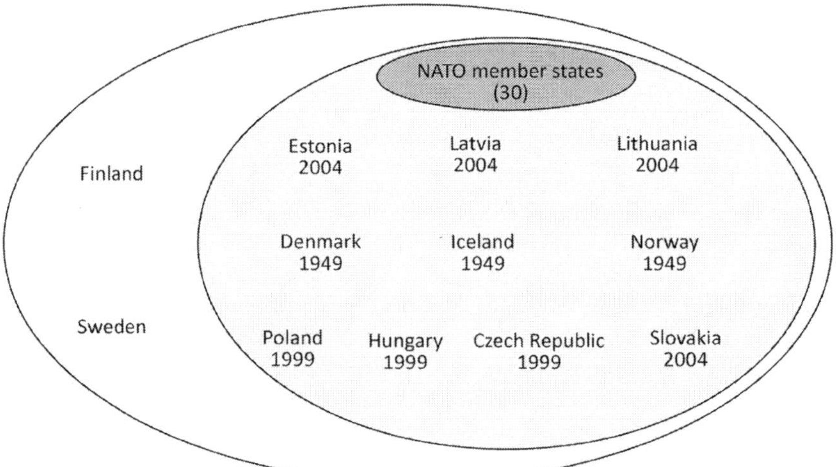

Figure 1.6 NATO membership among the Baltic, Nordic and Visegrád countries
Source: compiled by the author based on NATO (2021a).

Russia fiercely opposes any further expansion of NATO up to its borders as was demonstrated in 2008 at a NATO meeting held in Bucharest, Romania, when it was suggested that Georgia and Ukraine should become member states[11] (NATO 2008). Recently Russia insisted that Ukraine will never become a NATO member state, a guarantee that NATO has not been willing to provide arguing that as a sovereign country Ukraine can and should choose its own destiny. This dispute was the cause, or at least contributed to the Russian decision to invade Ukraine in February 2022.

But there are also disputes within NATO. European NATO member states have been criticized for failing to meet the target of 2% of GDP on defence expenditure. As Table 1.6 shows, all the Baltic states, Poland and Norway meet this target. All these countries border Russia. Estonia and Latvia lie to the east of Russia, Lithuania to the south and borders Kaliningrad (Russia), Poland is located on the northern borders with Kaliningrad (Russia) and Norway has a northern border with Russia. Although geography is not the only explanatory factor, it does explain a great deal about countries' defence strategies and foreign policies, including their choice of allies.

NATO was founded in 1949 by allied countries with the signing of the North Atlantic Treaty, more popularly known as the Washington Treaty (NATO 2021b).[13] Its original members were Belgium, Canada, Denmark, France, Iceland, Italy, Luxembourg, the Netherlands, Norway, Portugal, the UK and the US.[14] Three of its founding members were Nordic countries (see Table 1.5 and Figure 1.6).

Table 1.6 Defence expenditure as a share of GDP among the Baltic, Nordic and Visegrád countries based on 2015 prices[12]

	2013	*2014*	*2015*	*2016*	*2017*	*2018*	*2019e*	*2020e*
Czech Republic	1.03	0.95	1.03	0.96	1.04	1.12	1.18	1.43
Denmark	1.23	1.15	1.11	1.15	1.15	1.28	1.31	1.47
Estonia	1.90	1.92	2.01	2.07	2.02	2.00	2.03	2.38
Hungary	0.95	0.86	0.91	1.01	1.21	1.02	1.27	1.33
Latvia*	0.93	0.93	1.04	1.45	1.60	2.07	2.03	2.32
Lithuania*	0.76	0.88	1.14	1.48	1.71	1.98	2.02	2.28
Norway	1.50	1.55	1.59	1.74	1.72	1.74	1.86	2.03
Poland*	1.72	1.85	2.22	1.99	1.89	2.02	2.02	2.30
Slovakia	0.98	0.99	1.12	1.12	1.11	1.23	1.71	1.86

Source: compiled by the author based on NATO (2020).

Note: Figures for 2019 and 2020 are estimates.

*These allies have national laws and political agreements which call for 2% of GDP to be spent on defence annually; consequently, estimates are expected to change accordingly. For the past few years, allies' defence spending has been based on the then available GDP data and allies may, therefore, have met the 2% guideline when using those figures, (In 2018 Lithuania met the 2% target, according to November 2018 OECD figures).

NATO versus the Warsaw Pact

NATO's initial task was to address the Soviet threat in a bipolar world that was at the time dominated by two great powers, namely the US and the USSR. The Soviet Union and its allies joined a separate alliance under the Warsaw Pact[15] (see Table 1.7 and Box 1.3). The Warsaw Pact countries originally comprised the Soviet Union, Albania, Bulgaria, Czechoslovakia, East Germany, Hungary, Poland and Romania (see Table 1.7).

All the Visegrád countries were members of the Warsaw Pact. At the time, the Czech Republic and the Slovakia formed a single country, Czechoslovakia. All the Baltic states were parties to the Warsaw Pact under the umbrella of the Soviet Union as they were then Soviet republics.

The principle of collective defence is enshrined in Article 5 of the Washington Treaty. If one NATO member state is attacked, the others should come to its aid. The exact wording of Article 5 is as follows:

> The Parties agree that an armed attack against one or more of them in Europe or North America shall be considered an attack against them all and consequently they agree that, if such an armed attack occurs, each of them, in exercise of the right of individual or collective self-defence recognised by Article 51 of the Charter of the United Nations, will assist the Party or Parties so attacked by taking forthwith, individually and in concert with the other Parties, such action as it deems necessary, including the use of armed force, to restore and maintain the security of the North Atlantic area.
>
> Any such armed attack and all measures taken as a result thereof shall immediately be reported to the Security Council. Such measures shall be terminated when the Security Council has taken the measures necessary to restore and maintain international peace and security.
>
> (NATO 2021b)[17]

The Warsaw Pact also was a collective defence treaty. Formally it was known as the Treaty of Friendship, Co-operation and Mutual Assistance. The Warsaw Pact was created on 14 May 1955, immediately after the accession of

Table 1.7 Warsaw Pact membership, 1955–1991[16]

1955	Albania, Bulgaria, *Czechoslovakia*, East Germany, *Hungary*, *Poland*, Romania and the Soviet Union.
1968	Albania withdraws.
1991	The break-up of the Warsaw Pact was quickly followed by the dissolution of the Soviet Union in December 1991. Eventually all the Warsaw Pact Soviet satellite states and the Baltic states, previously Soviet republics, joined NATO.

Source: compiled by the author based on NATO (2021c).

Note: The names of the Visegrád countries are italicized.

West Germany to NATO. It complemented the Council for Mutual Economic Assistance, which was the regional economic organization established by the Soviet Union in January 1949 for the communist states of Central and Eastern Europe.

The Warsaw Pact embodied what was referred to as the Eastern bloc, while NATO and its member countries represented the Western bloc. NATO and the Warsaw Pact were ideologically opposed and, over time, built up their own defences thereby starting an arms race that lasted throughout the Cold War.

The fall of the Berlin Wall in November 1989 marked the end of the Cold War and communist governments in Poland, Hungary, Czechoslovakia, East Germany, Romania and Bulgaria started to collapse. The Warsaw Pact was declared at an end on 25 February 1991 and the President of Czechoslovakia, Vaclav Havel, formally declared an end to it on 1 July 1991.[18]

Former leader of the Soviet Union Mikhail Gorbachev's policy of openness ('glasnost') and restructuring ('perestroika'), together with other initiatives, paved the way for popular uprisings. The break-up of the Warsaw Pact was rapidly followed by the dissolution of the Soviet Union in December 1991. With the collapse of the Soviet Union the world ceased to be bipolar and instead became unipolar lead by the US. This followed the enlargement of the EU and NATO, including all the Baltic states and the Visegrád countries. (see Table 1.1).

The new EU member states and other states that had once been linked to the Soviet Union, either as Soviet satellite states or Soviet republics, view the US, NATO's largest military power, as their security guarantor. The major powers in the EU, Germany and France, do not play such an important role as the US does and in fact they too tend to view the US as their security guarantor in Europe. The UK usually also follows the US lead on security.

This situation is consistent with the US goal to dominate Europe and its being without a peer competitor in the region that could become a hegemon in Europe and challenge US authority. While Germany and Russia are both powerful European states, they can hardly dominate Europe as regional hegemons. Germany has wealth but an insufficient population for the task, while Russia lacks the wealth and its population is declining. Furthermore, the country's economy is too dependent on its oil and gas exports.

Box 1.3 The Warsaw Pact[19]

The Warsaw Pact (1955–91) was a treaty establishing a mutual defence organization known as the Warsaw Treaty Organization, and originally comprised the Soviet Union, Albania, Bulgaria, Czechoslovakia, East Germany, Hungary, Poland and Romania. The treaty provided for a unified military command and for the maintenance of Soviet military units on the territories of the other participating states.

The Warsaw Pact was the first step in a more systematic plan to strengthen the Soviet hold over its satellite states. The treaty also served as a lever to enhance the bargaining position of the Soviet Union in international diplomacy, an inference that may be drawn by the concluding article of the treaty, which stipulated that the Warsaw agreement would lapse when a general East-West collective security pact should come into force.

The Warsaw Pact, particularly its provision for the garrisoning of Soviet troops in satellite territories, became a target of nationalist hostility in Poland and Hungary during the uprisings in those two countries in 1956. The Soviet Union invoked the treaty when it decided to move Warsaw Pact troops into Czechoslovakia in August 1968 to bring the Czechoslovak regime back into the fold after it had begun lifting restraints on freedom of expression and had sought closer relations with the West.

After the democratic revolutions of 1989 in Eastern Europe, the Warsaw Pact became moribund and was formally declared 'non-existent' on 1 July 1991. Deployed Soviet troops were gradually withdrawn from the former satellite states, now politically independent countries. The decades-long confrontation between Eastern and Western Europe was formally rejected by members of the Warsaw Pact, all of which, with the exception of the Soviet successor state of Russia, subsequently joined NATO.

(Britannica 2021)

From unipolarity to multipolarity: the rise of China, Russian recovery post-Soviet Union and the Chinese-Russian partnership

Currently US power is being challenged as the world moves from unipolarity to multipolarity. A multipolar world dominated by great power rivalry is more dangerous than a unipolar world. And the problems no longer exist solely between states such as the US, Russia and China. Terrorism is now also a serious problem and terrorists are increasingly difficult to track down. A major terrorist attack was perpetrated against the US mainland on 11 September 2001 (known as 9/11), followed by a 20-year-long war in Afghanistan that proved very costly for the US and its allies. Wars have also taken place in other countries such as Iraq, Libya and the Syrian Arab Republic.

Arguably US engagement in wars since the collapse of the Soviet Union, when it gained the status of being the only remaining superpower in a unipolar world, has resulted in it overextending its economic and military power. In 2021 the US withdrew its troops from Afghanistan and the Taliban returned to power. Two decades of war with huge costs and losses on both sides have resulted in nothing. This was not a war within Europe or North America; however, NATO was involved, and its member states were under pressure from the US to take part in and contribute to this effort that was often called a 'war on terror'. Many American allies directed their bilateral development contributions to Afghanistan at least in part to please the US and in hope for NATO protection in return. They wanted to place themselves firmly under the US security umbrella.

The rise of China as a potential hegemon in Asia is serious challenge for US world dominance. China, with its huge population and growing wealth, is the most formidable competitor the US has ever seen. Although the US economy has grown in absolute terms it is relatively weaker than it was especially if one considers its position in the world in 1944 at the Bretton Woods conference or during the formation of NATO in 1949. Should China reach the per capita GDP of the Republic of Korea (South Korea), Hong Kong or Singapore it will become two to four times the size of the US economy. Fighting such an opponent would be a serious challenge for the US, already overextended economically and militarily, unless it has very powerful like-minded allies.

Donald Trump was elected president of the US in 2016. He entered the Oval Office with a more isolationist policy agenda than his predecessors in terms of military engagement, but also in international trade. During his election campaign he repeatedly stated that NATO was obsolete and that the level of burden-sharing among NATO member states was unfair. President Trump saw the US as being taken advantage of everywhere especially by rich European allies such as Germany.

In addition to frictions with NATO, President Trump was averse to forming trade agreements with either Europe or Asia. The refusal to proceed with a trade agreement in Asia, the Trans-Pacific Partnership, which excluded China, appears to be a major strategic mistake on the part of the US.[20] Negotiations towards a trade agreement with Europe, the Transatlantic Trade and Investment Partnership, were launched in 2013 and ended without conclusion at the end of 2016.[21]

For the Baltic, Nordic and Visegrád countries security in Europe remains the primary concern. At the Brussels NATO summit held on 14 June 2021 communiqué tensions with Russia received a lot of attention. According to the communiqué:

> Russia's growing multi-domain military build-up, more assertive posture, novel military capabilities, and provocative activities, including near NATO borders, as well as its large-scale no-notice and snap exercises, the continued military build-up in Crimea, the deployment of modern dual-capable missiles in Kaliningrad, military integration with Belarus, and repeated violations of NATO Allied airspace, increasingly threaten the security of the Euro-Atlantic area and contribute to instability along NATO borders and beyond.
>
> (NATO 2021d)[22]

Thus, Russia remains a key concern for NATO. However, with the rise of China and Chinese cooperation with Russia, Asian is also a growing concern for NATO:

> China's stated ambitions and assertive behaviour present systemic challenges to the rules-based international order and to areas relevant to Alliance [NATO] security. We are concerned by those coercive policies which stand in contrast to the fundamental values enshrined in the Washington Treaty … China is rapidly expanding its nuclear arsenal with more warheads and a larger number of sophisticated delivery systems to establish a nuclear triad. It is opaque in implementing its military modernisation and its publicly declared military-civil fusion strategy. It is also cooperating militarily with Russia, including through participation in Russian exercises in the Euro-Atlantic area.
>
> (NATO 2021d)[23] [24]

Under Joe Biden, elected to the presidency in 2020, the US is using NATO to further its own global interests outside Europe, especially in Asia. This is in contrast to the Washington Treaty that focused on security in Europe and North America. This twist to use NATO in Asia endangers NATO's credibility:

> We are enhancing political dialogue and practical cooperation with our long-standing Asia-Pacific partners – Australia, Japan, New Zealand, and the Republic of Korea – to promote cooperative security and support the rules-based international order. We will discuss common approaches to global security challenges where NATO's interests are affected, share perspectives through deeper political engagement, and seek concrete areas for cooperation to address shared concerns.
>
> (NATO 2021d)[25]

This comes in addition to US criticism that the NATO member states in Europe are not contributing fairly to NATO operations. Therefore, the question must be asked whether NATO member states should increase their contributions to NATO in order to engage in Asia, which is clearly not part of Europe or North America, that it was intended to defend.

Moreover, NATO's credibility in Europe is being questioned by the West. For example, in an interview conducted in 2019 the President of France, Emmanuel Macron, described NATO as 'braindead'.[26] President Macron questioned US commitment to the guarantees provided for under NATO's Article 5. Thus, Europe may need take its fate into its own hands and become a global power. However, this comes at a time when Europe is divided, and the EU and the euro area are confronting problems that have been exacerbated by the COVID-19 crisis and the ongoing war in Ukraine.

New EU member states such as the Baltic and the Visegrád countries have often supported the US and its operations outside Europe in the hope for

US-backed NATO security. Baltic involvement in Afghanistan is a good example of this. But these new EU member states are not of any significant strategic importance for the US. The Baltic states are, for example, more important for Russia than they are for the US. The US more interested in containing China and being in control of the Persian Gulf than in Europe. So, what should small states do?

China is showing more interest in Europe, including infrastructure investment. This could later translate into military influence. The US may be unwilling and unable to respond. Do smaller EU and European states want to rely on and be under German and French control against Russia?

Continued US dominance in Europe and European cooperation with China

From the US point of view, it made sense in 1949 to protect Europe via NATO given the threat posed by the Soviet Union. The Marshall Plan also was a great investment in the future of Europe and the US. Following the collapse of the Soviet Union, US interest in Europe waned and the growing threat of China in Asia further diminished US interest in Europe. Some would argue that the US is now overextended economically and militarily and that as a result the US has begun to use NATO to promote its own interests outside Europe. This trend was already visible in the communiqué released at the NATO summit held in Brussels in 2021 (NATO 2021d).[27] The US is already more interested in Asia and countries located in the Persian Gulf than in Europe. Arguably the conflict in Ukraine has delayed this process. However, it is expected that NATO will form an informal or formal alliance with Japan and South Korea, and also with Australia and New Zealand. Moreover, NATO may also want to form an alliance with India. These activities in Asia that are designed to counter China and those in the Persian Gulf to protect US oil interests are increasingly in US interests rather than providing support for the Baltic, Nordic and Visegrád countries. In fact, the new EU member states may in the longer term have an interest in cooperating with China for more trade and for much-needed infrastructure investment that they cannot afford themselves to bolster the eastern flank of Europe. The US may also in the longer term have an interest in forming better relations with Russia because of the competition with China. Russia could in the distant future be a valuable ally for the US in the Middle East, but this would not necessarily be welcomed by the Baltic states, not to mention Ukraine and Georgia, who seek membership of NATO for their protection.

Russia could also in the long term become a valuable ally for the US in the Arctic. In fact, Chinese interest and involvement in the Arctic could result in tensions between China and Russia. So, while the US and Western Europe's interests were compatible in 1949 this is less obvious in today's world. NATO may increasingly look obsolete especially if the US either cannot or does not want to engage in Europe anymore. But if the US leaves NATO another country could fill the void. This could also result in greater German and French domination in the EU. Smaller, weaker EU member states, especially those that joined from 2004 onwards, may look to China for more engagement, trade and investment. An example of this is the 17+1 Initiative (now 16+1 after the departure of Lithuania).

If the US loses it foothold in Europe, it may find it difficult or indeed impossible to regain it. An exit from Europe and NATO could result in current European partners viewing the US as an unreliable partner. If the US continues to support NATO it will probably want to engage NATO and NATO member states in areas of its own interest outside Europe where European countries have no obvious interest. Afghanistan is an example of this from which US recently withdrew. Engagement in Asia because of the rise of China is another example.

Major powers in Europe, Germany and France

For major powers in Europe, continued US dominance may no longer be feasible, especially for countries seeking a higher level of integration in Europe such as France and Germany. Indeed, some have called for the creation of a United States of Europe. For example, the French president has called for Europe to become a global power. The former chancellor of Germany, Angela Merkel, in response to remarks by the former US President, Donald Trump, that the fate of Europe lies in its own hands. Tensions with the US and a weaker NATO may be in the interests of those who want a bigger Europe in terms of closer integration, not only economically, but politically and with closer military cooperation through the development of a European army with more European military equipment. Despite the imposition of sanctions on Russia following its military invasion of Ukraine, Germany sought closer economic ties with Russia most notably through it support for the development of the key Nord Stream 2 gas pipeline. However, Russia's incursion into Ukraine brought the project to a halt.

Germany also has an interest in cooperation with China. It might be in Germany's long-term interest to drive the US and its interests out of Europe and for Germany to strive to become a regional hegemon in Europe empowered by its control of the EU that also creates an advantage for Germany vis-à-vis Russia. Tensions with the US may thus be regarded as advantageous for the large European powers. Why would Germany and France want to remain in thrall to the US?

What does this mean for small states/powers in Europe?

For small states in Europe, including those that are the focus of this book, continued US presence in Europe is feasible, especially for the vulnerable Baltic countries, small countries with a large Russian minority population, and those that share a border with Russia. Finland is also vulnerable and although it is not a NATO member state it is in close contact with NATO and NATO member states and has now applied for full membership.

For the Visegrád countries, Poland, which borders Russia (Kaliningrad), Belarus and Ukraine, the US presence in Europe is obviously important. Poland has historically had very tense relations with Russia. It is understandable that small states such as the Baltics regard the US as their security guarantor and are willing to take part in NATO missions in countries such as Afghanistan to please the US. It is unlikely that the Baltic countries would have participated in a war in this part of the world unless such military engagement was viewed positively by the White House. Arguably the US and NATO are exploiting the Baltic countries' vulnerability to encourage them to take part in activities that they would normally avoid. Even Poland – a large country by European standards – has been vulnerable historically given its position between two more powerful states, Germany and Russia. Poland too appreciates security guarantee offered by the US via NATO and the other three Visegrád countries are also all NATO member states. The Nordic countries also have an interest in maintaining a US military presence in Europe.

For all the countries in the three groups discussed in this book the rise of China means that they need to rethink their relationship with the US if it reduces its military presence in Europe and NATO is increasingly pushed to operate outside the Euro Atlantic area that it was initially intended to defend. This is not an easy task as the US as a democracy is closer to European values than China with its single-party system and Russia that is often considered an authoritarian regime. The new Cold War will not primarily be in Europe, but in East Asia. It is possible that Europe can continue its security cooperation with the US yet maintain good trade relations with China.

There is already competition between US and China in Europe. If one considers infrastructure investment in the eastern flank of Europe, the US backs the Three Seas Initiative that aims to promote cooperation for the development of infrastructure in the energy, transport and digital sectors, while China is pursuing the 17+1 (16+1) Initiative. Despite ongoing tensions between Russia, the Baltic states, Poland and Ukraine, Germany has enjoyed relatively good trade relations with Russia. Germany might also support the 17+1 initiative; it also provides generous bilateral development aid to China.

The different approaches to European integration and NATO membership

Clearly European integration is important for the the Baltic, Nordic and the Visegrád countries. NATO membership is also key to their security.

The Nordic countries

It is no coincidence that the Nordic group has the lowest level of European integration of the three country groups under study. Nevertheless, European integration is important for all the Nordic countries, especially access to the EU internal market. It is not surprising that Finland and Sweden joined the EU in 1995 following the collapse of the Soviet Union in 1991 and Finland went further and adopted the euro in 1999. The Soviet Union would not have welcomed the prospect of Sweden joining the EU or of Finland joining both the EU and the euro area, as the two countries have for a long time maintained a neutral status. EU membership has increased these two countries' safety, and Finland's decision to join the euro area provided additional security. An attack on the currency union would be considered a serious issue by leading countries in the EU such as Germany and France. Joining NATO remains a very sensitive issue especially in Finland with its long eastern border with Russia. Finland and Sweden cooperate with NATO but without having formal NATO membership. Finland is more vulnerable to an attack by Russia and it is also a buffer state for Sweden. The ongoing conflict in Ukraine encouraged both countries to apply for NATO membership.

Iceland and Norway participate in European integration via EFTA/EEA and both were founding member states of NATO in 1949. Denmark joined the EEC in 1973 and was also a founding member of NATO. European integration, especially access to the common market, can bring greater economic prosperity and stability to the Nordic countries as well as security. However, EU fiscal rules can be an obstacle for economic growth and stability as they hinder the activation of automatic stabilizers during recessions. However, such rules only apply to the Nordic EU member states, namely Denmark, Finland and Sweden, not to Iceland and Norway. Membership of NATO and other partnerships have helped to increase the security of Denmark, Iceland and Norway.

The Nordic countries are wealthier than the two other country groups, and a lower level of European integration allows for a more flexible economic policy given that Finland is in the euro area and the Nordic countries do not feel as threatened by Russia as the Baltics, with the exception of Finland with its long eastern border with Russia. Norway's northern border with Russia has not so far been viewed as a serious security threat for Norway. Prior to the collapse of the Soviet Union, the Nordic countries were all democracies, had well developed government institutions and a functioning market economy, and did not need EU integration and institutions to achieve the same goals as the Baltic states and the Visegrád countries (see below). They were more confident about making their own choices when the European integration process started and intensified over the years. They picked only what they wanted.

The Baltic states

The Baltic states were under Soviet rule until 1991. Thereafter, they needed to build new institutions, make the transition from a centrally planned to a market economy and introduce democracy in their national decision-making. EU accession helped them to get on track and EU membership in 2004 helped them to stay on track. Their commitment to joining the euro area brought stability but also reduced their flexibility in economic policymaking, and this became visible during the 2008/09 global financial crisis. Being members of a currency union (Estonia in 2011, Latvia in 2014 and Lithuania in 2015) brought more security to the Baltics. Becoming NATO member states in 2004 was also seen as key to increased Baltic security and survival. Given the threat posed by Russia it is understandable that the Baltic states have sought as much integration with the West as they can get. The Baltics have tried to develop a strong security relationship with the US, and as the largest military power in NATO the US is able to offer these countries guarantees under Article 5. The rise of China and the US pivot to Asia is likely to become a growing concern for Baltic security. The possible resumption of cooperation between Russia and Germany via the Nord Stream 2 pipeline once the war in Ukraine is over is also of great concern for the Baltic countries.

The Visegrád countries

In terms of European integration, the Visegrád countries go further than the Nordics, but are less integrated than the Baltics. All of them have been EU member states since 2004. Poland is the only Visegrád country that borders Russia, and it has the most tense relations with Russia of all the Visegrád countries. Slovakia borders Ukraine and is the only country in the group to have adopted the euro since 2009. Following the dissolution of the Soviet Union, the Visegrád countries had to make the transition to a market economy, reform their institutions and introduce representative democracy. EU accession and then EU membership supported this effort. All the Visegrád countries are NATO member states, Hungary, Poland and the Czech Republic since 1999 and Slovakia since the 2004. All the Visegrád countries are located close to and engage in extensive trade with Germany. The Visegrád countries have opposed EU immigration policies; Hungary is especially vulnerable due to its geographic location, including the southernmost border of Schengen, and recently Poland has faced a crisis at its border with Belarus. Like the Baltic countries, Poland was very concerned about the level of German-Russian cooperation on the Nord Stream 2 pipeline project.

Notes

1 www.efta.int/eea/eea-agreement.

2 https://ec.europa.eu/home-affairs/what-we-do/schengen-borders-and-visa/schengen-visa_en.
3 https://european-union.europa.eu/index_en.
4 www.efta.int/about-efta/the-efta-states.
5 https://ec.europa.eu/info/business-economy-euro/euro-area/what-euro-area_en.
6 www.nato.int/cps/en/natohq/topics_52044.htm.
7 www.economist.com/special-report/1999/10/21/my-continent-right-or-wrong.
8 Also known as a currency union or monetary union.
9 The Baltics, Finland and Slovakia.
10 NATO member states: www.nato.int/nato-welcome/index.html.
11 *Bucharest Summit Declaration Issued by the Heads of State and Government Participating in the Meeting of the North Atlantic Council in Bucharest on 3 April 2008*. See www.nato.int/cps/en/natolive/official_texts_8443.htm.
12 www.nato.int/cps/en/natohq/news_178975.htm.
13 The foundations of NATO were officially laid down on 4 April 1949 with the signing of the North Atlantic Treaty, more popularly known as the Washington Treaty. See www.nato.int/cps/en/natolive/topics_67656.htm.
14 www.britannica.com/topic/North-Atlantic-Treaty-Organization.
15 The Warsaw Pact, formally the Warsaw Treaty of Friendship, Cooperation, and Mutual Assistance, (14 May 1955–1 July 1991) treaty established a mutual defence organization (the Warsaw Treaty Organization). See www.britannica.com/event/Warsaw-Pact.
16 www.nato.int/cps/us/natohq/declassified_138294.htm.
17 www.nato.int/cps/en/natolive/official_texts_17120.htm.
18 www.nato.int/cps/us/natohq/declassified_138294.htm.
19 www.britannica.com/event/Warsaw-Pact; and www.nato.int/cps/us/natohq/declassified_138294.htm.
20 www.cnbc.com/2017/11/11/trans-pacific-trade-deal-advances-without-united-states.html.
21 https://ec.europa.eu/trade/policy/in-focus/ttip/.
22 www.nato.int/cps/en/natohq/news_185000.htm.
23 Ibid.
24 Ibid.
25 Ibid.
26 www.economist.com/europe/2019/11/07/emmanuel-macron-warns-europe-nato-is-becoming-brain-dead.
27 www.nato.int/cps/en/natohq/news_185000.htm.

References

Borger, J. (2016). Finland Says It Is Nearing Security Deal with US Amid Concerns over Russia. *The Guardian*. Available at: www.theguardian.com/world/2016/aug/22/finland-us-russia-military-security (accessed 5 August 2021).

Britannica (2021). *Warsaw Pact Europe 1955–1991*. Available at: www.britannica.com/event/Warsaw-Pact (accessed 5 August 2021).

Czinkota, M. R., Ronkainen, I. A., Moffett, M. H., Marinova, S. and Marinov, M. (2009). *International Business* (European edn). Chichester: John Wiley & Sons.

European Commission (2021a). *The Schengen Visa*. Available at: https://home-affairs.ec.europa.eu/schengen-borders-and-visa/schengen-visa_en (accessed 6 August 2021).

European Commission (2021b). *What Is the Euro Area?* Available at: https://ec.europa.eu/info/business-economy-euro/euro-area/what-euro-area_en (accessed 6 August 2021).

European Union (EU) (2021). *Country Profiles.* Available at: https://european-union.europa.eu/principles-countries-history/country-profiles_en (accessed 6 July 2021).

European Free Trade Association (EFTA) (2021a). *EEA Agreement.* Available at: www.efta.int/eea/eea-agreement (accessed 7 July 2021).

European Free Trade Association (EFTA) (2021b). *The EFTA States. Information about the EFTA Member States: Iceland, Liechtenstein, Norway and Switzerland.* Available at: www.efta.int/about-efta/the-efta-states (accessed 7 July 2021).

European Free Trade Association (EFTA) (2014). *This Is EFTA.* Available at: www.efta.int/sites/default/files/publications/this-is-efta/this-is-efta-2014.pdf (accessed 5 August 2022).

Hilmarsson, H. Þ. (2016). Iceland and the Challenge of European Integration: Is European Union Membership Feasible? In L. Briguglio (ed.) *Small States and the European Union. Europa Economic Perspectives.* London and New York: Routledge.

International Monetary Fund (IMF) (2022). *World Economic Outlook Database, April.* Available at: www.imf.org/en/Publications/WEO/weo-database/2022/April.

Keohane, R. O. (1969). Lilliputians' Dilemmas: Small States in International Politics. *International Organizations*, 23(2), 291–310. Available at: www.jstor.org/stable/pdf/2706027.pdf?refreqid=excelsior%3Af5064b8bf0d9dfbea87c5bb2eed8840b (accessed 9 June 2021).

Mankiw, N. G. and Taylor, M. P. (2020). *Economics* (5th edn). Andover: Cengage.

North Atlantic Treaty Organization (NATO) (2021a). *Member Countries.* Available at: www.nato.int/cps/en/natohq/topics_52044.htm (accessed 6 July 2021).

North Atlantic Treaty Organization (NATO) (2021b). *Founding Treaty.* Available at: www.nato.int/cps/en/natolive/topics_67656.htm (accessed 6 July 2021).

North Atlantic Treaty Organization (NATO) (2021c). *What Was the Warsaw Pact?* Available at: www.nato.int/cps/us/natohq/declassified_138294.htm (accessed 6 July 2021).

North Atlantic Treaty Organization (NATO) (2021d). *Brussels Summit Communiqué. Issued by the Heads of State and Government Participating in the Meeting of the North Atlantic Council in Brussels on 14 June 2022.* Available at: www.nato.int/cps/en/natohq/news_185000.htm (accessed 6 July 2021).

North Atlantic Treaty Organization (NATO) (2020). *Defence Expenditure of NATO Countries (2013–2020).* Available at: www.nato.int/cps/en/natohq/news_178975.htm (accessed 5 August 2021).

North Atlantic Treaty Organization (NATO) (2008). *Bucharest Summit Declaration. Issued by the Heads of State and Government Participating in the Meeting of the North Atlantic Council in Bucharest on 3 April 2008.* Available at: www.nato.int/cps/en/natolive/official_texts_8443.htm (accessed 6 July 2021).

2 Participation in global and regional institutions and international relations theories

Participation in global institutions

All the countries discussed in the book have pursued global integration via membership of international/global organizations such as the Organization for Economic Co-operation and Development (OECD), the World Trade Organization (WTO), the World Bank, the International Monetary Fund (IMF), and the United Nations. They joined these institutions at different times for reasons that will be discussed in this chapter (see Table 2.1). In addition to being under the US security umbrella as discussed in the previous chapter, they are now all part of the international world order lead by the US that fundamentally was established after the Second World War at the Bretton Woods conference. The rule-based international institutional framework they live in was primarily written in Washington, DC.

The OECD is an international organization that seeks to build better policies for better lives in its member states. Its goal is to shape policies that foster prosperity, equality, opportunity and well-being. The OECD seeks to establish evidence-based international standards and to find solutions to a range of social, economic and environmental challenges.[1] The OECD Convention came into force and the work of the organization officially began in 1961. All the Nordic countries, with the exception of Finland, were founding members in 1961. Finland followed in 1969. The Visegrád countries joined after the dissolution of the Soviet Union: the Czech Republic in 1995, Hungary and Poland in 1996, and Slovakia in 2000. The Baltic states followed suit after joining the European Union (EU): Estonia in 2010, Latvia in 2016 and Lithuania in 2018.[2]

It is not surprising that the Nordic countries that were an integral part of the West would be early members of the OECD, followed by the Soviet satellite states, the Visegrád group, and then the former Soviet republics, the Baltic states. Membership of the OECD was an important signal to both the Visegrád group and the Baltic states that they were joining a group of advanced nations and adhering to Western standards and policies.

The WTO is the only global international organization dealing with the rules of trade between nations. At its heart are the WTO agreements,

DOI: 10.4324/9781003212539-3

negotiated and signed by the bulk of the world's trading nations and ratified by their parliaments. Its goal is to ensure that trade flows as smoothly, predictably and freely as possible.[3] Among the main functions of the WTO is administering its trade agreements, being a forum for trade negotiations, handling trade disputes, monitoring national trade policies, providing technical assistance and training for developing countries, and cooperation with other international organizations. The WTO succeeded the General Agreement on Tariffs and Trade (GATT) in 1947, which is still in effect under the WTO framework, but subject to modifications since the WTO took over its role on 1 January 1995. All the Nordic and Visegrád countries, except Poland, joined the WTO in January 1995. Poland joined six months later. Estonia and Latvia joined in 1999 and Lithuania in 2001 (see Table 2.1). Clearly becoming a member of the WTO was important for all the countries, but especially for the Baltic and Visegrád countries that had previously been subject to the Soviet central planning system. For these countries free trade with other nations was key to their future growth and prosperity.

All the Baltic, Nordic and Visegrád countries are now members of the Bretton Woods institutions, namely the World Bank (called the International Bank for Reconstruction and Development at the Bretton Woods Conference) and the IMF. The Bretton Woods Conference, formally known as the UN Monetary and Financial Conference, took place in Bretton Woods, New Hampshire, US, on 1–22 July 1944[4] (Schuler and Bernkopf 2014). However, the countries became members of the institutions at different times. The Nordic countries, Iceland and Norway, sent a delegation. Denmark had observer status. Iceland and Norway joined in 1945, Denmark in 1946, Finland in 1948 and Sweden in 1951. The Union of Soviet Socialist Republics (USSR) sent a delegation to the Bretton Woods Conference, but all the Baltic states became members in 1992 after the dissolution of the Soviet Union. The Visegrád countries, Czechoslovakia (now two separate countries, the Czech Republic – Czechia – and Slovakia) and Poland, sent delegations to the Bretton Woods Conference (see Schuler and Bernkopf 2014).

All the Baltic, Nordic and the Visegrád countries are members of the UN (see Table 2.1).

Participation in regional institutions

In contrast to participation in global institutions, participation in regional institutions such as the regional development banks varies across the countries and country groups discussed (see Table 2.2). These development banks are regional in the sense that they have a regional focus in terms of their operations, in contrast with the World Bank that engages in operations globally, i.e. across continents. Nevertheless, one needs to keep in mind that membership of the regional development banks can be global as they have non-regional contributing member states. The Baltic states have the most limited representation in the regional development banks discussed in the

Table 2.1 Participation of the Baltic, Nordic and Visegrád countries in global institutions

		Organization for Economic Cooperation and Development (OECD)[5]	*World Trade Organization (WTO)*[6]	*World Bank/IBRD*[7]	*International Monetary Fund (IMF)*[8]	*United Nations (UN)*[9]
Baltics						
	Estonia	9 December 2010	13 November 1999	23 June 1992	26 May 1992	17 September 1991
	Latvia	1 July 2016	10 February 1999	11 August 1992	19 May 1992	17 September 1991
	Lithuania	5 July 2018	31 May 2001	6 July 1992	29 April 1992	17 September 1991
Visegrád						
	Czech Republic	21 December 1995	1 January 1995	1 January 1993	27 December 1945[10]	19 January 1993
	Hungary	7 May 1996	1 January 1995	7 July 1982	6 May 1982	14 December 1955
	Poland	22 November 1996	1 July 1995	27 June 1986	10 January 1946[11]	24 October 1945
	Slovakia	14 December 2000	1 January 1995	1 January 1993	27 December 1945[12]	19 January 1993
Nordics						
	Denmark	30 May 1961	1 January 1995	30 March 1946	30 March 1946[13]	24 October 1945
	Finland	28 January 1969	1 January 1995	14 January 1948	14 January 1948	14 December 1955
	Iceland	5 June 1961	1 January 1995	27 December 1945	27 December 1945[14]	19 November 1946
	Norway	4 July 1961	1 January 1995	27 December 1945	27 December 1945[15]	27 November 1945
	Sweden	28 September 1961	1 January 1995	31 August 1951	31 August 1951	19 November 1946

Source: compiled by the author based on OECD (2021); WTO (2021); World Bank (2021); IMF (2021) and United Nations (2021).

book. In fact, the Baltics only participate in the EBRD. All the Visegrád countries participate in the EBRD, but two, Hungary and Poland, are also members of the China-led Asia Infrastructure Investment Bank (AIIB). The Nordics, except for Iceland, have a much wider regional representation. Denmark, Finland, Norway and Sweden are members of the African Development Bank (AfDB), the Asian Development Bank (ADB), the AIIB, the EBRD and the Inter-American Development Bank (IDB) and have a higher international profile than any of the other countries thereby reflecting their own interests in international affairs, size and wealth, and their global ambitions.

When one considers the membership (non-regional) of the AIIB that was established in 2016 it is notable, but perhaps not surprising, that all the continental Nordic countries are members while none of the Baltic states are members. The continental Nordic countries are likely to have become members owing to their wide participation in regional development institutions. However, it is more surprising is that Iceland became a member of AIIB, but never seriously considered membership of the AfDB, the ADB and the IDB. It is also interesting to note the participation of Hungary and Poland in the AIIB; perhaps like many other member states these countries are preparing themselves for the growing influence of the People's Republic of China in the world.

The establishment of the China-led AIIB was seen by many as a challenge to the Bretton Woods institutions led by the US and the ADB led by Japan. In fact, the US would have preferred to see its allies rejecting membership of the AIIB. Following the establishment of the AIIB, Lawrence Summers, the former US Treasury Secretary, World Bank Group Chief Economist and Harvard president and professor, was quoted in the *Washington Post* thus:

> This past month may be remembered as the moment the United States lost its role as the underwriter of the global economic system … With China's economic size rivaling that of the United States and emerging markets accounting for at least half of world output, the global economic architecture needs substantial adjustment. Political pressures from all sides in the United States have rendered the architecture increasingly dysfunctional.[16]

The US decided not to become a member of the AIIB and did not view the establishment of the AIIB as a welcome development. It prefers to lead the World Bank established under US leadership at the Bretton Woods meeting in 1944. Japan also decided not to join the AIIB and instead focuses on the ADB where it has long been the leading country.

During the Cold War the US maintained a permanent military presence at the Keflavík Air Base in Iceland, and therefore it was less likely that at that time Iceland would seek membership of a China-led institution whose establishment was not welcomed by the US. However, following the establishment of the AIIB, the US air defence force left Iceland unilaterally, clearly against the wishes of the Icelandic government. The bilateral defence agreement in place between Iceland and the US since 1951 is still valid to this day and Iceland remains a member of NATO; however, the US could no longer provide credible and visible defence for Iceland once the fighter planes had left the Keflavík air base. Given this situation there was less need for the Icelandic government to consider the US when deciding to join the AIIB. Also, the Icelandic government and Icelandic business saw growing business interest in Asia where membership of AIIB might help in the future.[17]

It was also unsurprising that the Baltic states chose not to join the AIIB since they are not members of the regional development banks except those where they can directly benefit from their participation i.e. in the EBRD. They are now members of the Nordic Investment Bank where they have obvious interests as borrowers, like all the other EU member states they have joined the European Investment Bank. The Baltics regard the US as their security guarantor and are unlikely to take steps that might upset Washington. The Visegrád countries, Hungary and Poland, did become members of the AIIB. Both countries also regard the US as their guarantor of security in Europe, but they are larger than the Baltics and are geographically further away from the mainland of the Russian Federation than the Baltic states.

The UK's membership of the AIIB was perhaps particularly surprising, not least because the UK is widely regarded as the closest ally of the US in Europe. In 2015 the then British Chancellor of the Exchequer, George Osborne, stated:

> I am delighted to announce today that the UK will be the first major Western country to become a prospective founder member of the Asian Infrastructure Investment Bank, which has already received significant support in the region.
>
> This government has actively promoted closer political and economic engagement with the Asia-Pacific region and forging links between the UK and Asian economies to give our companies the best opportunity to work and invest in the world's fastest growing markets is a key part of our long term economic plan. Joining the AIIB at the founding stage will create an unrivalled opportunity for the UK and Asia to invest and grow together.[18]

From this statement one can see that the UK is preparing for greater involvement in Asia, not only politically and economically, but also for greater private sector cooperation. The UK has realized that it is in the country's best interests to diversify and not to rely solely on US global leadership.

Overseas development assistance

In terms of contributions to overseas development assistance (ODA) the performances of the countries discussed in the book vary greatly. Of the Nordic countries, Denmark, Norway and Sweden are some of the very few

Table 2.2 Participation of the Baltic, Nordic and Visegrád countries in some regional development banks

		African Development Bank (AfDB)[19]	*Asian Development Bank (ADB)*[20]	*Asian Infrastructure Investment Bank (AIIB)*[21]	*European Bank for Reconstruction and Development (EBRD)*[22]	*Inter American Development Bank (IDB)*[23]
Baltics						
	Estonia	no	no	no	yes	no
	Latvia	no	no	no	yes	no
	Lithuania	no	no	no	yes	no
Visegrád						
	Czech Republic	no	no	no	yes	no
	Hungary	no	no	yes	yes	no
	Poland	no	no	yes	yes	no
	Slovakia	no	no	no	yes	no
Nordics						
	Denmark	yes	yes	yes	yes	yes
	Finland	yes	yes	yes	yes	yes
	Iceland	no	no	yes	yes	no
	Norway	yes	yes	yes	yes	yes
	Sweden	yes	yes	yes	yes	yes

Source: compiled by the author based on AfDB (2021); ADB (2021); AIIB (2021); EBRD (2021); IDB (2021).

countries in the world that meet the UN target of contributing 0.7% of their gross national income (GNI) to ODA.[24] According to OECD figures, in 2019 Denmark contributed 0.71% of its GNI to ODA, Norway 1.02% and Sweden 0.99%. Finland and Iceland lagged behind, with Finland contributing 0.42% of its GNI to ODA and Iceland 0.27%. Of the Visegrád countries, Hungary contributed 0.22% of its GNI to ODA, followed by the Czech Republic with 0.13%, and Poland and Slovakia with 0.12%.[25] As a percentage of GNI the contributions of the Baltic states also are known to be very small especially in comparison to those of the Nordic countries, but they were not listed in the source referred to above.

Participation and priorities in bilateral development cooperation

It is interesting to consider the priorities of countries and country groups in development cooperation as reflected in their choice of priority ODA destinations. This can among other things reflect their own priorities, their regional location, history, development and transition experience, as well as the priorities of powerful allies. Strong support from both the Baltic and the Visegrád countries for Ukraine is notable. These countries, especially the Baltics, tend to include less advanced transition countries in their list of top ODA recipient countries, while the Nordic countries focus more closely on the poorest countries in the world, especially in Africa. Continental Nordic support for Afghanistan is notable and may also be linked to these countries' membership of or partnerships with NATO and the US. Denmark and Norway have both recently held the position of secretary-general of NATO. NATO is mostly funded and led by the US, and most of its military infrastructure comes from the US.

Table 2.3 The top 10 recipient countries of Baltic states' ODA, 2018

Estonia	*Latvia*	*Lithuania*
Ukraine	Türkiye (formerly Turkey)	Ukraine
Türkiye (Turkey)	Georgia	Belarus
Afghanistan	Ukraine	Türkiye (Turkey)
Georgia	Uzbekistan	Georgia
Moldova	China	Moldova
Syria	Azerbaijan	Mali
West Bank and Gaza Strip	Kazakhstan	Azerbaijan
Belarus	Kyrgyzstan	Armenia
Iraq	Moldova	West Bank and Gaza Strip
Uganda	Tajikistan	China

Source: compiled by the author based on OECD (2020).

If one considers the Baltic states (see Table 2.3), they tend to support transition countries that used to be part of the former Soviet Union and countries supported by the EU or the US. In 2018 there was strong support for Ukraine which was the largest recipient of Estonian and Lithuanian ODA; it was the third largest recipient of Latvian ODA. There is strong support for Türkiye (formerly Turkey) that could be reflected in Baltic EU and NATO memberships. Georgia and Moldova, both of which are less advanced transition countries, receive assistance from all the Baltic states. Lithuania and Estonia support Belarus. Estonian support for Afghanistan may be linked to NATO and alliance with the US.

In short, in 2018 Estonia's bilateral ODA was primarily focused on Eastern Europe. Latvia's bilateral ODA was primarily focused on ODA-eligible countries in Europe and Asia. Finally, in that year Lithuania's bilateral ODA was primarily focused on its own region.

The continental Nordic countries are large providers of ODA. Strong support for Afghanistan and the Syrian Arab Republic is notable when one considers Nordic ODA for 2018 (see Table 2.4). This prioritization could be NATO-related. Transition countries such as Ukraine, Georgia, Moldova and Belarus, all of which are supported by the Baltic states, are not the largest recipients of Nordic country ODA. There is support for some sub-Saharan countries such as Tanzania, Ethiopia, Kenya, Somalia, Mozambique, Uganda, Ghana and Malawi. While geographically dispersed, Norway's top 10 recipients of ODA reflect its policy focus on stabilization and conflict prevention, with seven of its top 10 recipients considered fragile.

Table 2.4 Top 10 recipients of Nordic countries' ODA, 2018

Denmark	*Finland*	*Iceland*	*Norway*	*Sweden*
Afghanistan	Ethiopia	Malawi	Syria	Afghanistan
Syria	Afghanistan	Uganda	Afghanistan	Tanzania
Tanzania	Nepal	Mozambique	Brazil	Somalia
Ghana	Kenya	Syria	West Bank and Gaza Strip	Ethiopia
Kenya	Tanzania	Yemen	South Sudan	Congo, Democratic Republic of
Burkina Faso	Indonesia	Sierra Leon	Somalia	Mozambique
Türkiye (Turkey)	Somalia	West Bank and Gaza Strip	Lebanon	Syria
Uganda	Mozambique	Liberia	Ethiopia	West Bank and Gaza Strip
Mozambique	Syria	Ethiopia	Malawi	Uganda
Bangladesh	Myanmar	Afghanistan	Colombia	Zambia

Source: compiled by the author based on OECD (2020).

In sum, bilateral ODA in 2018 from Denmark, Finland, Norway and Sweden was primarily focused on Africa, the Middle East and Asia. Iceland's bilateral ODA was primarily focused on Africa.

All the Visegrád countries have Ukraine among their top 10 ODA recipient countries and Ukraine is the leading recipient of ODA in Poland (see Table 2.5). Support for Bosnia and Herzegovina and for Serbia is to be expected given the ties that exist between the Visegrád countries and the Western Balkans. There is also support for less advanced transition countries such as Belarus, Moldova and Georgia, but less focus on Africa than that shown by the Nordics, but one can find ODA contributions for Kenya, Ethiopia, South Sudan and Zambia. Support for Syria and Türkiye (Turkey) may be related to EU and NATO membership and US relations. In short, in 2018 the Czech Republic's bilateral ODA was primarily focused on Europe. Hungary's bilateral ODA was primarily focused on Asia and the Middle East. Poland's bilateral ODA was primarily focused on Europe and Asia. Slovakia's bilateral ODA was focused on Africa, Europe and the Middle East.

If one considers the ODA provided by the EU institutions, France, Germany and the US, strong support from Germany for Asia is notable, with China being the third largest recipient of ODA (see Table 2.6). EU institutions' strong support for Türkiye (Turkey) and Syria may be related to the refugee crisis. There is common support from the EU and the US for Afghanistan that is related to cooperation among the EU, the US and NATO.

In 2018 the EU institutions' bilateral ODA was primarily focused on Africa, Europe and Asia. French bilateral ODA was primarily focused on Africa and

Table 2.5 Top 10 recipients of Visegrád group ODA, 2018

Czech Republic	*Hungary*	*Poland*	*Slovakia*
Bosnia and Herzegovina	Lao People's Democratic Republic	Ukraine	Kenya
Türkiye (Turkey)	Jordan	Myanmar	Ukraine
Ethiopia	Syria	Belarus	Iraq
Moldova	Iraq	Tanzania	Serbia
Ukraine	Ukraine	Türkiye (Turkey)	Moldova
Georgia	Türkiye (Turkey)	Kenya	Lebanon
Iraq	China	Lebanon	Syria
Afghanistan	India	Syrian Arab Republic	Georgia
Syria	Azerbaijan	Viet Nam	South Sudan
Zambia	Mongolia	Iraq	Bosnia and Herzegovina

Source: compiled by the author based on OECD (2020).

Table 2.6 Top 10 recipients of ODA from the EU institutions, France, Germany and the US, 2018

EU institutions	*France*	*Germany*	*The US*
Türkiye (Turkey)	Columbia	Indonesia	Jordan
Serbia	Indonesia	India	Afghanistan
Syria	Côte d'Ivoire	China	Nigeria
Afghanistan	Morocco	Syria	Kenya
Tunisia	Cameroon	Colombia	Ethiopia
India	India	Egypt	Syria
Morocco	Türkiye (Turkey)	Iraq	South Sudan
Egypt	Senegal	Türkiye (Turkey)	Tanzania
Ukraine	Egypt	Afghanistan	Uganda
Nigeria	China	Jordan	Yemen

Source: compiled by the author based on OECD (2020).

Asia. Germany's bilateral ODA was primarily focused on Asia, Africa and the Middle East. US bilateral ODA was primarily focused on Africa.

International organizations and the liberal world order

International organizations such as the World Bank, the IMF, the UN and the WTO have global membership and are global institutions. The OECD can be regarded as a club for advanced, richer nations. The international financial institutions discussed above can have a global membership and focus, i.e. they draw their membership from several continents and their operations are spread across several continents. This is the case with the World Bank and the IMF. Other international financial institutions have a global membership, but their operations primarily take place in one continent. In this sense they are also regional institutions. This is the case with the AfDB, the ADB and the IDB. Owing to their regional focus they are also called regional development banks. Similarly to the World Bank the regional development banks are also multilateral development banks. The international financial institutions that are also multilateral development banks work with and assist governments with loans, policy advice and technical assistance but also have instruments to work with the private sector including loans, equity contributions and various guarantees and risk mitigation instruments to promote cross-border investments (International Finance Corporation 2011).[26] For example, the World Bank and the EBRD assisted the Baltic states and the Visegrád countries in their transition to a market economy following the collapse of the Soviet Union.

If one considers the global organizations, the Bretton Woods institutions, the IMF, the World Bank and the UN, it is no coincidence that their headquarters are all based in the US. The Bretton Woods institutions are located in Washington, DC, close to the White House and the US Treasury, and the UN in New York. This reflects the status of the US as it emerged as the main superpower in a unipolar world after the ending of the Second World War. These institutions, along with the WTO (formerly GATT) and NATO, were part of the new liberal world order created by the US after this devasting war. Europe was in ruins, as was Japan. Having participated in the Bretton Woods Conference, the Soviet Union later emerged as a revival great power with its own institutions in a world that became bipolar with two great nuclear powers, namely the US and the USSR. This rivalry went on until 1991 when the Soviet Union fell and along with it the Warsaw Pact cooperation.

International financial institutions are multilateral institutions and allow for the membership and thus the participation of states, both large and small. However, they tend to be led by large states with smaller states having less weight. The rules for the Bretton Woods institutions, i.e. the IMF and the World Bank, were mostly written by the US where their headquarters are located. By tradition the president of the World Bank is always appointed by the president of the US and the managing director of the IMF is by tradition always a European. It was deemed impractical to appoint both heads of these institutions from the US, but the US's closest allies in Europe were chosen to head the IMF. The US has also by far the greatest voting power at the World Bank with about 16.7%[27] and 16.5%[28] at the IMF. This gives the US enormous leverage in the Bretton Woods institutions. The influence of the US is further strengthened by the location of those institutions practically next door to the White House and the US Treasury in Washington, DC (Wolfensohn 2010, p. 322).

If one considers the regional development banks, the IDB also has its headquarters in Washington, DC. The US is the largest shareholder with over 30% of the total voting power.[29] As a regional hegemon the US attaches great importance having control in the Americas, including South and Central America, and the IDB is thus of key importance to the US.

On the other hand, the ADB, located in the Philippines, is led by Japan and presidents of the ADB have always been Japanese. Japan and the US are by far the largest shareholders in the ADB[30] holding more than 12.7% of the total voting power each and 25.4% together. Japan and the US are allies in Asia and this increases Japan's influence in the ADB.

Things are different in the AfDB, located in Abidjan, Côte d'Ivoire, where Nigeria is the biggest shareholder followed by the US.[31] In the EBRD, located in London, UK, the US is the biggest shareholder but its holding is only marginally larger than that of the large counties in Europe, namely France, Germany, Italy and the UK, all of which have the same capital subscription.[32]

US control over the World Bank and the IMF increases US influence globally and the US also attaches great importance to its influence over the IDB and the ADB. For China, as a rising regional and potentially global power, this is not a favourable condition and China is by far the largest shareholder in the AIIB with about 26.6% of the total voting power; the US has 0.0% as it chose not to become a member of the AIIB.[33] The AIIB's headquarters are in Beijing, China. The headquarters of the New Development Bank (NDB) are based in Shanghai, China. The NDB was established by the BRICS countries (five emerging economies, namely Brazil, Russia, India, China and South Africa), all of which have an equal shareholding. The NBD is now expanding its country membership and membership in the bank is open to members of the UN.[34] The establishment of these two relatively new institutions have posed a challenge to the US-led liberal world order.

US power in the Bretton Woods institutions has continued to increase its influence globally. Having a strong position in the IDB continues to be important for the US as a regional hegemon in the Americas and also in the ADB as the US cares greatly about its influence in Asia. Furthermore, it is trying to contain its main rival, China. In this regard the US is not showing strong interest in Europe and much less in Africa. One reason is that in the Americas the US is, and wants to remain, the sole regional hegemon. In Asia the US wants to prevent China from dominating the region at all costs. In Europe there is no potential competitor to US authority. Germany does not have a sufficiently large population to enable it to control Europe, while Russia lacks a sufficiently strong economy to dominate the region. Furthermore, the US will retain its strong position in Europe so long as it maintains its leadership role in NATO. In Africa the US does not have obvious strategic interests compared to the other regions. China, on the other hand, sees opportunities including access to natural resources and invests substantially in Africa and is making good use of instruments such as the Belt and Road Initiative. Also, that fact that the US is not showing a strong interest in Africa creates room for a great power to expand without major conflict.

International relations theory: theoretical framework

Behind the establishment of the organizations discussed above and their operations lies a theoretical framework or belief system about what constitutes good governance and institutions and what constitutes good economic policies that will produce a good life for people, in particular democracy and individual liberty. These institutions were largely shaped by the US and its European allies. The US led the establishment of the Bretton Woods institutions as the Second World War drew to a close and greatly influences what these institutions preach. The regional development banks largely followed the US-led Bretton Woods institutions. Two exceptions to this rule are the China-led institutions, the AIIB and the NDB. As might be expected from a great power, China wants to establish its own institutions with its allies, particularly the BRICS, and to challenge the US rules-based world order supported by the international institutional architecture that it created.

The so-called Washington Consensus[35] of the 1980s was an economic policy framework created by the US and its allies. It was an attempt to summarize the outcome of a debate on the policy stances that are conducive to economic growth and development (for an in-depth discussion see, for example, Hilmarsson 2011). It is impossible to enact policy without some sort of theory and behind these Western institutions are liberal ideas, liberal theory or liberalism.

Following the dissolution of the Soviet Union in 1991 there was only one great power, the US, and thus no great power competition. Thereafter, the world became unipolar and was dominated by liberal principles until around 2017, when the world shifted to multipolarity with the rise of China and a more powerful Russia that is also allied with China.

Behind the liberalism led by the US there are three noteworthy theories in international relations: (i) the democratic peace theory; (ii) the economic dependency theory; and (iii) liberal institutionalism (see, for example, Mearsheimer 2003).[36] Each of the three theories will be discussed briefly below.

First, the *democratic peace theory* [37] is the idea that democracies do not fight other democracies. Therefore it is important to spread democracy all over the world. Democratic peace is the proposition that democracies are more peaceful in their foreign relations at least towards other democracies. The democratic peace theory has clear policy implications that drew the attention of the Bill Clinton administration and became the centrepiece of President George W. Bush's foreign policy in the wake of the '9/11' terrorist attacks (Gat 2005). According to the liberalism school of thought, every part of the world is important and the spread of democracy is key to liberal hegemony. After the fall of the Soviet Union, EU expansion was key to the spread of democracy, and the replacement of communism. This is despite the fact that the EU could economically rival the US and was therefore often viewed with suspicion by the US. EU enlargement included former Soviet republics such as the Baltic states and former Soviet satellite states such as the Visegrád countries; this is a pertinent example of the spread of democracy.

But there are other examples where this effort of spreading democracy has been less successful, such as the US-led endeavours in Iraq and Afghanistan. Gat (2005, p. 73), for example, notes that in shaping policy towards under-developed and developing countries it should be realized that democracy is difficult to institute and sustain where economic and social modernization has not taken root, nor does democracy in itself necessarily lead to democratic peace before such development has occurred. Furthermore, given that democracies such as the US and the UK have engaged in numerous wars one could argue that this contradicts the democratic peace theory. But one could also argue that the US and the UK have waged wars in countries that are not democracies and that they are less likely to go to war against democratic countries.

Second, the *economic interdependence theory* stipulates that if countries depend on one another for trade and investment, peace will follow. So according to this theory, extensive economic interdependence networks help to keep the peace between countries. A high degree of economic interdependence between two large economies would not only make war between them inconceivable, rather it would make such a war counterproductive. Concretely, even the 'winner' in a war between them would end up being worse off after the victory than before.[38]

But does growing economic interdependence among major powers actually increase or decrease the chance of conflict and war? Liberals argue that the benefits of trade give states an incentive to stay peaceful. Realists contend that trade compels states to struggle for vital raw materials and markets.

The EU common market and common currency makes EU and euro area member states interdependent economically and thus one can argue that EU, and euro area member states in particular, are unlikely to go to war against one another. Most notably major powers such as France and Germany that have historically fought devastating wars against one another are less likely to fight each other again given that they are EU member states and are also members of the same currency union. A war between the two powers would damage both severely and they are thus likely to find other means to settle their differences.

During the Soviet era there was little trade between the Soviet Union and the West including the US. If one considers the current global great powers, the US and China, there are extensive trade flows between those countries, so according to the theory this should reduce the likelihood of war breaking out between them because they engage in mutually beneficial trade and cross-border investments. As Cooper (2014, p. 19) pointed out, economic interdependence was much higher in 2013 than it was in 1913 for most countries, including China and the US and war would be extremely costly for both. Only history will tell if economic interdependence is sufficient to keep those countries from fighting one another. Currently tensions between the two powers are running high over Taiwan and the South China Sea, for example.

Economic interdependence does not necessarily produce stability in all cases. As Krickovic (2015) points out, contrary to the expectations of liberal theories, interdependence between Europe and Russia in the energy sphere has exacerbated security tensions between the two sides, leading to the competitive foreign policies that now see them at loggerheads in Ukraine. This energy interdependence is currently causing tensions between Russia and the West, especially with the EU and NATO, as well as tensions within those institutions. Such tensions include the construction of a natural gas pipeline, Nord Stream 2, by Germany and Russia that runs beneath the Baltic Sea bypassing a gas pipeline going via Ukraine. This serves the interest of those two countries, but the Baltic states, Poland and Ukraine in particular fiercely oppose this gas pipeline and Nord Stream 2 has now been put on hold because of the war in Ukraine.

Copeland (2014) demonstrated that when leaders have positive expectations of the future trade environment, they want to stay peaceful in order to secure the economic benefits that enhance long-term power. However, when these expectations turn negative, leaders are likely to fear a loss of access to raw materials and markets, giving them greater incentives to initiate crises to protect their commercial interests (see also Copeland 1996).

Economic interdependence between small powers can also cause tensions and conflicts of interest. An example of this is the banking interdependence between the Baltic states and the continental Nordic countries during the 2008/09 global financial crisis (see, for example, Hilmarsson 2018). The rescue of the mainly Swedish-owned banks in the Baltic states demanded austerity and fixed exchange rate policies in these countries. The Baltic states had little choice other than to follow Swedish and EU economic policies so that they were able to adopt the euro at a later date.

Third, *liberal institutionalism* stipulates that international organizations generate rules that nations obey. The Bretton Woods institutions are key examples of a liberal international order sometimes also referred to as the rules-based or the US-led international order. According to the theory, robust international institutions are important and nation-states should get involved in international institutions. The West, especially the US, has sought to integrate the rest of the world into this system of liberalism supported by the international institutions. This included the Soviet republics and satellite states when the Soviet Union fell in 1991 as well as China which has now become a major rival to US dominance. In fact, together China and Russia are currently challenging US supremacy with China developing its own institutions such as the AIIB and the NDB in tandem with the BRICS countries, but without US participation. The US has attempted to prevent Western countries from participating in the AIIB; however, the UK, the US's greatest ally, became a member of the AIIB, as did all the Nordic countries, as well as two Visegrád countries, Hungary and Poland. The Baltic states stayed out. One could argue that this was because they hesitated to irritate the US on foreign policy owing to their dependency on the US for their defence. One also needs to keep in mind that they are very small countries that have limited resources and will have limited economic interests in Asia.

There are exceptions to the US government policy of supporting and promoting liberal institutionalism. Former President Trump opposed the liberal world order and institutions such as the World Bank, the IMF and the WTO. He was also sceptical about the EU and NATO and considered traditional US allies in Europe to be free riders on the US in NATO. In his view, traditional US allies were taking advantage of the US in the very institutions it created after the Second World War. He was also against trade agreements such as the Trans-Pacific Partnership (TPP) in Asia and the Transatlantic Trade and Investment Partnership (TTIP) with Europe. His opposition to the TPP was considered odd by many allies given that it did not include China and thus was an opportunity for the US to form a coalition in Asia against China. This would have strengthened the US in its rivalry with China.

The EU, NATO and liberalism

The EU is a regional organization focusing on European integration for the benefit of member states while NATO is a defence alliance focusing on security in Europe and North America. Considering the theories discussed above the EU has sought to embrace the market economy and democracy, made countries interdependent on one another economically, most notably via a common market and common currency. EU member states commit themselves to following common EU laws and regulations since the EU is a rules-based organization. Those that are in the euro area follow the rules of the currency union. The EU member states are also integrated into the US-led Bretton Woods institutions. NATO embraces democracy and individual liberty and makes the member states dependent on one another for their security.

At the national level most EU member states embrace democracy but there is often talk of a democratic deficit within the EU institutional mechanism. For example, the European Commission consisting of unelected bureaucrats initiates EU legislation. Meanwhile, in EU member states parliaments consisting of elected officials normally initiate legislation at the national level, rather than unelected bureaucrats.

Despite European integration and interdependence, the EU remains a collection of nation-states that have their own institutions and political systems, and there is no common foreign policy, no common EU army, nor indeed a common police force. There is also considerable opposition to the EU as exemplified by the UK's decision to leave the Union (referred to as Brexit). There has also been opposition to the EU from the governments in Hungary and Poland, both of which feel that the EU is becoming too deeply involved in their internal affairs. For defence the EU relies on the NATO-backed Article 5 guarantee. Although there has been talk about the creation of a common European army, some EU member states fear that this could weaken NATO.

NATO and EU expansion towards the east in Europe was intended to spread democracy and to create a security zone along the eastern flank of Europe. Unlike the EU, NATO is dominated by the US, but it ties the West together and makes member states interdependent in terms of security. Support for the so-called colour revolutions, such as the Rose Revolution in Georgia and the Orange Revolution in Ukraine, is an example of the West attempting to promote democracy in potential NATO member states.

The expansion of NATO and the EU is naturally perceived as a threat in Russia. Potential membership of the EU and particularly NATO contributed to, or perhaps resulted in, the outbreak of war in Georgia in 2008 and in Ukraine in 2014. The Ukraine war started with the annexation of the Crimean Peninsula and subsequent conflict in Donbass but in February 2022 it escalated to a full-scale Russian military invasion of Ukraine. Russia has shown that it is prepared to destroy Georgia and Ukraine rather than allowing them to accede to the EU and especially NATO.

One needs to keep in mind that all the Warsaw Pact former Soviet satellite states are now NATO members, as are the Baltic states that were once Soviet republics. Had the Soviet Union survived and all NATO member states except the US had joined the Warsaw Pact countries, it is not hard to image that the US would feel threatened by that Soviet-led alliance. The Bush Doctrine of creating a sea of democracies with countries such as Afghanistan, Iraq, Iran, Libya and Syria proved to be a failure because none of these countries have a history of Western democracy.

The world is becoming more multipolar. The Chinese economy is becoming or perhaps already is bigger than that of the US. This depends whether one uses current prices to measure the size of the economy or purchasing power parity. Given its population size India could also become a bigger economy than that of the US. All it would take is for Indians to do as well in India as they do in the US. This is likely to result in tensions between the US and its competitors and the tensions with China are already visible. The irony is that the success of China can to a large extent be credited to the US by engaging China in the institutions that it created after the Second World War, including the Bretton Woods institutions and the WTO.

European and American interests do not necessarily always go together in this security competition. Countries in Europe and the EU could continue to maintain good relations with China and benefit from trade and investment. Germany and France may even export high technology products to China that could be used for military purposes. The first Cold War marked a period of geopolitical tension between the Soviet Union and its satellite states and the US and its Western European allies. Once the war in Ukraine is over a second Cold War is likely to emerge, but this time in Asia. Europe can hardly contribute much to a security competition between China and the US because it is preoccupied with its own security. But a growing security competition between the US and China could result in the US increasingly moving out of Europe. Thus, Russia could again be viewed as a major threat.

The Eastern and Central European countries, including the Baltic and Visegrád countries, see NATO as offering protection against Russia more than the EU. The US sees NATO also as an instrument to spread democracy and liberal policies that are different to those embraced by China and Russia. In the longer term the US may also see an enlarged NATO as an instrument to fight not only Russia but also China.

In a multipolar world the US and the EU will not be able to spread democracy in the same way as in a unipolar world. China and Russia will follow their own model of governance regardless of Western preferences. They may strive to reduce their economic interdependence with Western countries. The two countries will also create their own institutions but they will not be part of the liberal world order (such as the AIIB and the NDB, see above).

The EU member states have been integrated into the liberal institutions created by the US, but some of them are also members of institutions that challenge those institutions, most notably those recently created and led by China, such as the AIIB. One can thus argue that on the institutional front Europe is already preparing itself for China to assume a growing role in the world economy and in world politics.

Amid the current great power rivalry, China may calculate that a serious conflict between NATO and Russia could enhance its dominance in East Asia. Likewise, Russia might calculate that a serious conflict between China and the US could enhance its status in Europe and as a great power in a multipolar world. Russia wants to maintain a multipolar world in which it is the third great power, not a bipolar world dominated by the US and China. Meanwhile, the US wants to return to a unipolar world and China wants to ensure that this does not happen. Given the security competition between China and the US it seems very odd for the US to engage in a proxy war with Russia in Ukraine. At some point the normalization of relations between the US and Europe on the one hand and Russia on the other may be necessary. While the US and China will engage in intense security competition in the world, Europe might seek to maintain its distance in order to ensure beneficial trade flows with China.

Realism versus liberal institutionalism

Realism and liberal institutionalism are two competing schools in international relations theory. When the focus is on international institutions, realism is a view of international politics that stresses its competitive and conflictual side, whereas liberal institutionalism tends to emphasize the cooperation of nation-states within international institutions. According to the realist John Mearsheimer (1995), the most powerful states in the system create and shape institutions so that they can maintain their share of world power, or even increase it. In this view, institutions are essentially 'areas for acting out power relationships' (ibid., p. 13). In contrast, liberal institutionalists Robert Keohane and Lisa Martin maintain that '[w]hen states can jointly benefit from cooperation … we expect governments to attempt to construct such institutions' (1995, p. 42; see also Keohane 1984). Indeed, such institutions have been created. They ask 'what could be the rationale behind devoting resources to structures that will make no difference?' (Keohane and Martin 1995, p. 48).

Realists thus consider the principal actors in the international arena to be states, which are concerned with their own security, act in pursuit of their own national interests, and struggle for power.[39] Great powers compete for balance of power and the best strategy to survive is to be as powerful as possible. This is because states cannot call on a more powerful authority if they are attacked. There is no world government and states operate in anarchy. In contrast, according to liberal institutionalism, international institutions have rules that nations obey. Nations should get involved in international institutions for their own benefit.

With nations integrated into a host of post-Second World War institutions, namely the UN, the Bretton Woods institutions, NATO, the GATT (now the WTO), and others, liberal values and institutions became the foundation of the 'liberal world order'.[40] The OECD states were important American allies during the Cold War, and thus the US benefited strategically when they gained substantially in size and strength (Mearsheimer 1995, p. 21).

Liberal institutionalism has traditionally emphasized the need for institutional arrangements to initiate and sustain cooperation among states. The theory regenerated much interest in the capacity and potential of international institutions for sustained international cooperation and peace in the post-Cold War world.[41] In contrast, a realist might argue that the US wrote the rules of institutions such as the World Bank or the IMF for its own benefit in order to preach liberal views in the developing world and in an attempt to recreate other states in its own image. As Mearsheimer (1995) points out, the UN was established during the final days of the Second World War in order to provide collective security around the globe. However, the Soviet-American competition followed on the heels of that war, and the UN was therefore never seriously tested as a collective security apparatus during the Cold War (ibid., p. 33). The UN never gained the same momentum as the Bretton Woods institutions. At the UN each country has one vote, whereas at the World Bank and the IMF countries vote according to the size of their economies. This is one of the reasons why the UN is not as attractive to great powers such as the US as the Bretton Woods institutions.

The UN's most powerful institution, the UN Security Council, is now more representative of the old world than the world as it is today. There are no South American or African permanent member states in the council, nor are there any Muslim countries. There are 15 Council members. Five of these – China, France, Russia, the UK and the US – are permanent members and have veto power.[42] This makes decision-making hard and some would say that this most powerful unit within the UN system in ineffective.

Since the rise of China as an economic powerhouse and as a potential military competitor US priorities have changed, and the US has sought to increase its control over events in East Asia with less emphasis on Europe. The Persian Gulf is also of importance for the US because of its energy competition, especially with China. In Asia the US seeks to contain China and has strong relations with (and some would say dominates) potential great powers such as Japan and South Korea via its military presence in Asia.

In Europe the US still dominates the potential great powers, notably Germany, via its military presence in Europe and leadership role in NATO. As Mearsheimer puts it, NATO was essentially an American tool for managing power in the face of the Soviet threat (1995, p. 14). Now Russia and its ally China have become the main threat.

The US also remains influential in the World Bank and the IMF and continues to use those institutions to spread liberalism, market economy and democracy around the world.

The US also sought to engage China via the Bretton Woods institutions, and adoption of market economy in China, has made the country richer and more powerful and one could argue that the US played a role in creating its own rival that now competes with it for world dominance. More recently we are seeing the US grumbling about free riders and bad deals in a system the US itself constructed.

If one considers the future of the liberal world order created to a large extent by the US and supported by Europe there is hardly any question that wealth and power are moving from the North and the West to the East and the South, and the old order dominated by the US and Europe is giving way to one increasingly shared with non-Western rising states, most notably the BRICS.

It is also clear that liberal institutionalism has its limits. The theory is of little relevance in situations whereby states' interests are fundamentally conflictual and neither side thinks that it has much to gain from cooperation (Mearsheimer 1995, p. 15). Keohane and Martin recognize that 'institutionalists only expect interstates cooperation to occur if states have significant common interest' (1995, p. 39). They also maintain that the 'necessity for institutions does not mean that they are always valuable, much less that they operate without respect to power and interests, constitute a panacea for violent conflict, or always reduce the likelihood of war' (ibid., p. 50).

Americans who think seriously about foreign policy issues tend to dislike realism intensely, mainly because it clashes with their basic values. The theory stands opposed to how most Americans prefer to think about themselves and the wider world (Mearsheimer 1995, p. 47). Given that realism is largely alien to American culture, there is a powerful demand in the US for alternative ways of looking at the world, and especially for theories that square with American values. Institutionalist theories meet these requirements, and that is the main source of their appeal to policymakers and scholars. Whatever else one might say about these theories, they have one undeniable advantage in the eyes of their supporters: they are not realism. Not only do institutionalist theories offer an alternative to realism, they explicitly seek to undermine it. Moreover, institutionalists offer arguments that reflect basic American values. For example, they are optimistic about the possibility of greatly reducing, if not eliminating, security competition among states and creating a more peaceful world. They certainly do not accept the realist structure that war is politics by other means. Institutionalists, in short, purvey a message that Americans long to hear (Mearsheimer 1995, p. 49).

International institutions and small states/powers

One can argue that international institutions give small powers a voice around the table and thus enhance their influence, but one can also argue that those institutions are dominated by great powers that write the rules of those institutions and that international institutions are part of great power politics and competition. As Keohane and Martin (1995, p. 42) argue, '[i]nstitutions can provide information, reduce transaction costs, make commitments more credible, establish focal points for cooperation, and in general facilitate the operation of reciprocity'. This can be especially important for small states with small institutions and limited resources. Small powers can also form like-minded alliances among themselves to give themselves a stronger voice. But as Kenneth Waltz puts it, states operate in a 'self-help' system. This emphasis on self-help does not preclude states from forming alliances. But alliances are only temporary marriages of convenience, so that today's alliance partner might be tomorrow's enemy, and today's enemy might be tomorrow's alliance partner. States operating in a self-help world should always act according to their own self-interest, because it helps to be selfish in a self-help world (Waltz 1987; Mearsheimer 1995, p. 11).

The Visegrád cooperation was important for those countries to relink with the West, i.e. to help the member states achieve EU and NATO membership. This helped with much-needed economic transition and security. After that the purpose of the alliance became less obvious.

The Nordic-Baltic cooperation was important for the Baltic states when they were making a transition to a democratic market economy, and sought membership of both the EU and NATO. The Nordic countries supported them as it was in their own self-interest to promote security and prosperity in the region. During the 2008/09 global financial crisis the situation was different and the rescue of continental Nordic banks was costly for the Baltic states (Hilmarsson 2018).

Within large alliances such as the EU and NATO there are cases that surface that show that member states do not trust each other for historical reasons. As Mearsheimer (1995, p. 13) reminds us, states sometimes cooperate to gang up on a third state, as the Germans and the Soviets did against Poland in 1939. This has not been forgotten and within the EU and NATO Poland still has limited trust in Germany and relies more on the US-led NATO. Recently distrust between Germany and Poland has resurfaced because of the war between Russia and Ukraine and German-Russian cooperation in the Nord Stream 2 gas pipeline project. Poland is not a small state but compared to Russia and Germany it is a small power and like the other Visegrád countries and the Baltics states it relies on the US for its security.

Furthermore, given the US policy to pivot to Asia and away from Europe, small states can become concerned about guarantees they are given by US-led institutions such as Article 5. This is especially relevant to small states that are in close proximity to great powers, such as the Baltic states that border Russia. As Mearsheimer (1995, p. 23) comments, as impressive as the American efforts have been, threatened states are not likely to have much faith in a security system that tells them that help is likely to come, but that will arrive months after they have been conquered. This is naturally a concern in small countries where the US is unwilling to station its own troops to back up their defence commitments or removes its defence force unilaterally as it did in the case of Iceland.

Notes

1 www.oecd.org/about/.
2 www.oecd.org/60-years/timeline/.
3 www.wto.org/english/thewto_e/thewto_e.htm.
4 www.centerforfinancialstability.org/bw/Who_Was_at_Bretton_Woods.pdf.
5 www.oecd.org/about/document/list-oecd-member-countries.htm.
6 www.wto.org/english/thewto_/whatis_e/tif_e/org6_e.htm.
7 www.worldbank.org/en/about/leadership/members#1.
8 www.imf.org/external/np/sec/memdir/memdate.htm.
9 www.un.org/en/about-us/member-states.
10 Czechoslovakia became a member of the IMF on 27 December 1945 and ceased to be a member, effective 31 December 1954; Czechoslovakia was readmitted as a member of the IMF on 20 September 1990, and ceased to be a member, effective 1 January 1993. The Czech Republic and Slovakia succeeded to the membership of Czechoslovakia on 1 January 1993; see www.imf.org/external/np/sec/memdir/memdate.htm.
11 Among the original members (Article II, Section 1), which signed the Articles of Agreement by 31 December 1945. Poland became a member of the IMF on 10 January 1946 and withdrew from membership, effective 14 March 1950; Poland was readmitted as a member of the IMF on 27 June 1986; see www.imf.org/external/np/sec/memdir/memdate.htm.
12 Czechoslovakia became a member of the International Monetary Fund on December 27, 1945 and ceased to be a member, effective December 31, 1954; Czechoslovakia was readmitted as a member of the International Monetary Fund on September 20, 1990, and ceased to be a member, effective January 1, 1993. The Czech Republic and the Slovakia succeeded to the membership of Czechoslovakia on January 1, 1993, see further: https://www.imf.org/external/np/sec/memdir/memdate.htm.
13 Joined the Fund under the provisions for original members as extended to 31 December 1946 by Board of Governors Resolution IMF; see www.imf.org/external/np/sec/memdir/memdate.htm.
14 Among the 'original members' (Article II, Section 1), which signed the Articles of Agreement by 31 December 1945; see www.imf.org/external/np/sec/memdir/memdate.htm.
15 Ibid.
16 www.businessinsider.com/larry-summers-on-asian-infrastructure-investment-bank-2015-4?r=US&IR=T.
17 www.mbl.is/frettir/innlent/2015/03/31/gerist_stofnadili_ad_nyjum_banka/ and http://en.people.cn/n/2015/0401/c90883-8872167.html.
18 www.gov.uk/government/news/uk-announces-plans-to-join-asian-infrastructure-investment-bank.
19 www.afdb.org/en/about-us/corporate-information/members.
20 www.adb.org/about/members.
21 www.aiib.org/en/about-aiib/governance/members-of-bank/index.html.
22 www.ebrd.com/shareholders-and-board-of-governors.html.
23 www.iadb.org/en/about-us/how-are-we-organized.

24 https://public.tableau.com/views/ODA-GNI_15868746590080/ODA2019?:display_count=y&publish=yes&:origin=viz_share_link?&:showVizHome=no#1; and www.oecd.org/dac/development-cooperation-report/.
25 https://public.tableau.com/views/ODA-GNI_15868746590080/ODA2019?:display_count=y&publish=yes&:origin=viz_share_link?&:showVizHome=no#1.
26 www.adb.org/sites/default/files/publication/29108/ifi-development-private-sector.pdf.
27 https://finances.worldbank.org/Shareholder-Equity/Top-8-countries-voting-power/udm3-vzz9.
28 www.imf.org/en/About/executive-board/eds-voting-power.
29 www.iadb.org/en/about-us/capital-stock-and-voting-power.
30 www.tandfonline.com/doi/abs/10.1080/03050629908434952?journalCode=gini20.
31 www.afdb.org/fileadmin/uploads/afdb/Documents/Financial-Information/AfDB_Financial_Overview_Jan_2016.pdf.
32 www.ebrd.com/shareholders-and-board-of-governors.html.
33 www.aiib.org/en/about-aiib/governance/members-of-bank/index.html.
34 www.ndb.int/about-us/organisation/shareholding/.
35 www.britannica.com/topic/Washington-consensus.
36 For a detailed discussion see, for example, Mearsheimer (2003).
37 www.oxfordbibliographies.com/view/document/obo-9780199756223/obo-9780199756223-0014.xml; and www.jstor.org/stable/4F060125?seq=1.
38 https://scholar.harvard.edu/files/cooper/files/wwi.rev_.pdf.
39 https://plato.stanford.edu/entries/realism-intl-relations/; and https://journals.sagepub.com/doi/pdf/10.1177/1474885110374001.
40 www.brookings.edu/blog/future-development/2018/07/18/liberal-institutionalism-its-threatened-past-its-threatened-future/.
41 https://journals.sagepub.com/doi/pdf/10.1177/002088170904500302.
42 www.un.org/en/model-united-nations/security-council.

References

African Development Bank (AfDB) (2021). *Member Countries.* Available at: www.afdb.org/en/about-us/corporate-information/members (accessed 5 October 2021).

Asian Development Bank (ADB) (2021). *Who We Are.* Available at: www.adb.org/who-we-are/about#members (accessed 5 October 2021).

Asian Infrastructure Investment Bank (AIIB) (2021). *Members and Prospective Members of the Bank.* Available at: www.aiib.org/en/about-aiib/governance/members-of-bank/index.html (accessed 6 October 2021).

Britannica (2022). *Washington Consensus.* Available at www.britannica.com/topic/Washington-consensus (accessed 8 October 2021).

Cooper, R. N. (2014). *Economic Interdependence and War.* Available at: https://dash.harvard.edu/bitstream/handle/1/34903181/CooperEconomicInterdependenceandWar2014.pdf;jsessionid=B0386826A0BEC6957FF2EE5C1F81511C?sequence=3 (accessed 2 July 2022).

Copeland, D. C. (2014). Economic Interdependence and War. In *Economic Interdependence and War.* Princeton, NJ: Princeton University Press.

Copeland, D. C. (1996). Economic Interdependence and War: A Theory of Trade Expectations. *International Security*, 20(4), 5–41. Available at: https://doi.org/10.2307/2539041 https://www.jstor.org/stable/2539041?seq=1 (accessed 2 July 2022).

European Bank for Reconstruction and Development (EBRD) (2021). *EBRD Shareholders and Board of Governors.* Available at: www.ebrd.com/shareholders-and-board-of-governors.html (accessed 5 October 2021).

Gåsemyr, H. J. (2018). *China and Multilateral Development Banks Positions, Motivations, Ambitions*. Available at: https://nupi.brage.unit.no/nupi-xmlui/bitstream/handle/11250/2580352/China%2Band%2BMDBs%2BIMF%2BNUPI_Report_8_2018_Gaasemyr.pdf?sequence=2&isAllowed=y (accessed 7 October 2021).

Gat, A. (2005). The Democratic Peace Theory Reframed: The Impact of Modernity. *World Politics*, 58(1), pp. 73–100. Available at: www.jstor.org/stable/40060125?seq=1 (accessed 27 October 2021).

Hilmarsson, H. Þ. (2018). *The Economic Crisis and Its Aftermath in the Nordic and Baltic Countries: Do as We Say and Not as We Do*. Abingdon and New York: Routledge.

Hilmarsson, H. Þ. (2011). How Can the Baltic States as Non-DAC Donors Best Contribute to International Development Cooperation? *Baltic Journal of Economics*, 11(2), 27–40. Available at: www.tandfonline.com/doi/abs/10.1080/1406099X.2011.10840499 (accessed 27 October 2020).

Inter-American Development Bank (IDB) (2021). *Member Countries*. Available at: www.iadb.org/en/about-us/how-are-we-organized (accessed 5 October 2021).

International Finance Corporation (IFC) (2011). *International Finance Institutions and Development through the Private Sector*. Available at: www.adb.org/sites/default/files/publication/29108/ifi-development-private-sector.pdf (accessed 19 October 2021).

International Monetary Fund (IMF) (2021). *List of Members*. Available at: www.imf.org/external/np/sec/memdir/memdate.htm (accessed 19 October 2021).

Keohane, R. O. (1984). *After Hegemony: Cooperation and Discord in the World Political Economy*. Princeton, NJ: Princeton University Press.

Keohane, R. O. and Martin, L. L. (1995). The Promise of Institutionalist Theory. *International Security*, 20(1), 39–51. Available at: www.jstor.org/stable/2539214 (accessed 14 October 2021).

Krickovic, A. (2015). When Interdependence Produces Conflict: EU–Russia Energy Relations as a Security Dilemma. *Contemporary Security Policy*, 36(1). Available at: www.tandfonline.com/doi/abs/10.1080/13523260.2015.1012350?journalCode=fcsp20 (accessed 14 October 2021).

Mearsheimer, J. J. (2003). *The Tragedy of Great Power Politics* (Rev. edn). New York and London: W. W. Norton.

Mearsheimer, J. J. (1995) The False Promise of International Institutions. *International Security*, 19(3), 5–49. Available at: www.jstor.org/stable/2539078 https://doi.org/10.2307/2539078 (accessed 14 October 2021).

Organisation for Economic Co-operation and Development (OECD) (2021). *Our Global Reach*. Available at: www.oecd.org/about/members-and-partners/ (accessed 8 October 2021).

Organisation for Economic Co-operation and Development (OECD) (2020). *Development Co-operation Report 2020: Learning from Crises, Building Resilience*. OECD Publishing. Available at: https://doi.org/10.1787/f6d42aa5-en (accessed 7 October 2021).

Organisation for Economic Co-operation and Development (OECD) (2018). *Development Co-operation Report*. Available at: www.oecd.org/dac/development-cooperation-report/ (accessed 8 October 2021).

Schuler, K. and Bernkopf, M. (2014). *Who Was at Bretton Woods?*New York: Center for Financial Stability. Available at: https://centerforfinancialstability.org/bw/Who_Was_at_Bretton_Woods.pdf (accessed 1 January 2022).

Steil, B. (2013). *The Battle of Bretton Woods: John Maynard Keynes, Harry Dexter White, and the Making of a New World Order*. Princeton, NJ: Princeton University Press.

United Nations (UN) (2021). *Member States*. Available at: www.un.org/en/about-us/member-states (accessed 16 October 2021).

Waltz, S. K. (1987). *The Origins of Alliances*. Ithaca, NY: Cornell University Press.

Wolfensohn, J. D. (2010). *A Global Life: My Journey among Rich and Poor, from Sydney to Wall Street to the World Bank*. New York: Public Affairs.

World Bank (2021). *Member Countries*. Available at: www.worldbank.org/en/about/leadership/members#1 (accessed 16 October 2021).

World Trade Organization (WTO) (2021). *Members and Observers*. Available at: www.wto.org/english/thewto_e/whatis_e/tif_e/org6_e.htm (accessed 15 October 2021).

3 Some small power alliances in Europe

The Baltic, Nordic and the Visegrád groups

The alliances of small states discussed in this chapter comprise the Baltic states (Estonia, Latvia and Lithuania) that are former Soviet republics, the Nordic countries (Denmark, Finland, Iceland, Norway and Sweden) that are often labelled Western welfare states, and finally the Visegrád group (Hungary, the Czech Republic, Poland and Slovakia) that are former Soviet satellite states. These groups all have a distinct history and organization, but their participation in European integration and security cooperation brings them together in the European Union (EU), the North Atlantic Treaty Organization (NATO) and also in the framework of the Nordic-Baltic Eight (NB8) and the Visegrád group (V4) cooperation.[1] The Nordics and Baltics also sometimes meet with the Visegrád group.

The Nordic countries have the longest history of partnership, and they are composed of rather homogenous populations with a shared history and culture. The Baltic states rekindled their alliance after the fall of the Soviet Union and their cooperation is influenced by the Nordic model of cooperation. In fact, as the Baltic states regained their independence in 1991 the Nordic countries can be considered to serve informally as their mentor within Europe. This is not to say that the Baltic states always follow the Nordic way of doing things. The Baltic economic and social systems, for example, are very different from those of the Nordic countries (Hilmarsson 2018). The Visegrád group is a cultural and political alliance that seeks to advance member states' cooperation in military, cultural, economic and energy matters with one another and to further their integration into the EU and cooperation with NATO.

The Baltic, Nordic and Visegrád alliances can be viewed as platforms for like-minded countries that seek to promote their common interests within larger groups, most notably the EU and NATO. They often come together as a small group before the larger groupings such as the EU27 or meetings of all 30 NATO member states. The effectiveness of such small groups within larger alliances depends to a large extent on their ability to form a common agenda. The Nordic and the Baltic countries seem to have a more formal cooperation than the Visegrád group with common institutions such as the

DOI: 10.4324/9781003212539-4

Nordic Council and the Baltic Assembly. There is also the Nordic Council of Ministers and the Baltic Council of Ministers. Cooperation among the Visegrád group seems less formal mostly without institutions comparable with the Nordics and the Baltics, but this does not prevent ministers from meeting to discuss issues of common interest. The Nordics have sought to integrate the Baltics into their regional cooperation format under the NB8 umbrella, for example, with shared offices at the World Bank and the International Monetary Fund, as well as at the European Bank for Reconstruction and Development. The Nordic and the Baltic countries have also formed smaller groups such as the NB6, which is a coalition of EU member states from the Nordic and Baltic region. Of these three groups of 12 countries, only five (the three Baltic states, Finland and Slovakia) are members of the euro area.

If one considers the wealth and population of nation-states as a measure of power the Baltic states comprise the smallest, the least powerful and the most vulnerable group. The Nordic countries are the wealthiest group, while and the Visegrád countries have the largest populations of the three groups (see Tables 3.1, 3.2 and 3.3).

The Baltic states' weakness is their small and declining populations. They have been occupied by larger powers over the centuries and remain vulnerable. However, the Baltic states have been successful in integrating themselves firmly into Western structures such as the EU and NATO that are important for their security, and despite recording a severe decline in their respective

Table 3.1 Gross domestic product at current prices in US $ billions and population in millions

Baltic states	*GDP (2019)*	*Population (2019)*
Estonia	31.475	1.325
Latvia	34.121	1.920
Lithuania	54.225	2.783
Total	119.821	6.028

Source: IMF (2020).

Table 3.2 Gross domestic product at current prices in US $ billions and population in millions

Nordic countries	*GDP (2019)*	*Population (2019)*
Denmark	347.031	5.806
Finland	269.327	5.518
Iceland	24.224	0.357
Norway	403.336	5.357
Sweden	530.884	10.328
Total	1,574.802	27.366

Source: IMF (2020).

Table 3.3 Gross domestic product at current prices in US $ billions and population in millions

Visegrád group	*GDP (2019)*	*Population (2019)*
Czech Republic	250.681	10.650
Hungary	160.957	9.773
Poland	592.401	37.973
Slovakia	105.434	5.450
Total	1,109.473	63.846

Source: IMF (2020).

gross domestic product (GDP) during the 2008/09 global financial crisis they have also been successful economically in comparison to other former Soviet republics such as Ukraine and Georgia.

The Nordics have earned the reputation of being rich countries in Europe with a relatively even income distribution, relatively generous welfare policies and progressive tax systems. The Nordic countries all have growing populations.

The Visegrád countries have the largest populations of the three groups and given their increasing GDP they have the potential jointly to become a more powerful force within Europe and the EU. The Visegrád group is, however, different from the other two country groups in that one of its member states, Poland, is larger than the three remaining member states combined, both in terms of GDP and size of population. According to Gyarfášová (2018, p. 111), 'Poland is a regional power, a key political actor, and the Poles feel that they are in a different league'.

Following their accession to the EU, the Visegrád countries have been at odds with some of the other EU member states in terms of their strict immigration policies. Democracy and the freedom of the press have also been questioned, especially in Hungary and Poland.

Nordic cooperation[2]

Over the past 1,000 years, the Nordic countries have fluctuated between periods of war and peace but have worked more closely together in the last two centuries. Significant features of relations between the Nordic countries throughout their history have been alliances and wars.[3]

Around 1000 CE, kingdoms began to form in the Nordic regions. Up until then the Vikings ruled the whole area. As Christianity began to take root the Viking period ended. For centuries, rivalry for control raged between the Nordic countries, especially Denmark and Sweden. After the Great Northern War at the beginning of the 18th century, Sweden was no longer an imperial power after its defeat. Instead, Russia and Prussia became the ruling states around the Baltic Sea. Today's Russian Federation is still viewed as the primary security threat for Scandinavia and the Baltic states. Indeed, Russia attacked and occupied Finland, taking it from Sweden in 1809.

The union between Sweden and Norway was dissolved in 1905, with Norway declaring its independence. Finnish independence followed in 1917. In 1918 Iceland attained a major degree of autonomy. However, it was still a part of the Danish monarchy and subject to Danish foreign policy until 1944, when it became fully independent with its own president. In 1919 the Nordic Association was founded and comprised Denmark, Norway and Sweden, with Iceland and Finland following in 1922 and 1924. Since then, the Nordic Association has been essential in encouraging closer Nordic cooperation.

Denmark, Iceland and Norway joined NATO in 1949, while Finland and Sweden remained neutral (NATO 2021a). The Nordic Council was formed by Denmark, Iceland, Norway and Sweden in 1952. Finland, which was still under Soviet influence, did not join until 1955. In 1960 Sweden, Norway and Denmark joined the European Free Trade Association (EFTA). Finland became an associate member of EFTA in 1961 and a full member in 1986, while Iceland joined EFTA in 1970 (EFTA 2015, p. 5). Thus, for a brief period all the Nordic countries were part of the same free trade area.

A Treaty of Co-operation (known as the Helsinki Treaty) between Denmark, Finland, Iceland, Norway and Sweden was signed and entered into force in 1962. The Nordic Council was established in 1971. The purpose of the Nordic Council of Ministers was to support and maintain cooperation between all the Nordic countries.

In 1973 Denmark joined the European Economic Community (EEC), the only Nordic country to gain membership (EU 2021). At the time there was concern that Denmark's membership of the EEC would result in it neglecting Nordic cooperation. Anker Jørgensen, Prime Minister of Denmark, disputed this notion: 'On the contrary, we tried in a way – and in accordance with the wishes of the other Nordic countries – to build bridges between the Nordic Region and Europe'.[4]

The fall of the Berlin Wall in 1989 radically changed the political landscape of Northern Europe. Democracy was introduced in Poland at the end of 1989. East and West Germany were reunited in 1990 and the Soviet Union collapsed in 1991. The Baltic states regained the complete independence they had enjoyed between the First and Second World Wars. In 1994 Finland, Norway and Sweden held national referendums on EU membership. Finland and Sweden voted 'yes' and joined in 1995, but Norway again voted 'no' to EU membership (Hilmarsson 2019, p. 48). Arguably the dissolution of the Soviet Union made it easier for Sweden and Finland in particular to join the EU. A weakened Russia was in no position to retaliate.

All the Baltic littoral states, with the exception of the Russian enclave of Kaliningrad and the area around St Petersburg, are now part of the EU. Close contact continues between the Nordic and Baltic countries, but only time will tell what the future will bring for Nordic cooperation. Clearly, the two country groups' different approaches to European integration, security and membership of NATO make cooperation more complex (Hilmarsson

2016). At the time of writing, both Finland and Sweden had applied for membership of NATO, largely as a consequence of the Russian invasion of Ukraine. As the Russian army is seen as being weaker than many expected, one can imagine that Finland and Sweden have seen and seized an opportunity to strengthen their security by joining NATO. Prior to submitting a formal application for NATO membership in 2022, both Finland and Sweden had participated in NATO military exercises. They also positioned themselves firmly in the ranks of Western countries with their participation in EU integration.

Nordic cooperation has been institutionalized via the Nordic Council and the Nordic Council of Ministers. The Nordic Council for interparliamentary cooperation is run by a presidium comprising elected parliamentarians from all the Nordic countries. At an annual summit meeting during a session of the Nordic Council, members discuss important issues and the future of Nordic cooperation with the member states' prime ministers. The Nordic Council of Ministers is the forum for intergovernmental cooperation. The ministers for Nordic cooperation are in charge of the work of the Nordic Council of Ministers. Nordic co-operation is based on the Helsinki Treaty, which specifies that the ministers for Nordic cooperation assist their prime ministers in coordinating Nordic issues.[5]

Nordic cooperation seeks a robust Nordic voice in European and international forums and indeed throughout the world. The Nordic countries' shared values help to make the region one of the most innovative and competitive in the world. In terms of European integration, these countries have taken different approaches, which in turn makes it more complicated for them to form a common agenda. Three of the Nordic countries are members of NATO, but two had originally opted to stay out – although, as discussed earlier, this is about to change. The Nordic countries regularly coordinate their foreign and security policies, which helps them to speak with one voice internationally; it can also make them more influential in NATO (see, for example, Bjarnason 2020; Haugevik and Sverdrup 2019; Stoltenberg 2009).

Baltic cooperation

Cooperation among the Baltic states is based on the common interests and goals of the three countries in foreign and security policy as well as welfare policy and economic development. All three countries are members of the EU, the euro area and NATO. Among the three country groups discussed in this book the Baltic states have the highest level of integration in EU structures (Hilmarsson 2018). The Baltics cooperate intensively in the energy sectors and on transport infrastructure projects, and this is related to their economic development and security.[6]

A common approach to EU integration facilitates Baltic cooperation as the countries share common interests and similar goals. This is different from the other groups, especially the Nordic countries that participate in

European integration, but in different ways, and also the Visegrád group, of which only one country, Slovakia, is in the euro area; the others have decided to stay out and use their own currency. The initial steps in cooperation between Estonia, Latvia and Lithuania were taken in the 1920s, soon after the three countries gained their independence. The three countries were independent until the outbreak of the Second World War and then became part of the Soviet Union at the end of the war.

The cooperation of the Baltic states became visible again in the late 1980s and early 1990s during the fight for the return of their independence and the Baltic Way[7] in 1989. Baltic independence was restored in 1991.

After regaining their independence, the Baltic states received the support of the Nordic countries, and the Baltic Assembly was created based on the model of the Nordic Council. The Baltic Council of Ministers was based on the model of the Nordic Council of Ministers. In addition to advancing cooperation among the Baltic states these bodies also advanced Baltic and Nordic cooperation,[8] including among the NB8. According to Rūse (2014), the NB6 member states interact during the pre-negotiations stage in the EU Council, thus enhancing their bargaining power. However, we cannot speak of a permanent regional 'bloc' in the EU owing to member states' interest differences (Rūse 2014, p. 229). The Baltics and the Nordics also conduct cooperation and consultation meetings with the Visegrád group. Interestingly, as Havelka (2021, p. 111) notes, Poland prioritizes communication with its neighbours, especially the Baltic states.

Within the framework of Baltic cooperation, dialogue is ongoing at the level of presidents, parliamentary speakers, heads of government, ministers and experts. Baltic parliamentary collaboration takes place in the Baltic Assembly,[9] which was established in 1991. The Baltic Assembly is an entity under international law, with the headquarters of its secretariat located in Rī ga, Latvia (Baltic Assembly 2021). It has its own symbols and a flag. Each year one of the Baltic states assumes the rotating presidency. Intergovernmental cooperation between the Baltic states takes place in the Baltic Council of Ministers, founded in 1994. The Baltic Council of Ministers provides a direct link to the executive power of the Baltic states.

Visegrád cooperation[10]

The Visegrád group was formed in 1991 on the initiative of Václav Havel, President of the Czechoslovak Republic, Lech Wałęsa, President of the Republic of Poland and József Antall, Prime Minister of the Republic of Hungary (Visegrád Group 2021). This high-level meeting in the town of Visegrád, Hungary, created a historical link with a similar meeting in 1335. Then the participants were John of Luxembourg, King of Bohemia; Charles I of Anjou (Charles Robert), King of Hungary; and Casimir III, King of Poland. The main goal of the two meetings was a wish to intensify mutual collaboration and friendship among the three Central European states.[11]

Apart from the idea of forming an alliance between the countries of Central Europe, the establishment of the Visegrád group in 1991 was clearly motivated by different factors from those in 1335. In 1991 several factors had decisive relevance, including (i) the wish to remove the remnants of the communist bloc in Central Europe when the Visegrád countries were satellite states of the Soviet Union; (ii) the desire to overcome historical animosities between the Central European countries; (iii) the belief that through joint efforts it would be easier to reach the set goals, namely to successfully conclude social transformation; and (iv) a wish to participate in the European integration process with the goal of joining the EU and on the security front by joining NATO. Thus since 1991, after the fall of the Soviet Union, the Visegrád countries have worked together during their transition to democracy and a market economy, as well as effecting swift EU and NATO integration. Following the V4 states' accession to both organizations by 2004, the Visegrád group became an essential framework for representing the members' joint interests in the EU, launching joint projects and bringing the four nations closer together.

In the initial period of its existence from 1991–93 the Visegrád group played its most significant role during talks with NATO and the EU. In the years that followed, the strength of cooperation between the V4 countries began to fade due to acceptance of the idea that individual steps towards accession to Euro-Atlantic integration formations would be more efficient. However, Visegrád cooperation was later resumed in 1998.

Following the disintegration of Czechoslovakia in 1993, the Visegrád group comprised four countries, as both the Czech Republic and Slovakia, remain members.

Recently the Visegrád group has had issues with the EU. Controversies surrounding the Visegrád group include its opposition to EU immigration policy.[12] Concerns have also arisen about democracy, the rights of minority groups and freedom of the judiciary, especially in Poland and Hungary.

According to Nič (2016), the internal flexibility of the group was tested to the limit by deep divisions at the outset of the Ukrainian crisis that started in 2014. The positions taken range from Poland's strong anti-Russian stance and Hungary's privileged partnership with Moscow, with the Czech Republic and Slovakia standing somewhere in between (ibid., pp. 284–85).

The Visegrád group also cooperates with the two other groups discussed in the book in the form of the NB8 + the V4.[13] This is a format that allows the ministers of foreign affairs from NB8 countries and the Visegrád countries to meet. In 2013, Polish Foreign Minister Radosław Sikorski and Swedish Foreign Minister Carl Bildt came up with a proposal for a meeting of both cooperation formats. The meetings are co-organized by the country holding the rotating presidency of the V4 and the coordinating country of the NB8.[14]

The Visegrád group today

Visegrád cooperation is probably the most clearly profiled initiative in Central Europe. The foundation of this cooperation consists of joint contacts at all levels – from the highest-level political meetings through expert and diplomatic meetings, to activities of the region's non-governmental organizations (NGOs), think tanks and research bodies, cultural institutions or various networks of individuals.[15]

Cooperation among the different ministries constitutes a significant part of the activities within the V4 framework, either in the form of mutual expert teams or at ministerial level. Several mutual projects are currently being implemented, particularly in the fields of culture, the environment, internal security, defence, science, and education. This is in addition to growing cooperation in the fields of justice, transportation, tourism, energy and information, and communications technologies.

The member states of the Visegrád group seek to cooperate with other countries, organizations or regional formations interested in cooperating in specific areas found to be in the common interest and in the spirit of pan-European cooperation.

In this context the Visegrad group cooperates with other regional bodies, as well as with individual countries in the region and beyond on an ad hoc or regular basis. The Benelux countries, the countries of the Nordic Council of Ministers,[16] the countries within the EU's Eastern Partnership and the Western Balkans form part of the group's priorities.[17]

Differences also exist within the Visegrád group. For example, the Czech Republic has always valued its relationship with neighbouring Germany as being more important than that with any of its Visegrád allies. Likewise, Slovakia is part of the euro area, making it more integrated with Germany and the core European countries than with the other Visegrád countries – indeed, it is ready to push ahead with greater fiscal integration (Nič 2016, p. 288).

The structure of Visegrád cooperation

Unlike Nordic and Baltic cooperation, Visegrád cooperation is not institutionalized in any manner.[18] There is no Visegrád Council or Assembly, nor a Visegrád Council of Ministers. Visegrád cooperation is based on the principle of regular meetings of its representatives at diverse levels, from the high-level summits of prime ministers and heads of state to expert consultations. Official summits of V4 prime ministers take place annually. Between those summits, one of the V4 countries holds the rotating presidency of the group, part of which involves leadership in drafting a one-year plan of action: the Programme of the Presidency. The most recent programme, entitled *Recharging Europe*, was published by the Hungarian Ministry of Foreign Affairs and Trade in 2021 (Hungarian Ministry of Foreign Affairs and Trade 2021).

The only organization within the V4 platform is the international Visegrád Fund (2021). The fund, established in 2000, aims to support the development of cross-border cooperation in culture, scientific exchange, research, education, student exchanges, and tourism, thereby representing the civic dimensions of V4 cooperation. In the majority of cases, the fund provides financing for the activities of NGOs and individual citizens. In addition to grant programmes, the fund awards personal scholarships and artist residencies which contribute to the exchange of ideas in the V4 region and neighbouring countries.

The role of states in the international system

The Princeton professor and political scientist, Robert Keohane, suggested that we should focus on the systemic role that states' leaders see their countries playing. They are as follows: *system-determining* states play a critical role in shaping the international system; *system-influencing* states cannot expect individually to dominate the international system, but may nevertheless be able to influence it through unilateral or multilateral actions; *system-affecting* states are those that cannot hope to affect the international system if acting alone but can exert significant impact on the system if working through small groups or alliances or through universal or regional international organizations; and finally *system-ineffectual* states are those that can do little to influence the system-wide forces that affect them, except in groups which are so large that each state has minimal influence (ibid., pp. 295–96).

Arguably the US was a system-determining state among Western countries after the Second World War. It was the prime architect of key institutions such as the Bretton Woods institutions that were formed during the war, but which became operational after the war, alongside the General Agreement on Tariffs and Trade that later became the World Trade Organization. NATO, still the world's most powerful security alliance, was also created under US leadership in 1949. But after the Second World War a revival emerged with the Soviet Union and its own military alliance under the Warsaw Pact. The world was thus divided between the US and the Soviet Union which shaped the eastern bloc until around 1991 when it collapsed. After the dissolution of the Soviet Union there was a period in which the US was dominant as the sole superpower until recently with the rise of China as a great economic and military power and Russia re-emerging as a military power.

One can hardly speak about a global hegemon today that is system-determining for the entire international system. China has created its own international institutions, the Asia Infrastructure Investment Bank and the New Development Bank. The latter was established by the BRICS countries (five emerging economies, namely Brazil, Russia, India, China and South Africa), all of which have an equal shareholding. There are also powerful states in Europe that strongly influence the EU and can be classified as system-influencing. Germany and France fit this category within the EU. The contemporary world has shifted from a unipolar or bipolar system to multipolarity with more than two great powers competing for power.

But how can this categorization contribute to our understanding of the behaviour of small states in international organizations? As Keohane (1969,

p. 297) observes, 'a major function of international organizations perceived by many small and middle powers is to allow these states acting collectively to help shape developing international attitudes, dogmas and codes of proper behaviour'.

Smaller groups such as the Baltic, Nordic and Visegrád countries can form groups as Keohane discussed if they feel that they cannot affect the international system when acting alone but can exert significant impact on the system when working through small groups or alliances or through universal or regional international organizations such as the EU. Acting alone they would risk becoming system-ineffectual states that can do little to influence the system-wide forces that affect them, except in groups which are so large that each state has minimal influence. This applies to all the states in the groups discussed in the country groups if they act alone, except perhaps Poland that could become system-affecting via the Visegrád group or the Three Seas initiative if the other countries in these groups share a common interest and agree to have a larger state leading the group. One might argue that Sweden could be system-affecting in the EU via the Nordic group of countries, but the latter take a different approach to European integration which complicates cooperation and the formation of a common agenda.

The Baltics states on their own would be system-ineffectual within the EU or the euro area. As a group the EU is a too large overall and there are too many much larger states within the Union for the Baltics to exert their influence therein. In the euro area the Baltics could cooperate with Finland, but would still have limited influence given the small size of that group in terms of population and wealth. During the 2008/09 global financial crisis it became clear that the Baltic states did what they were told to do in terms of their exchange rate policies and fiscal austerity to be able to fulfil the necessary conditions to adopt the euro. The terms were set by other more powerful states (Hilmarsson 2018).

The Nordic countries could perhaps be system-affecting within the EU in certain matters, but not in the euro area of which only one country, Finland, is a member. The NB8 and the NB6 chould, if they are well organized, be able to be system-affecting within the EU, but less so in the euro area given that there only four Nordic and Baltic member states.

The Visegrád group could in some cases be system-affecting within the EU, but less so in the euro area as only Slovakia is a member. As Havelka (2021, p. 112) comments,

> All four member states agree on a common position towards the Eastern Partnership, Enlargement, and Western Balkans … One might argue that these areas are the only where the V4 can positively influence the European discourse, and even manage to set the agenda. It must be stressed, though, that in other issues – such as EU policy towards Russia – the Visegrád states fail to agree. In this sense, relations with Russia break the otherwise strong tandem of Poland and Hungary. Whereas Polish policy

on Russia has always been cautious, Hungary tends to position itself as a 'bridge' between Russia and the rest of the EU. Czechia and Slovakia somehow oscillate between these rather extreme positions.

One might add that the Visegrád countries can be system-affecting when it comes to EU migration policies.

Meetings between the Nordic, Baltic and Visegrád groups

There are also occasions when the NB8 and the V4 meet to discuss issues affecting all the countries and country groups, such as the COVID-19 pandemic or the situation in Ukraine and Georgia. All 12 countries to some extent feel threatened by Russia and have a common interest in discussing such issues and formulating a common position that can be communicated at EU and NATO meetings. However, as noted above the V4 member states' position on Russia is not identical.

The Nordic, Visegrád and Baltic countries in particular rely on NATO for their defence. Given that NATO is backed by the US the relationship with the US government is critically important. All the counties fall under the US security umbrella. For individual countries it could be difficult to get the attention of the president of the US, but as a group they are more likely to do so, as testified by meetings between the White House and presidents of the Baltic states,[19] leaders of the Nordic countries,[20] and as Poland has done while also inviting other Visegrád leaders to attend.[21]

When meeting with the US president the Nordic countries like to highlight the Nordic welfare model and the Nordic way of managing global challenges as well as their international contributions. For example, the continental Nordic countries contribute generously to international development cooperation. Gender equality and income equality perspectives are discussed as well as global challenges such as climate change and the transition to green technology. Individually the Nordic countries are small and quite insignificant on an international scale, but together they command considerable power. Despite accounting for just 0.3% of the world's population they represent nearly 2% of global domestic product (GDP). In Russia meetings with the Nordic countries and the other groups are often seen as an attempt by the US to create a united front against Russia.[22]

Poland wants to establish itself as a regional leader in Central and Eastern Europe, including the Three Seas Initiative. This group is not intended to replace the Visegrád group, but its focus is on joint infrastructure projects, especially a new north–south interstate highway, in the structurally underdeveloped regions along the EU's eastern border. The group also seeks to improve the free flow of natural gas and other forms of fuel in the interest of energy security and competition.

When meeting with the US president the Baltic heads of state are likely to want to focus on the security threat posed by Russia, while economic cooperation is also likely to be on the agenda more for the formality. The security focus reflects Baltic vulnerability and uncertain US commitment to NATO and fears about the reliability of the guarantees offered under Article 5 of the Washington Treaty. In a 2018 meeting with US President Donald Trump the Baltic heads of state praised the American leadership, touted their own contributions to NATO and noted that the US had been a strong ally during the half-century during which they were under Soviet occupation. A 2018 press conference between President Trump and the Baltic heads of state was described as 'a hastily assembled Motown covers band more than an event involving four heads of state'.[23] Elsewhere, the event was described as a 'distinction' that was granted to the Baltic states and was by all accounts was very 'dignified'.[24]

Siding with the US or China?

In addition to participation in European integration via the EU and security cooperation via NATO, the rise of China and relations with China are a challenge for the countries in the Baltic, Nordic and Visegrád groups. The need for infrastructure investments beyond what the EU can support in the Baltic and the Visegrád countries makes China an attractive partner. But partnerships with China come at a cost since too close partnerships with Beijing will not be welcomed in Washington. The current security competition between the US and China in East Asia is likely to affect relations between the US and Europe and could cause tensions in the EU and NATO. In fact, as a recent Brussels Summit communiqué issued by the NATO heads of state and of government from 14 June 2021 shows the US is dragging European member states into the East Asia conflict, although these states have primarily viewed Russia as the main threat to their security (NATO 2021b). This could divide the EU and NATO further as some Central and Eastern European member states that participate in the 17+1 initiative[25] (now 16 +1 after the departure of Lithuania) are supported by China and while others favour the Three Seas Initiative that is now supported by the US.[26]

The two greatest powers in the world, China and US, consider each other as a primary threat. China is likely to become a regional hegemon in Asia, and is building up its military capacity to back this position. South-East and East Asian nations are under pressure to choose a side, be that China or the US. Australia is also facing pressure to choose between the two great powers.

University of Chicago Professor and offensive realist, John Mearsheimer, published a book in 2001 entitled *The Tragedy of Great Power Politics* predicting many things we see today in US-China relations (Mearsheimer 2001). In a recent interview John Mearsheimer argued that there are two factors that are pushing China towards aggression. One, it is almost impossible for any country as it grows more powerful not to become somewhat more aggressive in its foreign policy. The second factor is that China's neighbours and the US are pushing back. In fact, the US began to contain China regionally with the 2011 pivot to Asia.[27] According to Mearsheimer, a balancing coalition against China is taking shape. He suggests that Japan, India, Singapore, and Viet Nam will eventually ally themselves with the US. And one could probably add the Republic of Korea. On the Chinese side the likely candidates are Pakistan, the Democratic Republic of Korea, Cambodia, the Lao People's Democratic Republic and probably Myanmar. There will thus be two alliance structures, much like there were two alliance structures during the Cold War: NATO on one side and the Warsaw Pact on the other.[28] The question to be asked here is how will this affect NATO and the European nations that rely on the US in Europe to provide a counterbalance against Russia? Will they find themselves being dragged into the China–US conflict?

Lithuania's tensions with Russia and China and the blind reliance on the US

The Baltic states have long had tensions with Russia particularly since the collapse of the Soviet Union. They view the US as their security guarantor, are NATO member states, and have also sought close ties with the EU, also by being euro area member states. Recently Lithuania has experienced tensions with China owing to the Republic of China (Taiwan). After Taiwan announced plans to open a new representative office in Lithuania, the Chinese government responded by ordering Lithuania to withdraw its ambassador in Beijing[29] and stated that it would recall China's ambassador in Vilnius. The Lithuania incident is notable as it was the first time that China had recalled an ambassador from an EU member state since the EU's establishment in 1993 and it follows the EU's criticisms of China on its human rights record.

This incident was followed by Lithuania's withdrawal from the 17+1 Initiative,[30] whose goals are to promote the Chinese Belt and Road Initiative and to enhance cooperation in the fields of infrastructure, transportation and logistics, and trade and investment chiefly with the Central and Eastern European countries. Moreover, Lithuania is currently experiencing serious tensions with Russia[31] as are the Baltic states.[32] At the same time there are reports that both NATO and the US are ill-prepared to defend the Baltics states, including Lithuania, in the event of a war against Russia.[33]

It seems odd that when it is doubtful that NATO can successfully defend the territory of its most exposed members, the Baltics, Lithuania is not only having serious problems with Russia, but also with a rising great power, China. It may well be that Lithuania sees the benefit in making these moves assuming that fuelling tensions with Russia as well as initiating tensions with China will please the US. But the question remains whether this strategy is viable. Newt Gingrich, former Speaker of the US House of Representatives, once claimed that '40% of Estonia is Russian … I'm not sure I would risk nuclear war over some place that is the suburb of St Petersburg'.[34] Many US politicians are ill-informed about the Baltic states and the US has no obvious interest there. It is therefore questionable if it makes sense for a country like Lithuania to irritate China on top of tense relations with Russia when there is no obvious benefit to the US in coming to the aid of Lithuania or any of the other Baltic states during an emergency when such an operation would be costly for the US. Willingness to defend the Baltic states also depends on who is the incumbent president of the US at any given time.

Can the Baltic states rely on the US for their defence? Can they rely on the EU?

Given the rise of China the US may in the longer term want to make peace with Russia, although the war in Ukraine has made this more complicated. If Russia and China have disputes in the Arctic, Russia may seek cooperation and support from the US. While it makes sense for the Baltic states to encourage the US to stay in Europe and lead NATO this cannot be taken for granted as the US seeks to strengthen its position in Asia and ensure its access to the Persian Gulf.

EU support depends on the actions or inactions of the largest EU member states, particularly Germany and France. When the war in Ukraine is over Germany may have greater interest in cooperating with Russia than in supporting Ukraine, Georgia or the Baltic states. Prior to the outbreak of war in Ukraine Germany went ahead with the Nord Stream 2 project despite opposition from those countries as well as Poland. Once the war in Ukraine is over German industry interest, including cheap gas from Russia, maybe become stronger than Germany's interest in keeping some of the smaller EU member states or EU candidate countries happy and secure.

Notes

1 www.stjornarradid.is/media/utanrikisraduneyti-media/media/gunnar-bragi/NB8-VN4-statement-Narva-FINAL.pdf.
2 www.norden.org/en.
3 www.norden.org/en/information/history-nordic-co-operation.
4 www.norden.org/en/information/history-nordic-co-operation.
5 Ibid.
6 www.mfa.gov.lv/en/co-operation-among-baltic-states.
7 As a show of unity in their pursuit of freedom, almost two million people joined hands on 23 August 1989 to form the 600-km Baltic Way that spanned Lithuania, Latvia and Estonia.
8 www.mfa.gov.lv/en/policy/baltic-sea-region/co-operation-among-the-baltic-states-13464-en.
9 www.baltasam.org/en/structure/how-do-we-work.
10 www.visegradgroup.eu/about.
11 www.visegradgroup.eu/about/history.
12 www.france24.com/en/20180621-visegrad-anti-immigrant-eastern-eu-states-boycott-eu-summit-merkel-orban-kurz.

13 See, for example, www.visegradgroup.eu/documents/official-statements/joint-press-release-of.
14 www.visegradgroup.eu/documents/official-statements/meeting-of-foreign.
15 www.visegradgroup.eu/about/aims-and-structure.
16 See, for example, www.visegradgroup.eu/documents/official-statements/joint-press-release-of.
17 www.visegradgroup.eu/about/cooperation.
18 www.visegradgroup.eu/about/aims-and-structure.
19 See, for example, www.lrp.lt/en/media-center/photos/21462/meeting-with-baltic-presidents-and-u.s.-president-barack-obama/a1675; and https://news.err.ee/693410/baltic-presidents-to-meet-with-u-s-president-donald-trump-on-tuesday.
20 www.norden.org/is/node/4262.
21 www.dw.com/en/in-poland-donald-trump-meets-the-new-europe/a-39540960.
22 www.norden.org/is/node/4262.
23 www.theguardian.com/us-news/2018/apr/03/trump-baltic-leaders-press-conference.
24 www.baltictimes.com/baltic_presidents__meeting_with_trump_to_be_followed_by_luncheon/.
25 https://thediplomat.com/2021/02/how-chinas-171-became-a-zombie-mechanism/.
26 https://3seas.eu/; and https://3seas.eu/media/news/political-leaders-from-europe-and-usa-will-discuss-smart-growth-in-central-and-eastern-europe-on-monday.
27 Former US Secretary of State Hillary Clinton announced the pivot to Asia in 2011. At that time the US was beginning to think about containing China; see www.dw.com/en/chinas-rise-and-conflict-with-us/a-55026173.
28 www.dw.com/en/chinas-rise-and-conflict-with-us/a-55026173.
29 https://thediplomat.com/2021/08/whats-behind-lithuanias-outreach-to-taiwan/.
30 www.politico.eu/article/lithuania-pulls-out-china-17-1-bloc-eastern-central-europe-foreign-minister-gabrielius-landsbergis/.
31 https://neweasterneurope.eu/2021/01/07/after-years-of-animosity-is-russia-ready-2-talk-with-lithuania/; https://foreignpolicy.com/2017/03/24/russia-lithuania-nato-grybauskaite-putin-trump-interview/.
32 www.neweurope.eu/article/how-real-is-the-russian-threat-to-the-baltic-states/.
33 www.rand.org/pubs/research_reports/RR1253.html; and www.euractiv.com/section/politics/short_news/nato-ill-prepared-for-large-scale-war-finds-swedish-report/.
34 www.bbc.com/news/world-us-canada-38051155.

References

Baltic Assembly (2021). *Baltic Assembly.* Available at: www.baltasam.org/ (accessed 10 September 2021).

Bjarnason, B. (2020). Nordic Foreign and Security Policy 2020: Climate Change, Hybrid & Cyber Threats and Challenges to the Multilateral, Rules-based World Order. In *Reykjavik: Nordic Foreign and Security Policy.* Available at: www.stjornarradid.is/library/02-Rit–skyrslur-og-skrar/NORDIC_FOREIGN_SECURITY_POLICY_2020_FINAL.pdf (accessed 23 July 2022).

European Free Trade Association (EFTA) (2015). *This Is EFTA*. Available at: www.efta.int/sites/default/files/publications/this-is-efta/this-is-efta-2015.pdf (accessed 10 September 2021).

European Union (EU) (2021). *EU Member Countries in Brief.* Available at: https://europa.eu/european-union/about-eu/countries/member-countries_en (accessed 10 September 2021).

Gyarfášová, O. (2018). Public Opinion in the V4 about Visegrad and Beyond. In Péter Stepper (ed.), *Central Europe and the Visegrád Cooperation: Historical and Policy Perspectives.* Budapest: Antall József Knowledge Centre.

Haugevik, K. M. and Sverdrup, U. (2019). *Ten Years On: Reassessing the Stoltenberg Report on Nordic Cooperation.* Available at: www.fiia.fi/wp-content/uploads/2019/05/ten-years-on-reassessing-stoltenberg.pdf (accessed 23 July 2022).

Havelka. V. (2021). Visegrád Group. In Tamás Levente Molnár (ed.), *Minilateral Cooperation in the EU: Internal Cohesion, Group Dynamics, and Voting Behaviour of Selected State Blocks.* Budapest: Institute for Foreign Affairs and Trade.

Hilmarsson, H. Þ. (2018) *The Economic Crisis and its Aftermath in the Nordic and Baltic Countries: Do as We Say and Not as We Do.* Europa Economic Perspectives. Abingdon: Routledge.

Hilmarsson, H. Þ. (2016). *Iceland and the Challenge of European Integration: Is European Union Membership Feasible?* In Lino Briguglio (ed.) *Small States and the European Union.* Europa Economic Perspectives. Abingdon: Routledge.

Hungarian Ministry of Foreign Affairs and Trade (2021). *Recharging Europe, Hungarian Presidency 2021/2022 of the Visegrád Group.* Available at: https://v4.mfa.gov.hu/asset/view/139043/Programme_of_the_HU_V4_Presidency_2021-22.pdf (accessed 8 July 2022).

International Monetary Fund (IMF) (2020). *World Economic Outlook Database.* Available at: www.imf.org/en/Publications/WEO/weo-database/2020/October.

Keohane, R. O. (1969). Lilliputians' Dilemmas: Small States in International Politics . *International Organizations,* 23(2), 291–310.

Mearsheimer, J. J. (2001). *The Tragedy of Great Power Politics.* New York: W. W. Norton. Available at: https://samuelbhfauredotcom.files.wordpress.com/2015/10/s2-mearsheimer-2001.pdf (accessed 10 September 2021).

Nič, M. (2016). The Visegrád Group in the EU: 2016 as a Turning-Point? *European View,* 15(2), 281–290.

North Atlantic Treaty Organization (NATO) (2021a). *What Is NATO?* Available at: www.nato.int/nato-welcome/index.html (accessed 10 September 2021).

North Atlantic Treaty Organization (NATO) (2021b). *Brussels Summit Communiqué. Issued by the Heads of State and Government Participating in the Meeting of the North Atlantic Council in Brussels 14 June 2021.* Available at: www.nato.int/cps/en/natohq/news_185000.htm (accessed 11 September 2021)

Rūse, I. (2014). Nordic-Baltic Interaction in European Union Negotiations: Taking Advantage of Institutionalized Cooperation. *Journal of Baltic Studies,* 45(2), 229–246.

Stoltenberg, T. (2009). *Nordic Cooperation on Foreign and Security Policy. Proposals Presented to the Extraordinary Meeting of Nordic Foreign Ministers in Oslo on 9 February 2009.* Available at: www.regjeringen.no/globalassets/upload/ud/vedlegg/nordicreport.pdf (accessed 23 July 2022).

Visegrád Fund (2021). *Advancing Ideas for Sustainable Regional Cooperation in Central Europe.* Available at: www.visegradfund.org/ (accessed 10 September 2021).

Visegrád Group (2021). *History of the Visegrád Group.* Available at: www.visegradgroup.eu/about/history (accessed 10 September 2021).

4 Economic and social performance after the 2008–09 global financial crisis and during the COVID-19 pandemic

All the Baltic states and the Visegrád countries have grown economically since becoming members of the European Union (EU) in 2004. Figures 4.1 and 4.3 show the countries' gross domestic product (GDP) per capita at constant prices on a purchasing-power parity (PPP) basis. The Nordic countries that are either in the EU or in the European Free Trade Association (EFTA)/European Economic Area (EEA) have also grown economically (see Figure 4.2). Nevertheless, it can be seen from Figure 4.4 that neither the Baltic states nor the Visegrád countries have caught up with the Nordic countries, which remain well ahead of both the Baltic and the Visegrád countries more than 30 years after the collapse of the Soviet Union and after nearly two decades of being members of the EU. All the Nordic countries are well above the EU average in terms of GDP per capita (on a PPP basis), while the Baltic states and the Visegrád countries remain well below the EU average on this indicator (see Figures 4.1–4.4). However, one also needs to keep in mind that the EU average declined when poorer EU countries such as Bulgaria and Romania became members of the EU in 2007.

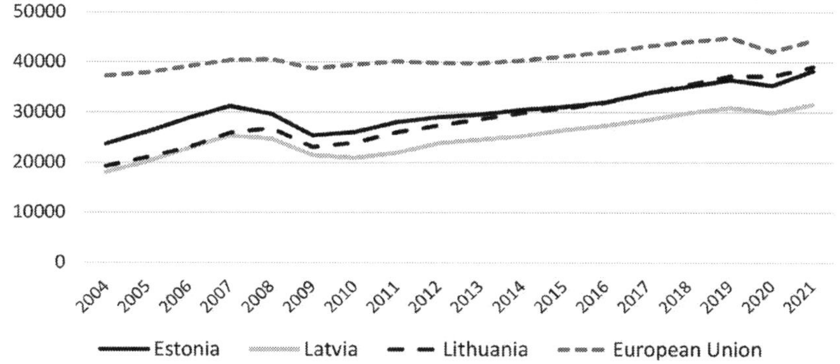

Figure 4.1 Baltic states' GDP per capita in constant prices on a PPP basis (in 2017 international dollars), 2004–21
Source: IMF (2022).

DOI: 10.4324/9781003212539-5

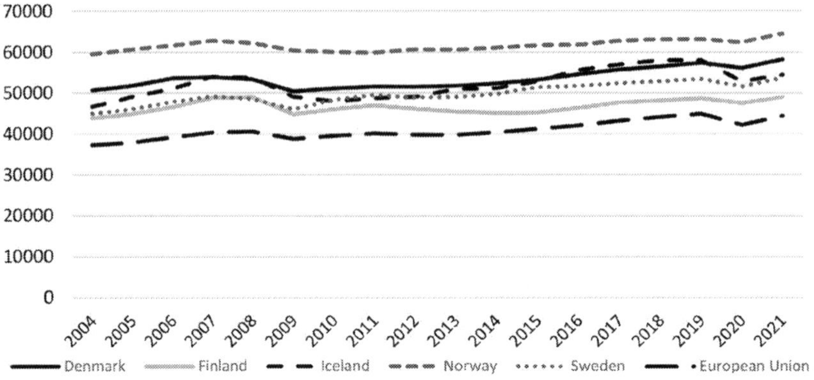

Figure 4.2 Nordic countries' GDP per capita in constant prices on a PPP basis (in 2017 international dollars), 2004–21
Source: IMF (2022).

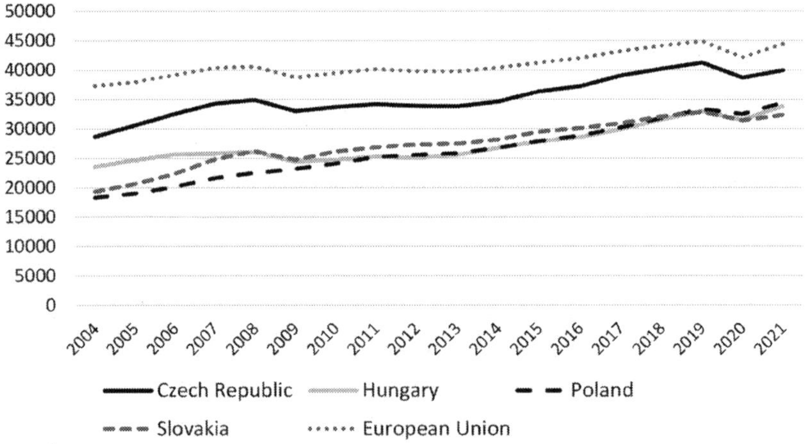

Figure 4.3 Visegrád countries' GDP per capita in constant prices on a PPP basis (in 2017 international dollars), 2004–21
Source: IMF (2022).

There have been challenges along the way. The 2008/09 global financial crisis hit all the Baltic states very hard and all the member countries implemented severe fiscal austerity programmes during the crisis and kept their exchange rates fixed to facilitate adoption of the euro. This meant that they were affected more deeply by the crisis. Among the Nordic countries, both Finland and especially Iceland were severely affected by the crisis, while the other Nordic countries experienced a recession. All the Visegrád countries

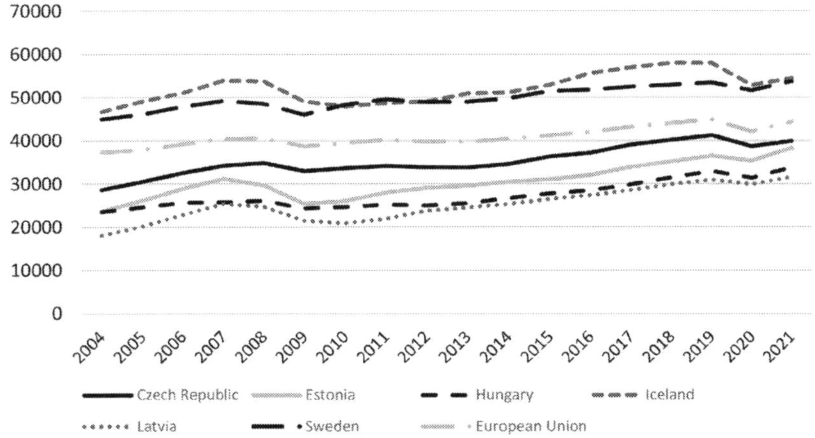

Figure 4.4 Baltic and Visegrád countries' GDP per capita in constant prices on a PPP basis (in 2017 international dollars), 2004–21
Source: IMF (2022).

reported a decline in their GDP per capita (on a PPP basis) during the 2008/09 global financial crisis, except Poland which maintained positive growth throughout the crisis while Hungary experienced the sharpest recession among the Visgrád countries. All the countries were negatively affected by the COVID-19 pandemic and from now on to varying degrees they will be affected by the war in Ukraine that started on 24 February 2022. The war in Ukraine is now halting recovery in all the countries and fuelling inflation.

Unemployment

All the Baltic states experienced a steep increase in unemployment during the 2008/09 global financial crisis (see Figure 4.5). In 2010 unemployment in all the Baltic states stood at more than 15%; it was close to 20% in Latvia. Unemployment then declined from 2010 onwards partially due to GDP growth but also partially due to large outward migration from the Baltics states mainly to wealthier EU member states. During the COVID-19 crisis all the Baltics again experienced an increase in unemployment.

All the Nordic countries experienced an increase in unemployment during the 2008/09 global financial crisis (see Figure 4.6). The increase was especially steep in Iceland and Denmark, but Norway was the least affected of the Nordic countries. Since then, unemployment has remained high particularly in Finland and Sweden and to a lesser extent in Denmark. From 2010 unemployment declined sharply in Iceland. During the COVID-19 crisis all the Nordic countries experienced an increase in unemployment, especially Iceland that has become increasingly dependent on the tourism industry.

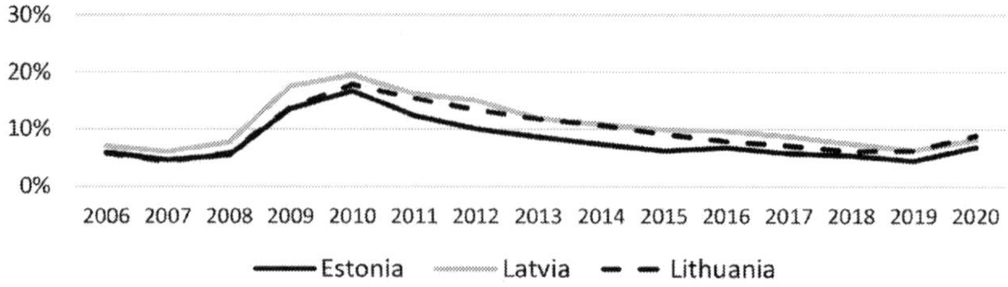

Figure 4.5 Unemployment in the Baltic states (% of the total labour force)
Source: IMF (2021d).

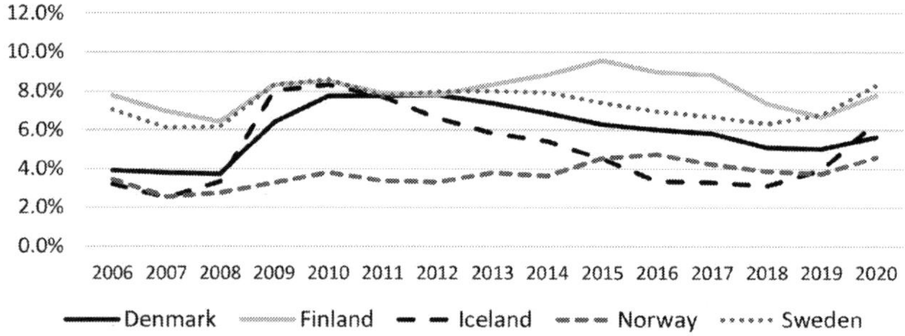

Figure 4.6 Unemployment in the Nordic countries (% of the total labour force)
Source: IMF (2021d).

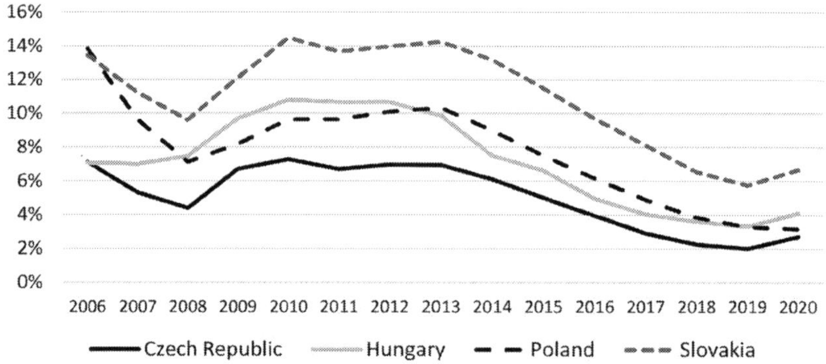

Figure 4.7 Unemployment in the Visegrád countries (% of the total labour force)
Source: IMF (2021d).

Prior to the 2008/09 global financial crisis unemployment had been declining in the Visegrád countries except Hungary (see Figure 4.7). Unemployment then increased and reached particularly high levels in Slovakia in 2010, at about 14%, close to the level experienced by the Baltic states. Unemployment remained rather stable in the Visegrád group until 2013. Thereafter unemployment declined in all the countries until the COVID-19 crisis hit and it rose again, except in Poland (see Figure 4.7).

Market economy versus Keynesian welfare state: the Nordic versus the Baltic model

All the countries in the Baltic, Nordic and Visegrád groups have adopted a market economy, democracy and have taken part in European integration. The Nordic and Baltic peoples have been in contact for centuries despite interruptions – most recently the Soviet occupation of the Baltics. Nevertheless, after their separation from the Soviet Union, the economic, welfare and tax policies developed in the Baltic states were very different from the Nordic welfare model. Post-independence, the Baltic states went from one extreme to another: from a communist centrally planned economy to a neoliberal free market economy and were – at least in Estonia – influenced by the University of Chicago economist, Milton Friedman. The Visegrád countries appear to have found a middle ground with better social outcomes than the Baltic states, as will be discussed below and shown empirically.

Economic and welfare policies are often fiercely disputed within countries and the Baltic, Nordic and Visegrád countries are no exception. The renowned British economist John Maynard Keynes (n.d.) once commented that '[c]apitalism is the astounding belief that the most wickedest of men will do the most wickedest of things for the greatest good of everyone'. When discussing the 2008/09 global financial crisis in his book *The Price of Inequality*, Stiglitz states that '[t]he wealth given to the elites and the bankers seemed to arise out of their ability and willingness to take advantage of others' (2013, p. xliv). This comment appears to fit the Baltic states' transition to a market economy. Government assets were captured by the Baltic elite and during the 2008/09 global financial crisis for and Swedish banking interests were more important than the wellbeing of ordinary Baltic people. Austerity policies then resulted in massive outward migration (see, for example, Hilmarsson 2018, 2020 and 2014).

But capitalism can be a useful system if governments can successfully and democratically intervene for the common good. The Nordic countries are known worldwide as welfare states and, while their welfare systems are undergoing constant review and reform, these systems remain among the key characteristics of Nordic societies and the Nordic welfare model (see further Hannibalsson 2017). According to Ingebritsen, 'Scandinavians remain committed to the provision of universal benefits and to playing a role in international society consistent with the golden age of welfare capitalism' (2006, p. 12). For the Baltic states the question arises as to whether or not they are likely to become members of this group of like-minded northern European social welfare states or whether they will remain at the other end of the spectrum as neoliberal societies with high income inequality and weak welfare systems, implementing austerity programmes during recessions.

The Nordic countries certainly allow market forces to play a big role in their societies, but governments do intervene to correct what they perceive as market failures, and they redistribute income through a progressive income tax, tax property owners and maintain social safety nets to help the most vulnerable. This is what they call welfare capitalism, which is not as wicked as the capitalism Keynes talked about.

In contrast, Baltic capitalism was founded on flat income taxes and low taxes on wealthy property owners; this seems wicked in the Keynesian sense, in that burden-sharing seems unfair. The Nordic countries have learned how important economic and social justice is and perhaps it is now time for the Baltic states to consider taking steps towards becoming more inclusive societies. This will be a challenge especially since many of their young and best educated inhabitants, who could have become taxpayers, have chosen to immigrate to other countries partly because of the weak welfare systems and income inequality. It is noteworthy that the Visegrád countries seem to have managed to find a middle ground here with social outcomes close to those of the Nordics but a per capita GDP level similar to the Baltics. The Visegrád countries, such as the Czech Republic (Czechia) and Slovakia, have been able to avoid the massive outward migration of young and well-educated people that Latvia and Lithuania have been faced with (see Figure 4.10).

The Nordic welfare model and collective risk sharing

As pointed out in a comprehensive report by Andersen et al. (2007) entitled *The Nordic Model: Embracing Globalization and Sharing Risks*, the Nordic model is widely regarded as a benchmark for other countries. As the authors state, the Nordic countries are often seen to have succeeded better than other countries in combining economic efficiency and growth with a relatively peaceful labour market, a fairly even distribution of income, and social cohesion (ibid.). The Nordic model could thus be a source of inspiration for other nations in their search for a better economic and social system, including perhaps the Baltic states.

During a meeting between the author of this book and officials at the IMF some years ago, during which economic and social progress in the Baltic states was discussed and compared with that of the Nordic countries, a senior IMF official commented that 'it is hard to look good if you are compared with the Nordics'. This is how the Nordic countries are frequently seen. As Ingebritsen notes, 'Scandinavia provides examples of how power and wealth can be distributed more equitably; how gender and class differences can be minimized; and how state authority can be used in a positive way to temper markets and social injustice' (2006, p. 2).

Scandinavians have not hesitated to intervene with market forces and have used government institutions and systems to produce results that are regarded as being more equitable than those achieved by neoliberal hands-off policies. To correct the 'wickedness' in capitalism that Keynes spoke of, Andersen et al. (2007) argue that the Nordic countries have embraced both globalization and the welfare state, and that the security offered by collective mechanisms for sharing risks has been instrumental in enhancing a favourable attitude to globalization and competition.

Collective risk-sharing can thus continue to offer a safety net that helps workers and their families to cope with risks and to adapt to new requirements during times of crisis, transition and change. At the same time, the Nordic welfare model is widely seen as being consistent with a good business and investment climate with a vibrant private sector and foreign investment, research and innovation. This can, for example, be seen in the World Bank's *Doing Business* reports, which constantly rank the Nordic countries among the top performers worldwide for creating a favourable investment and business climate (World Bank 2020).

Furthermore, as Anderson et al. point out: 'Professional economists have often been puzzled by the relatively good economic performance of the Nordic model, given its high taxes and its generous social protection systems as well as the role of strong labour unions and wage coordination' (2007, p. 16). Clearly, reductions in economic efficiency must be caused by some of the characteristics of the Nordic welfare model, and numerous studies have been devoted to analysing the economic costs of a large welfare state.

Meanwhile, numerous factors appear to have made up for these disadvantages. Arguably the Nordic model has become a venue for generating political support for growth-enhancing technical change, free trade and open markets by creating systems through which the winners emerging from structural transformation compensate the losers, at least to some extent (see Andersen et al. 2007, p. 18). In the future, the pressure will be on European countries to deliver their preferred mix of public and private goods more efficiently. As Eichengreen points out, the Scandinavian countries are widely cited as examples of societies that have already started to move in this direction by successfully maintaining essential social protection while enhancing the efficiency of their provision (2008, pp. 421–22). A reasonable degree of social and political cohesion would also seem of importance in the Baltic states for their political stability and growth sustainability. It could reduce ethnic strife and political tensions, while improving their security profile.

The Baltic neoliberal revolt against the welfare state

Although the Baltic states have sought cooperation with the Nordic countries in international organizations, also engaging with them in trade, investment and financial sector cooperation, they have to a lesser degree followed them in terms of economic policy. Moreover, they do not follow the Nordic welfare model in the design of their tax and welfare systems. Since regaining their independence in 1991, the Baltic states have followed a very different political, economic and social path from their wealthier Nordic neighbours. Adopting the Nordic welfare model on a full scale would be out of reach and unsustainable at their income level. Nor is there reason for them to copy the Nordic countries on every account. Nevertheless, they could attempt to approach the Nordic model if that was their wish and move closer to the welfare systems of some of the other wealthier European countries, perhaps with EU support. This could also help them to keep a higher proportion of their young people within their borders. Currently the Baltics are closer to the free market neoliberal Anglophone model (see Table 4.2 for a comparison of the different country groups).

Mart Laar became prime minister of Estonia in 1992 and served in that capacity until 1994 and again from 1999–2002. In an interview with the *Brussels Journal* during the Baltic boom in 2005 and before the global financial crash in 2008 he commented as follows:

> It is very fortunate that I was not an economist …I had read only one book on economics – Milton Friedman's *Free to Choose.* I was so ignorant at the time that I thought that what Friedman wrote about the benefits of privatisation, the flat tax and the abolition of all customs rights, was the result of economic reforms that had been put into practice in the West. It seemed common sense to me and, as I thought it had already been done everywhere, I simply introduced it in Estonia, despite warnings from Estonian economists that it could not be done. They said it was as impossible as walking on water. We did it: we just walked on the water because we did not know that it was impossible.
>
> (Laar 2005)

Laar thus decided to implement neoliberal policies in Estonia in a more orthodox way than any other country in the world had ever done, based on the assumption that this was common practice 'in the West' (ibid.). The neoliberal era started in the 1980s as a revolt against the welfare state and was based on a belief in market infallibility. Markets self-corrected, and governments should get out of the way. The results of this policy became clear on a global scale in 2008, including in the Baltic states.

We should keep in mind that this happened in a country that was once a Soviet republic and Estonians were not well-informed about economic and welfare policies in other countries when Laar took office, not even in Scandinavia in spite of their close geographic proximity. This shows how isolated the country was and how ill-prepared it was during the early days of independence. Nevertheless, Estonia is often seen as the Baltic state that initiates reforms which the other Baltics, Latvia and Lithuania, follow.

Thus, after the Baltic states had regained their independence, reforms in those countries were characterized by the creation of an ultra-liberal, business-friendly environment that sought to attract foreign investment. A balanced fiscal budget and strict monetary policy with fixed exchange rates was to give the Baltic states a strong reputation as reliable borrowers. A fully open trade regime led to rapid reorientation of foreign trade towards the West, especially the EU common market. The social system should, on the other hand, inspire 'people to assume responsibility for their own future' (Laar 2007, p. 9; see also Bohle and Greskovits 2012).

Visegrád group

The Visegrád countries were never Soviet republics like the Baltic states. They were called satellite states and one could therefore expect that they would be able to exercise more independence in their policymaking. The economic and social transformation strategy of the Baltic states, as discussed above, was much more radical than that pursued by the Visegrád countries, as the former intended to make a radical break from the Soviet Union and the socialist legacy. According to Bohle and Greskovits,

> The common factor in the Visegrád success stories of building democratic market societies – relatively high initial levels of economic development and social welfare, geographic and cultural proximity to the West, and presocialist experiences with democracy and the market – are often mentioned in the literature.
>
> (2012, p. 154)

Unlike the Baltic states that emphasized the benefits of a free market ultraliberal business-friendly environment, the Visegrád countries seem to have been able find a middle ground between the Baltic neoliberal policies and the Nordic welfare state. As Bohle and Greskovits state,

> Built on existing policy and institutional legacies, the Visegrád countries' welfare states stand out in the region for the generosity of their provisions – including education, health care, pensions, labour market policies, family and child care and social housing – whether measured by the social spending share of GDP or by the absolute volume of benefits.
>
> (Ibid.)

Thus, much more than the reformers of the Baltic states, policymakers in the Visegrád group built on existing state legacies. They drew heavily on the expertise of social policymakers and bureaucrats and kept a high degree of continuity in the institutional set-up of the welfare state. The Latvian minister of welfare is cited as addressing pensioners as follows: 'You do not need [a] big pension, because you worked under the Communist regime, and your work accomplished nothing' (Bohle and Greskovits 2012, p. 116). In contrast, according to Hungary's first democratically elected premier, József Antall,

> pension is a right acquired by work; the security of pensioners can only be guaranteed in a renewed insurance system ... All those who are powerless and disadvantaged should be able to count on society's and the state's help by means of a social safety net.
>
> (Ibid., p. 155; see also Inglot 2008)

Meanwhile, according to the Polish Minister of Labour and Social Affairs, Jacek Jan Kuroń,

> I believe that you cannot take away certain social rights from people, you can modify them, change the method of implementation, make them more rational ... but to simply say you are not entitled to them any more cannot be done.
>
> (Ibid.)

As will be discussed below income equality, the level of poverty and social exclusion are, according to Eurostat data, all remarkably similar to those of the Nordic countries that have a much higher per capita GDP than the Visegrád countries.

Social justice in the Baltic, Nordic and Visegrad countries

Solidarity, social inclusion and safety nets for the most vulnerable were not on the agenda when the Baltic states became independent from the Soviet Union. It was the survival of the fittest and the fittest had accumulated wealth that in some cases was based on the privatization of government property in a corrupt environment. A World Bank working paper reported that Latvia is among the high state capture economies (Helman et al., 2000).

A free market, fiscal discipline, fixed exchange rates and economic integration were some of the key priorities. The Baltic states' reforms were not intended to be soft with a human face. It should not come as a surprise that, in terms of indicators such as the at-risk-of-poverty rate, the Gini coefficient or the income quintile share ratio, the Baltics do not have a strong record in the EU, the euro area or the EEA. Income inequality is particularly high in Latvia and Lithuania (see Table 4.1). Estonia is close to the EU average on this indicator as measured by the Gini coefficient.

The Gini coefficient/index[1] is a standard measure of inequality. If income were shared exactly in proportion to population, for example, with both the bottom and top 10% obtaining 10% of a country's income, then the Gini index would be zero. If, on the other hand, all the income was to accrue to the wealthiest inhabitant, the Gini index would be 100. So, the lower the Gini index, the greater the income equality. More equal societies, such as the Nordic and the Visegrád countries (see Table 4.1), have a Gini index of 30 or below. In more unequal societies, such as the Baltic states and the south-eastern European countries Bulgaria and Romania, the Gini index is above

Table 4.1 GDP per capita (current prices, US$) and selected social indicators, 2019

	GDP per capita (current prices, US$)	*Proportion of people at-risk-of-poverty or social exclusion*[2]	*At-risk-of-poverty rate*[3]	*The Gini index/ coefficient*[4]	*Income quintile share ratio*[5]
Baltics					
Estonia	23,720	24.3	21.7	30.5	5.08
Latvia	17,739	27.3	22.9	35.2	6.54
Lithuania	19,552	26.3	20.6	35.4	6.44
Nordics					
Denmark	60,299	16.3	12.5	27.5	4.09
Finland	48,749	15.6	11.6	26.2	3.69
Iceland	69,572	13.3*	8.8*	n.a.	3.21*
Norway	75,700*	16.1	12.7	n.a.	3.81
Sweden	51,443	18.8	17.1	27.6	4.33
Anglophone countries					
Ireland	80,481	20.6	13.1	28.3	4.03
The United Kingdom	42,416	24.8*	18.6*	33.5*	5.63*
Central Europe (Visegrád countries and Slovenia)					
Czech Republic	23,539	12.5	10.1	24.0	3.34
Hungary	16,725	18.9	12.3	28.0	4.23
Poland	15,689	18.2	15.4	28.5	4.37
Slovenia	26,036	14.4	12.0	23.9	3.39
Slovakia	19,281	16.4	11.9	22.8	3.34
South-eastern Europe					
Bulgaria	9,863	32.8	22.6	40.8	8.10
Romania	12,867	31.2	23.8	34.8	7.08
EU28		21.4	16.8	30.7	5.09

Source: IMF (2021d) and Eurostat (2021).

Note: * Data are from 2018.

30 and close to 35 in Latvia, Lithuania and Romania; in the case of Bulgaria it is above 40.

It is perhaps not surprising that in comparison to the Nordic welfare states the Baltics have an uneven income distribution, weak safety nets and weak welfare systems, which together made their citizens vulnerable during the 2008/09 global financial crisis. However, poverty, social exclusion and income inequality remain serious problems, even in comparison to countries with similar income levels, such as the Czech Republic, Hungary, Poland and

Slovakia (see Table 4.1 and Figures 4.11, 4.13, 4.14 and 4.16) Measured by the Gini index income distribution in Latvia and Lithuania is also more uneven than in the European Anglophone countries, Ireland and the United Kingdom (see Tables 4.1 and 4.2). To see developments over the past decade, time series data with graphs are discussed later in this chapter for income inequality and poverty and social exclusion.

Public spending in the Baltic states is relatively low and their governments remain relatively small, particularly with respect to transfer payments. General government expenditure is lower than in the Visegrád or Nordic countries (see Figure 4.8.) and the share of GDP devoted to social benefits is substantially lower. According to the IMF, the Baltic states are closer to the Anglophone countries than the Nordic countries in the structure of their private sectors (IMF 2014, p. 4). In fact, in terms of poverty (measured by the at-risk-of-poverty rate) and income inequality (measured by the Gini

Table 4.2 Comparator country groups

Baltic states	*Nordic countries*	*Anglophone countries*	*Visegrád countries*	*South-eastern European countries*
Estonia	Denmark	Australia	Czech Republic	Bulgaria
Latvia	Finland	Canada	Hungry	Romania
Lithuania	Iceland	Ireland	Poland	
	Norway	New Zealand	Slovakia	
	Sweden	The UK		
		The US		

Source: compiled by the author based on IMF (2014).

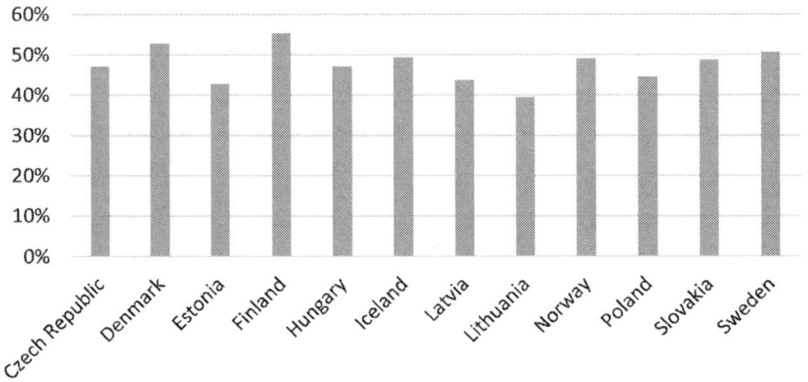

Figure 4.8 General government expenditure of the Baltic, Nordic and Visegrád countries (% of GDP), 2021
Source: IMF (2022).

coefficient) Latvia and Lithuania are close to Romania, a less advanced country and at lower income level (see Table 4.1).

General government expenditure in 2021 was lowest in the Baltic states at around 40% of GDP. General government expenditure in the Nordic countries was around or above 50% and close to 50% in the Visegrád countries, except for Poland where was slightly lower. The Nordic countries thus spent a higher proportion of their GDP on this indicator but in addition to that their GDP per capita is much higher than in the other countries so their expenditure is much higher per capita than in the Visegrád countries and especially compared to the Baltic states.

The Baltic states have had a relatively high labour taxation and a low profit taxation. In contrast to their weak performance on social indicators, they rank relatively highly on business indicators, according to the World Bank (2020). In fact, as stated above, low taxes and a liberal economic regime introduced following the restoration of independence in the 1990s aimed at attracting foreign investment and promoting investment growth and thus GDP growth. Social cohesion was not a priority.

EU emphasis on fiscal discipline made matters worse during the 2008/09 global financial crisis. Extreme austerity was implemented with cuts in health care and education. Internal devaluation was enforced since depreciation of the local currencies could result in the exclusion of the Baltic states from the euro area, which these countries perhaps wanted to join for reasons of security more than economics.

Had the Baltic states wanted to implement more Nordic policies they could, for example, have introduced more a progressive income tax, instead of a flat-rate tax and a higher property/capital gains tax, in order to have the rich carry some of the burden. It should be noted that a progressive income tax has now been introduced in Latvia.[6] Having regained their independence in 1991 the Baltic states could have used this revenue to help the most vulnerable, including their young people, who as a consequence might have stayed in the country rather than fleeing the policies imposed by neoliberal governments. It is a sad story of states that became independent but lost the opportunity to become inclusive and more humane. The Baltics had a very low level of government debt when the 2008/09 global financial crisis struck (see Figure 4.9).

Government debt subsequently increased, not as a means of creating social safety nets, but rather to facilitate foreign bank recovery. This was not the first time that unregulated capitalism was saved from capitalists by the state. It amounted to a bailout of the financial system by the taxpayers, and the creation of a welfare system for banks, not the poorest, most vulnerable segment of the population. Thus the Baltic states embraced neoliberalism and monetarism, while the wealthier Nordic countries followed Keynesianism. Arguably the austerity policies in the Baltics, especially in Latvia and Lithuania, contributed to large outward migration which was not, however, experienced by Visegrád countries such as the Czech Republic and Slovakia, whose populations have in fact increased (see Figure 4.10).

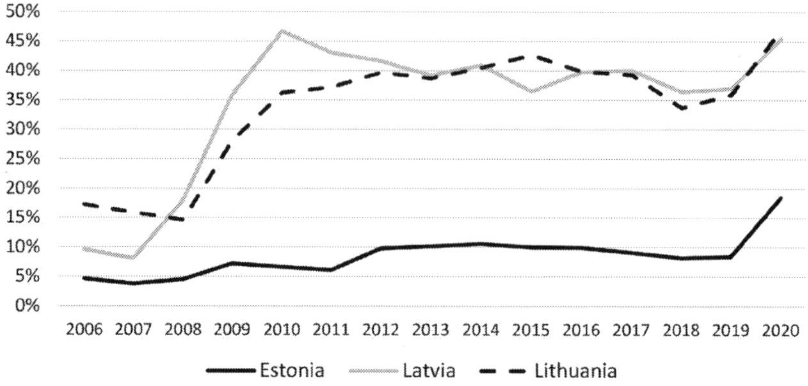

Figure 4.9 Baltic states' general government gross debt (% of GDP), 2006–20
Source: IMF (2021d).

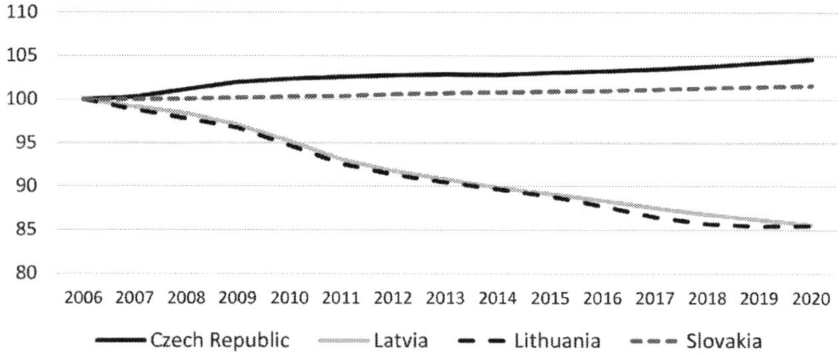

Figure 4.10 Population index (2006 = 100), 2006–20
Source: IMF (2021d).

The performance of welfare systems: the Baltic States lagging behind

When discussing recent developments in the Baltic, Nordic and Visegrád countries one needs to keep in mind that all these countries have been impacted by the COVID-19 pandemic. Also, the war in Ukraine will halt recovery in those countries and has fuelled inflation. Poland, which shares a long eastern border with Ukraine, has been severely affected by the war, and 'there will be additional public spending to manage the large influx of displaced people from Ukraine' (World Bank 2022, p. 88). Both Hungary and Slovakia, which also share eastern borders with Ukraine, have also been affected.

Among the country groups discussed in this volume the greatest inequality, poverty and exclusion can be found in the Baltic states. Social policies are under constant review and change frequently. In recent Article IV consultations with Estonia, the IMF commented that '[d]espite good progress in reducing several social gaps over time, there remain long-standing challenges related to relative poverty, inequality, and gender pay disparities' (2021a, p. 7). Furthermore 'Estonia has made welcome progress in reducing general inequality, with its Gini coefficient moving close to the euro-area average in 2019. However, data on at-risk poverty suggest substantial pockets of relative inequality [in Estonia], particularly among the elderly' (ibid., p. 20). Finally, '[to] manage potential social scarring risks, policies should continue to reduce inequality and gender gaps and further protect the elderly' (ibid., p. 26).

According to the IMF, in Latvia

> [p]overty and inequality levels remain high, especially among the elderly and those with lower education levels. Social protection is limited, partly given the relatively large informality. Taxes and social benefits in Latvia have a low redistributive impact compared to other EU countries, weighing on income inequality.
>
> (2021b, p. 4)

Furthermore, '[i]ncome inequality is one of the highest in the EU. Poverty rates are one of the highest in the EU, especially among the elderly and those with lower education' (ibid., p. 26). According to the OECD, 'the social safety net in Latvia is limited, poverty rates are high compared to the EU average and poor households suffer the most from rising energy and food prices' (2022a, p. 171).

In its Article IV consultations with Lithuania the IMF highlighted the fact that '[d]irectors stressed the importance of implementing structural reforms to address long-standing economic and social challenges, including high poverty rates and regional disparities, which have increased budget rigidities' (2021c, p. 2). Furthermore, '[r]educing social disparities and poverty will require larger and more effective social programs' (ibid., p. 23). Finally that '[t]he authorities are revisiting the tax system to improve the structure of taxes and social benefits, thus contributing to the reduction of income inequality, as well as planning to develop an action plan to reduce the shadow economy and the VAT gap' (ibid., p. 70).

When discussing Lithuania, the OECD calls for '[s]upport for vulnerable households to cope with surging energy prices includes an increase in non-taxable income, an extension of means-tested heating compensation and higher pensions' (2022b, p. 174).

Thus, while the Baltic states have made progress economically in terms of growing their GDP per capita it is clear that they still need to implement further urgent social reforms. On this front the Nordic and the Visegrád countries are more advanced.

Income inequality, poverty and social exclusion in the Baltic, Nordic and the Visegrád groups during the past decade

The following section provides an overview of recent trends in income inequality as well as poverty and social exclusion in the Baltic, Nordic and the Visegrád countries (see Figures 4.11– 4.16). For this purpose, reference will be made to the Gini coefficient as an indicator measuring income inequality. When measuring poverty or social exclusion the Eurostat indicator shows the proportion of people at-risk-of-poverty or social exclusion. For both indicators the EU average is provided.

Regarding income inequality measured by the Gini coefficient the Baltic states have the highest income inequality and remain above the EU average, while the Nordic countries have the lowest income inequality and are all well below the EU average (see Figures 4.11 and 4.12). Finally, in recent years income inequality in the Visegrád countries has been below the EU average (see Figure 4.13). In the Baltic states income inequality is very high and since 2017 it has been higher in Latvia and Lithuania than in Romania, which has a lower income level. In the Nordic countries income inequality is highest in Denmark and Sweden and lowest in Iceland and Norway. In the Visegrád countries income inequality is lower than in the EU except in Poland from 2010–14. Income inequality is highest in Hungary and Poland and lowest in the Czech Republic and Slovakia.

According to Figure 4.11, there is much more income inequality in Latvia and Lithuania than in the EU as measured by the Gini coefficient. Estonia's

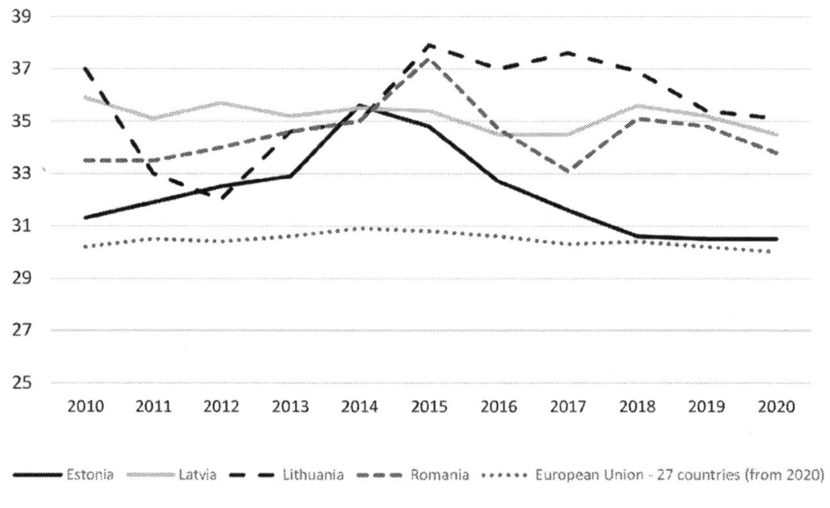

Figure 4.11 The Gini coefficient of equivalized disposable income in Baltic states and Romania, 2010–20

Source: Eurostat (2021).

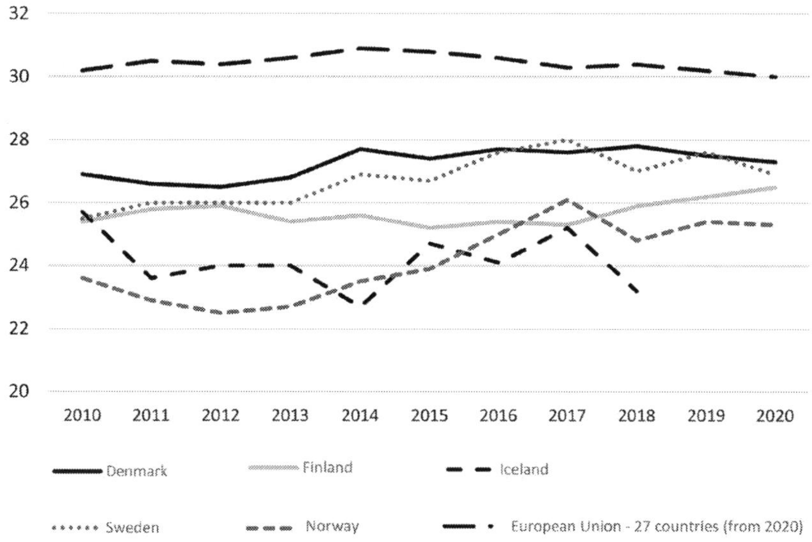

Figure 4.12 The Gini coefficient of equivalized disposable income in the Nordic countries and the EU, 2010–20
Source: Eurostat (2021).

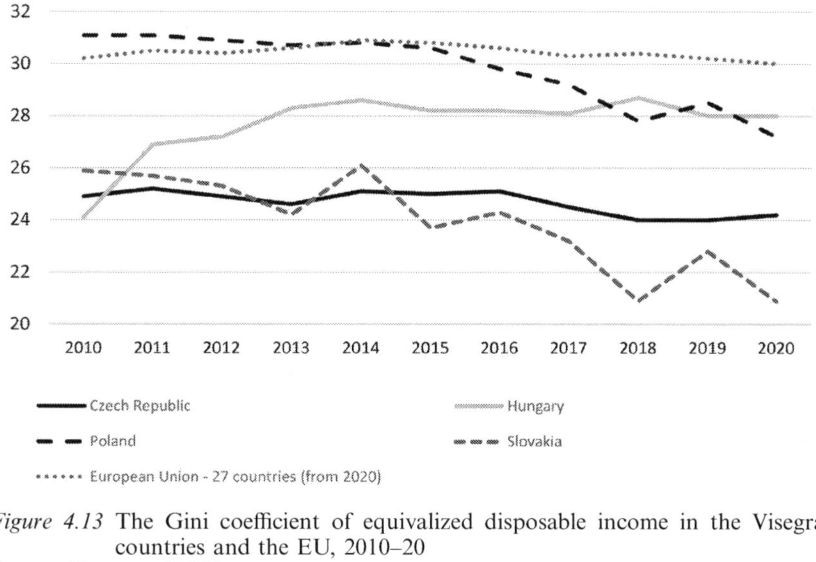

Figure 4.13 The Gini coefficient of equivalized disposable income in the Visegrád countries and the EU, 2010–20
Source: Eurostat (2021).

income inequality declined from 2014–18 when it reached about the same level as that of the EU. It is also noteworthy that since 2017 there has been more income inequality in Latvia and Lithuania than in Romania.

Figure 4.12 shows that there is less income inequality in all the Nordic countries than in the EU as measured by the Gini coefficient. On this measure income inequality is highest in Denmark and Sweden and lowest in Norway and Iceland.

However, according Figure 4.13, there is less income inequality in the Visegrád countries than in the EU as measured by the Gini coefficient. The only exception is Poland from 2010–14.

Poverty or social exclusion?

In recent years the proportion of people at risk of poverty or social exclusion has been higher in the Baltic states than in the EU on average (see Figure 4.14). In all the Nordic countries the proportion of people at risk of poverty or social exclusion has been much lower than the EU average (see Figure 4.15). In recent years the proportion of people at risk of poverty or social exclusion in the Visegrád countries has been lower than the EU average, except in Hungary from 2010–18 and Poland from 2010–14 (see Figure 4.16).

In the Baltic states, Latvia and Lithuania, the proportion of people at risk of poverty or social exclusion declined from 2010–20, while it remained more stable in Estonia and closer to the EU average on this indicator.

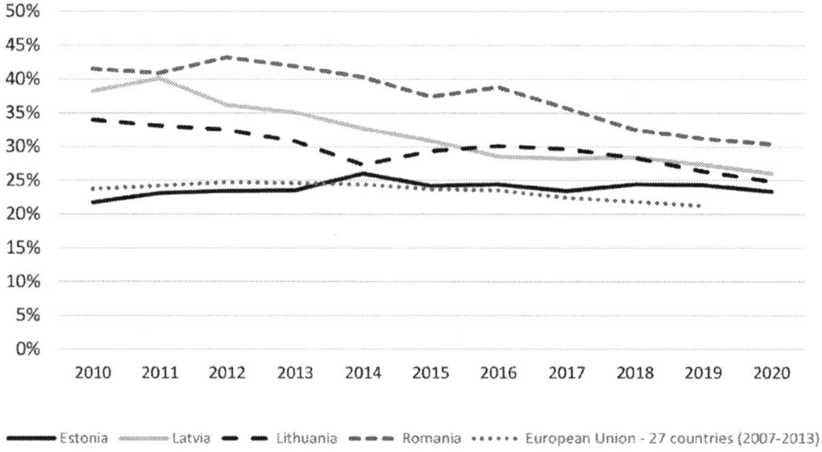

Figure 4.14 People at risk of poverty or social exclusion in the Baltic states (%), 2010–20

Source: Eurostat (2021).

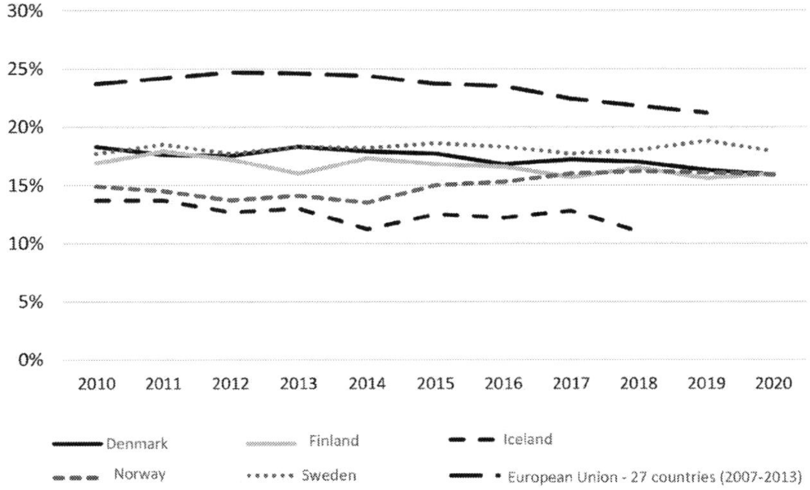

Figure 4.15 People at risk of poverty or social exclusion in the Nordic countries (%) 2010–20

Source: Eurostat (2021).

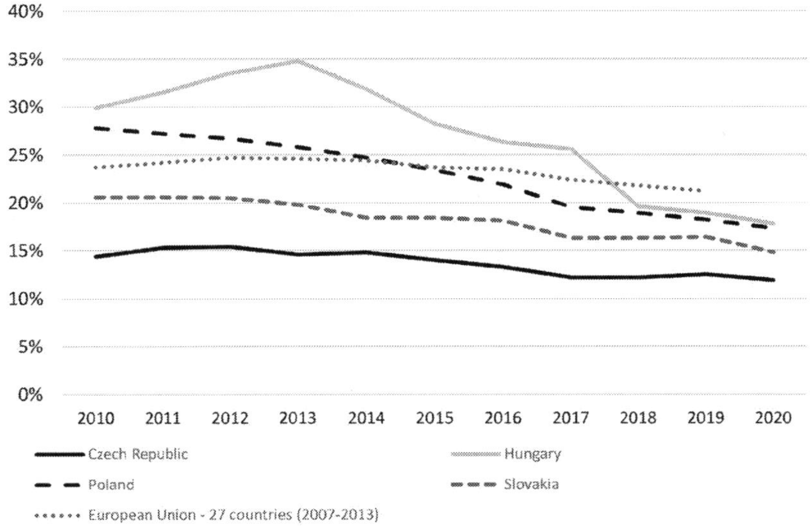

Figure 4.16 People at risk of poverty or social exclusion in the Visegrád countries (%), 2010–20

Source: Eurostat (2021).

The Nordic welfare states have similar income or GDP levels per capita, except Norway which is the wealthiest country. The number of people at risk of poverty or social exclusion has fluctuated but it was similar in the continental Nordic countries from 2010–20, although Sweden has recorded the highest rate since 2015 and Norway the lowest from 2010–17. Iceland has the lowest proportion of people at risk of poverty or social exclusion, according to the data provided by Eurostat (data for the period 2018–20 were not available at the time of writing). All the Nordic countries are well below the EU level of people at risk of poverty or social exclusion which was slightly over 20% in 2019.

The Visegrád countries have similar levels of GDP per capita. The proportion of people at risk of poverty or social exclusion followed a downward trend in all the Visegrád countries from 2010–20, except in Hungary from 2010–13, but from 2013–20 the proportion of those at risk declined from 35% to 18%. Since 2018 all the Visegrád countries have recorded a lower proportion of people at risk of poverty or social exclusion than in the EU on average. The Czech Republic and Slovakia have been well below the EU average on this indicator since 2010.

Health care expenditure and COVID-19 cases and deaths

Following the outbreak of the COVID-19 pandemic in 2020, it is interesting to know how much individual countries are spending on health care. The statistics from Eurostat on current health care expenditure (public and private) show how this varies across the EU and the EEA (see Table 4.3).

On average health care expenditure in the EU amounted to 9.9% of GDP in 2018 (€3,076.80 per capita). Among the EU countries under study, health care expenditure in euros per capita was highest in Denmark and Sweden in 2018, while it was lowest in Romania and Bulgaria. The EFTA/EEA countries, Iceland and Norway, spend more on health care per capita than any of the other EU countries under study (Table 4.3).

It is perhaps not surprising that health care expenditure as a percentage of GDP is higher in the Nordic countries than in the Baltic states, given that the Nordics are welfare states whereas the Baltics have pursued neoliberal policies. Health care expenditure in euros per capita is also much higher in the Nordics than in the Baltics reflecting the fact that they spend more on health care as a percentage of GDP and enjoy a much higher GDP per capita.

Health care expenditure as a percentage of GDP and health care expenditure in euros per capita is not that different in the Visegrád countries compared to the Baltic states. Health care expenditure in euros per capita in Romana and Bulgaria is lower than in Baltic and the Visegrád countries, thereby reflecting a lower level of GDP per capita in these countries (see Tables 4.1 and 4.3).

If one considers the number of confirmed cases of COVID-19 and the number of deaths per 100,000 of population (see Table 4.4) it is hardly

Table 4.3 Health care expenditure in selected countries as a percentage of GDP and health care expenditure in euros per capita, 2018

	Healthcare expenditure as % of GDP[7]	*Health care expenditure in euros per capita*[8]
Baltics		
Estonia	6.66	1,312.18
Latvia	6.21	936.28
Lithuania	6.57	1,061.15
Nordics		
Denmark	10.10	5,255.75
Finland	9.04	3,828.64
Iceland	8.54	5,279.54
Norway	10.05	6,960.03
Sweden	10.90	5,041.30
Anglophone countries		
Ireland	6.93	4,612.74
The UK	10.00	3,645.78
Central Europe (Visegrád countries and Slovenia)		
Czech Republic	7.65	1,493.13
Hungary	6.70	916.93
Poland	6.33	829.54
Slovenia	8.30	1,830.93
Slovakia	6.69	1,099.99
South-eastern Europe		
Bulgaria	7.35	586.55
Romania	5.56	583.95
EU28	9.89	3,076.80

Source: Eurostat (2021).

surprising that the Nordic countries, with the exception of Sweden which pursued a herd immunity strategy against the virus, fared much better than the Baltic states. The Nordics have well-funded public health care systems and spend many times more per capita on health care than either the Baltics or the Visegrád countries. What is surprising, however, is the relatively poor performance of the Visegrád countries compared to the Baltic states in terms of the number of COVID-19-related deaths. If one considers the number of deaths per 100,000 population in November 2021 the worst performing country among the Baltic states on this indicator, Lithuania, had a slightly worse level of COVID-19-related fatalities than Poland but a better level than all the other Visegrád countries and Slovenia. Using this same indicator, the Czech Republic and Hungary are close to Romania and Bulgaria, countries that have much lower

Table 4.4 COVID-19 cases and deaths: cumulative total per 100,000 population,[9] 9 July–22 November 2021[10]

	Cases: cumulative total per 100,000 population, July 2021	*Deaths: cumulative total per 100,000 population, July 2021*	*Cases: cumulative total per 100,000 population, November 2021*	*Deaths: cumulative total per 100,000 population, November 2021*
Baltics				
Estonia	9,887.01	95.56	16,259.21	128.97
Latvia	7,223.30	132.88	12,819.85	204.49
Lithuania	9,986.22	157.33	16,186.59	231.24
Nordics				
Denmark	5,110.00	43.59	7,536.13	47.95
Finland	1,767.35	17.66	3,164.05	22.60
Iceland	1,833.12	8.24	4,513.45	9.34
Norway	2,469.87	14.83	4,383.86	18.56
Sweden	10,576.60	141.78	11,499.36	146.30
Anglophone countries				
Ireland	5,561.63	100.84	10,387,70	112.98
UK	7,399.02	189.05	14,320.95	211.47
Central Europe (Visegrád countries and Slovenia)				
Czech Republic	15,605.95	283.63	18,307.72	298.10
Hungary	8,275.09	307.12	10,220.43	335.53
Poland	7,589.07	197.99	8,701.81	211.81
Slovakia	7,178.86	229.32	10,869.47	252.50
Slovenia	12,291.80	226.78	18,688.20	254.17
South-eastern Europe				
Bulgaria	6,075.73	260.87	9,614.68	388.19
Romania	5,593.58	176.92	9,080.62	281.15

Source: WHO (2021).

income levels and much lower health care expenditures in euros per capita (see Tables 4.1 and 4.3). Furthermore, the Baltic states are also not far away from the Anglophone countries. As of November 2021 Estonia recorded similar levels of COVID-19-related fatalities as Ireland, and Latvia and Lithuania similar levels as the UK, despite the fact that the Anglophone countries have a much higher level of GDP per capita than the Baltic states and spend more on health care (see Tables 4.1. 4.3 and 4.4).

On the website of the European University Institute one can find the following statement:

> Europe's East has been conspicuously absent from the daily news on COVID-19. Much of the region took restrictive policy measures relatively early and seem (so far) to have avoided exponential case growth. Yet, the region is particularly vulnerable to the outbreak and its consequences. Neoliberal reforms and austerity have left healthcare systems chronically underfunded; shortages of medical equipment, expertise and personnel are worsened by free movement of labour in the EU. The region's economies are highly dependent on the West such that disruptions in international production and mobility have disproportionate impact. Finally, a shift towards 'illiberal democracies' in the region leaves political systems uniquely unprepared to face the crisis.
>
> (European University Institute n.d.)

The Visegrád group's relatively poor performance may be linked to policymakers' unwillingness in the second and third waves of the COVID-19 pandemic to implement tougher measures and to close down their economies. All the Visegrád and Baltic countries imposed strict lockdowns before the first wave actually arrived and had therefore no real first wave to contend with. But policymakers were very reluctant to do the same in the second or third waves, as measures intended to curb the spread of the pandemic were unpopular, and some countries feared the dramatic economic fallout. Some part of the explanation might be populist governments. Population density might be a factor, explaining why the Baltics are performing better than the Visegrád countries as the Baltic states are very small and sparsely populated. Age and family structure should be similar. But further research is needed and it will be interesting to see how the fourth wave plays out; thus far it has been particularly difficult for the Baltic states.

There are no reasons to believe that there are systematic differences between the health care sectors among the Baltic and Visegrád countries, and expenditure on health care per capita is not dramatically different across the Baltic and the Visegrád countries (see Table 4.3).

Concluding remarks

The countries in the country groups under study follow different policies when it comes to economic and social policies. Most dramatic is the difference between the Nordic welfare states and the Baltic states that have followed neoliberal policies after regaining their independence from the Soviet Union in 1991. The Visegrád countries fall somewhere in between.

The Nordic countries tend to follow more Keynesian economic policies, while the Baltic states prefer fiscal austerity. This was quite visible during the 2008/09 global financial crisis when strict fiscal discipline was demanded as a condition for the adoption of the euro by the Baltic states. Among the EU and euro area countries the Baltic states have been particularly successful in following the fiscal rules expected from candidate member states. The Visegrád countries tend to tolerate higher fiscal deficits and are more indebted than the Baltics.

When one considers indicators of poverty, social exclusion and income equality it is perhaps not surprising that the Baltic states, especially Latvia and Lithuania, do not perform as well as the Nordic countries, but it is noteworthy that they also perform poorly in comparison to the Visegrád countries which have similar levels of GDP per capita. In fact, Latvia and Lithuania are not that far from Romania when considering these indicators, a country that is poorer than any of the Baltic states.

If one considers health care expenditure as a percentage of GDP, and health care expenditure in euros per capita, the Baltic states lag far behind the Nordic countries, because they spend a smaller amount on health care as a percentage of GDP, and also because their GDP per capita is still much lower than that of the Nordics. In terms of the number of confirmed cases of COVID-19 (cumulative total per 100,000 population) and the number of COVID-19-related deaths (cumulative total per 100,000 population) the Baltics do not perform as well as the Nordics, except for Sweden. However, overall the Baltics have performed better in comparison to the Visegrád countries with fewer deaths per 100,000 of population.

Further research is needed to better understand why the Visegrád countries perform much better on social indicators in comparison to the Baltic states (see Table 4.1), but why the Visegrád group have performed relatively poorly in comparison to the Baltics in terms of fighting COVID-19 (see Table 4.4).

Notes

1 The Gini index/coefficient is defined as the relationship of cumulative shares of the population arranged according to the level of equivalized disposable income, to the cumulative share of the equivalized total disposable income received by them; https://ec.europa.eu/eurostat/databrowser/view/tessi190/default/table?lang=en.

2 This indicator corresponds to the sum of persons who are at risk of poverty after social transfers, severely materially deprived or living in households with very low work intensity. Persons are counted only once even if they are affected by more than one of these phenomena. Persons are considered to be at risk of poverty after social transfers, if they have an equivalized disposable income below the risk-of-poverty threshold, which is set at 60% of the national median equivalized disposable income. Severely materially or socially deprived persons have living conditions that are severely constrained by a lack of resources, they experience at least seven out of 13 following deprivations items: cannot afford (i) to pay rent or utility bills; (ii) to keep their homes adequately warm; (iii) face unexpected expenses; (iv) eat meat, fish or a protein equivalent every second day; (v) a week's holiday away from home; (vi) have access to a car/van for personal use; (vii) replace worn-out furniture; (viii) replace worn-out clothes with some new ones; (ix) have two pairs of properly fitting shoes; (x) spend a small amount of money each week on him/herself ('pocket money'); (xi) have regular leisure activities; (xii)

get together with friends/family for a drink/meal at least once a month; and (xiii) have an internet connection. People living in households with very low work intensity are those aged 0–64 living in households where the adults (aged 18–64) worked 20% or less of their total work potential during the past year. In order to measure child poverty, the indicator is available for the age group 0–17; see https://ec.europa.eu/eurostat/databrowser/view/SDG_01_10__custom_1356881/default/table?lang=en.

3 The at-risk-of-poverty rate is the share of people with an equivalized disposable income (after social transfers) below the at-risk-of-poverty threshold, which is set at 60% of the national median equivalized disposable income after social transfers. This indicator does not measure wealth or poverty, but low incomes in comparison to other residents in that country, which does not necessarily imply a low standard of living; https://ec.europa.eu/eurostat/databrowser/view/tespm010/default/table?lang=en.

4 https://ec.europa.eu/eurostat/databrowser/view/tessi190/default/table?lang=en.

5 http://appsso.eurostat.ec.europa.eu/nui/show.do?dataset=ilc_di11&lang=en.

6 From 2018 a progressive personal income tax system replaced the earlier flat tax rate. See www.oecd-ilibrary.org/sites/94dd720b-en/index.html?itemId=/content/component/94dd720b-en.

7 https://ec.europa.eu/eurostat/databrowser/view/HLTH_SHA11_HF__custom_227597/bookmark/table?lang=en&bookmarkId=1530a1e6-767e-4661-9e15-0ed2f7fae0d5.

8 https://ec.europa.eu/eurostat/databrowser/view/HLTH_SHA11_HF__custom_227597/bookmark/table?lang=en&bookmarkId=948e46d8-6423-4775-afe1-ade53d902db3.

9 https://covid19.who.int/table.

10 https://covid19.who.int/table?tableChartType=heat.

References

Andersen, T. M., Holmström, B., Honkapohja, S., Korkman S., Söderström H. T. and Vartiainen, J. (2007). *The Nordic Model: Embracing Globalization and Sharing Risks*, Helsinki: Yliopistopaino. Available at: https://economics.mit.edu/sites/default/files/2022-09/Nordic%20Model%20Book%20-%20with%20cover_0.pdf (accessed 23 July 2022).

Bohle, D. and Greskovits, B. (2012). *Capitalist Diversity on Europe's Periphery*. Cornell Studies in Political Economy. Ithaca, NY: Cornell University Press.

Eichengreen, B. (2008). *The European Economy since 1945: Coordinated Capitalism and Beyond*. Princeton, NJ: Princeton University Press.

European University Institute (n.d.). *East Central Europe COVID-19 Monitor*. Available at: www.eui.eu/research-hub?id=east-central-europe-covid-19-monitor (accessed 22 June 2021).

Eurostat (2020). *Eurostat Database*. https://ec.europa.eu/eurostat/data/database.

Hannibalsson, J. B. (2017). What Can We Learn from The Nordic Model? *Social Europe*. Available at: www.socialeurope.eu/what-can-we-learn-from-the-nordic-model (accessed 23 September 2021).

Hellman, J. S., Jones, G. and Kaufmann, D. (2000). *Seize the State, Seize the Day: State Capture, Corruption and Influence in Transition*. Policy Research Working Paper. https://documents1.worldbank.org/curated/en/537461468766474836/pdf/multi-page.pdf.

Hilmarsson, H. Þ. (2020). The Dangers of Banking Interconnectedness during Times of Crisis: The Nordic-Baltic Case. *Journal of Applied Management and Investments*, 9(4), 153–161.

Hilmarsson, H. Þ. (2018). *The Economic Crisis and Its Aftermath in the Nordic and Baltic Countries: Do as We Say and Not as We Do*. Abingdon: Routledge.

Hilmarsson, H. Þ. (2014). Managing Financial Crisis: The Case of Iceland and Latvia. *Review of International Comparative Management*, 15(2), 200–214.
International Monetary Fund (IMF) (2022). *World Economic Outlook Database.* Available at: www.imf.org/en/Publications/WEO/weo-database/2022/April.
International Monetary Fund (IMF) (2021a). *Republic of Estonia 2021 Article IV Consultation: Press Release and Staff Report.* IMF Country Report No. 21/160. Available at: www.imf.org/en/Publications/CR/Issues/2021/07/20/Republic-of-Estonia-2021-Article-IV-Consultation-Press-Release-and-Staff-Report-462375 (accessed 7 August 2022).
International Monetary Fund (IMF) (2021b). *Republic of Latvia 2021 Article IV Consultation: Press Release; and Staff Report; and Statement by the Executive Director for the Republic of Latvia.* IMF Country Report No. 21/194. Available at: www.imf.org/en/Publications/CR/Issues/2021/08/31/Republic-of-Latvia-2021-Article-IV-Consultation-Press-Release-Staff-Report-and-Statement-by-465002 (accessed 7 August 2022).
International Monetary Fund (IMF) (2021c). *Republic of Lithuania 2021 Article IV Consultation: Press Release; and Staff Report; and Statement by the Executive Director for the Republic of Lithuania.* IMF Country Report No. 21/192. Available at: www.imf.org/en/Publications/CR/Issues/2021/08/30/Republic-of-Lithuania-2021-Article-IV-Consultation-Press-Release-Staff-Report-and-Statement-464874 (accessed 7 August 2022).
International Monetary Fund (IMF) (2021d). *World Economic Outlook Database.* Available at: www.imf.org/en/Publications/WEO/weo-database/2021/April.
International Monetary Fund (IMF) (2014). *Baltic Cluster Report.* IMF Country Report No. 14/117, May. Available at: www.imf.org/en/Publications/CR/Issues/2016/12/31/Baltic-Cluster-Report-Selected-Issues-41541 (accessed 30 September 2021).
Ingebritsen, C. (2006). *Scandinavia in World Politics*, Lanham, MD and Oxford: Rowman & Littlefield.
Inglot, T. (2008). *Welfare States in East Central Europe, 1919–2004.* Cambridge: Cambridge University Press.
Keynes, J. M. (n.d.). *John Maynard Keynes Quotes.* Available at: www.brainyquote.com/quotes/john_maynard_keynes_137774 (accessed 23 July 2022).
Laar, M. (2007). *The Estonian Economic Miracle.* The Heritage Foundation. Available at: www.heritage.org/report/the-estonian-economic-miracle (accessed 7 January 2022).
Laar, M. (2005). Walking on Water: How to Do It . *The Brussels Journal.* Available at: www.brusselsjournal.com/node/202 (accessed 23 June 2022).
Organisation for Economic Co-operation and Development (OECD) (2022a). *Latvia Economic Snapshot.* Available at: www.oecd.org/economy/latvia-economic-snapshot/ (accessed 7 August 2022).
Organisation for Economic Co-operation and Development (OECD) (2022b). *Lithuania Economic Snapshot.* Available at: www.oecd.org/economy/lithuania-economic-snapshot/#:~:text=Economic%20Forecast%20Summary%20(June%202022,markets%20and%20intensifies%20supply%20bottlenecks (accessed 7 August 2022).
Stiglitz, J. (2013). *The Price of Inequality: How Today's Divided Society Endangers Our Future.* New York and London:W. W. Norton & Company.
World Bank (2022). *War in the Region. Europe and Central Asia Economic Update.* Spring. doi:doi:10.1596/978-1-4648-1866-0 (accessed 7 August 2022).
World Bank (2020). *Doing Business 2020.* Available at: www.doingbusiness.org/en/reports/global-reports/doing-business-2020 (accessed 7 June 2021).
World Health Organization (WHO) (2021). *WHO Coronavirus (COVID-19) Dashboard.* Available at: https://covid19.who.int/table (accessed 9 July 2021).

5 Great powers influencing Europe in a changing world

From bipolar to unipolar to multipolar

From a bipolar to a unipolar to a multipolar world: how does this affect Europe?

From 1945–91 we lived in a bipolar world with two major superpowers dominating the system, namely the US and the Union of Socialist Soviet Republics (USSR). During the so-called Cold War the US exercised what could be labelled as Europe's first policy. Europe had been the most important ally of the US ever since the ending of the Second World War. Important alliances were built during the Bretton Woods Conference, known as the United Nations Monetary and Financial Conference, held in 1944, followed by the US-funded Marshall Plan and the establishment of the US-led North Atlantic Treaty Organization (NATO) in 1949. The transatlantic alliance was key to US-European security cooperation with the European countries relying on the principle of collective defence that is enshrined in Article 5 of the North Atlantic Treaty (or Washington Treaty).

The Berlin Wall fell in 1989 and then the Soviet Union fell in 1991. A unipolar system emerged between 1991 and 2017 with the US remaining the only global superpower. This period came to be known as the 'unipolar moment'. Given the fall of the USSR, and with a weak Russian Federation, US interest in Europe diminished. The US supported EU expansion, not only to incorporate the former satellite states of the Soviet Union, but also the former Soviet republics, the Baltic states. No nation state in the EU, not even the largest EU member states, Germany and France, had sufficient wealth and population to dominate Europe and challenge the US which also led NATO and supported its expansion to the east in parallel with EU expansion. Even to date it is unknown how far the EU and NATO intend to expand.

Recently we have entered an era of a multipolar system with at least three great powers: (i) the US which remains the most powerful country economically and militarily; (ii) the People's Republic of China which is a rising economic and now also a fast-growing military power;[1] and finally (iii) Russia which is still a military power covering a huge landmass with vast natural resources and with nuclear capabilities.[2] Prior to the Russian military

DOI: 10.4324/9781003212539-6

invasion of Ukraine, Russia was perceived as being stronger than it was after dissolution of the Soviet Union, but weaker than either the US or China.

India has population whose size is comparable to that of China, but it does not have sufficient wealth to become a major power. However, if per capita incomes in India were to increase so that they became comparable to the average incomes of Indians living in the US, then India will become a larger economy than that of the US, and that economic power could then develop into military power. Meanwhile, Germany has the necessary wealth to become an economic power, but its population is not large enough for it to be able to dominate Europe or other regions.

Prior to the outbreak of war in Ukraine, US interest in Europe declined, but grew in two areas of the world: (i) East Asia primarily because of the rise of China; and (ii) the Persian Gulf because of its vast reserves of oil. If China continues to rise it will compete with the US not only as it currently does in Asia, but increasingly in other parts of the world, including the Persian Gulf, for the same reason as the US – energy.

Given these changes will the US from now on increasingly want to abandon Europe, and if so who will fill the vacuum? Does a stronger China mean less US interest in Europe and a weaker NATO, followed by growing Chinese influence in Europe? How should European small powers and small power alliances behave in this changing world?

The US pivot to Asia may be delayed due to the war in Ukraine. Nevertheless, Russia neither has the population nor the wealth to dominate the world, as the US did during the 'unipolar moment'. But as a great power Russia wants to maintain its status in a multipolar world where it is an important player and can influence Europe and other regions, in areas such as energy. The US, on the other hand, wants to regain its supremacy in a unipolar world. If China continues to grow economically it has a good chance of dominating all the other great powers and becoming a new hegemon in a unipolar world. In other words, Russia can only hope for a multipolar world, while the US and China dream of a unipolar world.

The goal of the US, China and Russia is not only to survive as great powers, but also to dominate their respective regions and eventually, if possible, the other regions of the world. A key reason why the US became so dominant after the dissolution of the Soviet Union was the fact that it already dominated its own region, the Americas. It borders Canada to the north, Mexico to the south and the oceans to the west and east. No other country poses a physical threat to the US and this has given the US the necessary unthreatening environment needed if it wishes to be able to interfere in the affairs of other regions, including Europe, Asia and the Middle East. The US became a balancing power in Europe against the USSR during the Cold War up until the collapse of the Soviet Union. This left a power vacuum in Europe. At the same time the rise of China increasingly became a threat to the US as a security guarantor in Asia and resulted in its pivot to Asia policy. China poses the main threat to US global supremacy, but the war in Ukraine has at least for some time diverted its attention from Asia to Europe.

China does not have a comparable situation in Asia to that which the US has in the Americas. China borders many countries and unlike the US is in proximity with military powers. There are important countries in Asia that individually or in groups can challenge Chinese dominance.

Japan is an economic and technological power and has one of the largest economies in the world. It has disputes with China in the East China Sea and will seek to defend its interests alone or more likely in partnership with allies, particularly the US. India has a population comparable to that of China, but it does not have the necessary wealth to compete with China. However, as its per capita income grows India can in the longer term challenge Chinese power.

Then there are smaller emerging powers in Asia such as Viet Nam, the Philippines, Thailand, Malaysia and Singapore that do not have the same interests as China and often oppose policies of the Chinese government including its border disputes and control over the South China Sea. There are border disputes between China and India, disputes about the Senkaku Islands (also known as the Diaoyu Islands) that lie between China and Japan, and disputes in the South China Sea with countries such as Viet Nam, the Philippines and Thailand. In addition, the Republic of Korea (South Korea) is a rising power that has disputes with the Democratic Republic of Korea (North Korea) which is supported by China. Furthermore, there are countries outside Asia such as Australia and New Zealand that play an important role and influence China's status in Asia. Australia is one of the strongest allies of the US.

Given this situation China is not a regional hegemon in Asia in the same sense as the US in the Americas. There are several issues that China must resolve before it can dominate Asia and then focus on influencing or interfering in the affairs of other regions, such as Europe, like the US has done. Also, it needs to worry about US alliances in Asia that do not welcome Chinese dominance and are prepared to take action to contain China. Finally, the US has a strong and growing military presence in Asia that continues to challenge China.

Russia would like to drive the US out of Europe just as China would like to drive the US out of Asia. However, Russia does not have the population or the wealth to dominate Europe, and a number of wealthy European countries that have allied with the US via NATO are also willing to buy US military equipment to defend themselves. The US is willing to provide poorer European countries with military equipment as it has done for Ukraine.

A reduced US military presence in Europe, because of the rise of China, could provide both Russia and China with opportunities in Europe. Russia can put more pressure on Europe, especially on countries on its borders such as the Baltic states and Finland. It can continue to use Europe's energy dependency to pressure Europe including the most powerful European country, Germany.[3] The Nord Stream 2 Baltic Sea gas pipeline project, designed to double the flow of Russian gas to Germany, had faced opposition within the EU and NATO and from the US on the grounds that it would increase Europe's energy dependence on Russia. However, in early 2022 Germany halted the project following the Russian military invasion of Ukraine and this posed a threat to European energy security.

China's growing interest in Europe and the US pivot to Asia

China is already extending its interest in European affairs via its Belt and Road Initiative (BRI). In 2018 Greece formally joined the BRI when China made a large investment that could transform the port of Piraeus into the biggest harbour in Europe.[4] This development must be alarming for other EU member states as well as the US. Another example is Chinese investment in the expansion of the port of Trieste, Italy.[5] One of the Visegrád countries, Hungary, was the first European country to participate in the BRI.[6] In addition to being a member of the EU and NATO, Hungary has developed good relations with both China and Russia.

Given that its economy is based on export-led growth, access to the EU internal market is critical for China so entering the market via Hungary is invaluable and for Russia it is important to have an ally within the EU. China investment in the Baltic states, including the construction of the 100-km Tallinn–Helsinki undersea tunnel, forms part of Beijing's BRI.[7] China has also shown interest in Baltic ports.[8] China claims that the initiative is a 'win-win' cooperation for the countries involved and the EU, while others maintain that China is using a 'divide and conquer' strategy that benefits China at Europe's expense. Many Central and Eastern European countries view EU-Chinese relations as mutually beneficial and they have formed a platform to enable them to work closely with China.[9]

Some leading international relations experts such as John Mearsheimer, an American political science professor at the University of Chicago, maintain that the US should leave Europe militarily.[10] This is understandable given the demands faced by the US in Asia with the rise of China, but one could also argue that the US needs to maintain a sufficient presence in Europe to balance power there as Russia could become stronger. If the US withdraws from Europe, it may lose its credibility among the EU countries, and may be viewed as an unreliable partner that cannot necessarily return to Europe again as a trusted ally. The European countries need to be careful in their dealings with the US. For example, the US is beginning to show an interest in using NATO to oppose China, as testified by the Brussels Summit communiqué dated 14 June 2021:

> China's stated ambitions and assertive behaviour present systemic challenges to the rules-based international order and to areas relevant to Alliance security. We are concerned by those coercive policies which

> stand in contrast to the fundamental values enshrined in the Washington Treaty. China is rapidly expanding its nuclear arsenal with more warheads and a larger number of sophisticated delivery systems to establish a nuclear triad. It is opaque in implementing its military modernisation and its publicly declared military-civil fusion strategy. It is also cooperating militarily with Russia, including through participation in Russian exercises in the Euro-Atlantic area. We remain concerned with China's frequent lack of transparency and use of disinformation. We call on China to uphold its international commitments and to act responsibly in the international system, including in the space, cyber, and maritime domains, in keeping with its role as a major power.
>
> (NATO 2021)

Europe should avoid open confrontation with China. It is highly questionable whether European NATO member states should allow themselves to be drawn into the US-Chinese security competition in East Asia. And Europe is divided on the issue. The President of France, Emmanuel Macron seeks the establishment of a European army and has expressed hopes that Europe will emerge as a major power in a multipolar world that is independent of the US. This view is not widely supported by other EU and European NATO member states that have placed greater trust in the US for their defence than in European powers such as Germany and France. And why should a country like Poland trust Germany to defend it against Russia?

NATO's frequent demand that China and Russia should follow the rules-based international order sounds naïve as those great powers, especially China, will want to write their own rules and will object to following directives from Washington.

Small states' behaviour in a multipolar world

How should small powers and small power alliances in Europe behave in a changing world dominated by great power rivalry? First, small states must find their place in a world that has shifted from unipolarity to multipolarity. In this new era policymakers must address the decreasing influence of the US in many countries around the world including those in the Pacific region, as well as the increasing power of China and the instability that Russia imposes on Europe. A less powerful US means that it may no longer be able or willing to serve as a security guarantor in Europe owing to tensions in the Pacific that it needs to attend to, and consequently it eventually may also be unable to serve as a security guarantor in the Pacific.

Second, while small European states should continue to maintain good relations with the US they should not neglect the opportunities that can be found in China. Some of the countries discussed in this book may see China as a potential source of funding, especially countries in the Visegrád group and perhaps the Baltic states, Estonia and Latvia, all of which participate in the 17+1 Initiative (now the 16+1 Initiative following the departure of Lithuania), since the EU may not be able to supply them with the grants and loans that they need in the future. The 16+1 Initiative seeks to promote business and investment relations between China and the 16 participating Central and Eastern European countries, namely Albania, Bosnia and Herzegovina, Bulgaria, Croatia, the Czech Republic (Czechia), Estonia, Greece, Hungary, Latvia, Montenegro, North Macedonia, Poland, Romania, Serbia, Slovakia and Slovenia. The initiative brings together EU and non-EU states into one group which may be a source of irritation for the EU. As Pendrakowska (2018) points out, 'Brussels tends to emphasize that the 16+1 platform undermines the EU unity by rule and divide tactics'. Then there is a question whether policymakers in those countries should strive to attract greenfield investments or rather make acquisitions of national companies that can be more sensitive.

Third, the possibility of gaining better access to the Chinese market is important and should be included in the discussion about small states' participation in the BRI. Meanwhile, Europe must continue to engage in talks with the US in the wake of the failure of the Transatlantic Trade and Investment Partnership.[11] Trade discussions between Europe and China may put pressure on the US.

There will be obstacles along the way especially as regards investment since the EU and China operate under different systems, e.g. rules for procurement as well as environmental standards. While the Chinese are willing to undertake large projects from start to finish, EU systems do not allow this as countries are expected to allow companies from other countries to participate in a competitive bidding process. Projects in Europe need to follow EU standards that are different from those in China. China prefers to undertake large projects rather than small, insignificant projects. There are also differences in planning in European democracies where elected officials serve for a few years compared to China which has a single-party government and leaders who are allowed to remain in power for life. In China actions are planned at least a decade ahead, whereas in Europe they are often planned to take place by the next election. In such situations the main activities of the parties concerned are concentrated on maintaining power. The concern here is not only that China thinks and plans decades ahead and Europe thinks mostly months ahead, but that these two standpoints need to be brought together and need to form a common strategy.

Another important phenomenon is the asymmetry of expectancies that could perhaps be reduced by promoting communication between scientists, academics and journalists. This could help to prevent misunderstanding and build a more shared view between European countries and China's counterparts as to what is realistic and to help to manage expectations. European policymakers tend to concentrate on short-term goals, whereas the Chinese political system allows more time in which to achieve a bigger success with grand plans that take decades to implement.

The Three Seas Initiative, also known as the Baltic, Adriatic, Black Sea Initiative or simply as the Three Seas, is a forum of 12 EU states, running along a north–south axis from the Baltic Sea to the Adriatic and Black Seas in Central and Eastern Europe. The Initiative aims to create a regional dialogue on questions affecting the member states and seeks to facilitate interconnectivity on energy and infrastructure projects in Central and Eastern Europe. Lead by Poland and Romania the participating counties are Austria, Bulgaria, Croatia, the Czech Republic, Estonia, Hungary, Latvia, Lithuania, Poland, Romania, Slovakia and Slovenia. The Three Seas Initiative is supported by the US. Unlike the China-supported 16+1 Initiative, the Three seas Initiative only includes EU member states. Some EU countries, namely Bulgaria, Croatia, Czech Republic, Estonia, Hungary, Latvia, Poland, Romania, Slovakia and Slovenia, participate in both initiatives.

This demonstrates that the Baltic states, Estonia and Latvia, and all the Visegrád countries are willing to work with both China and the US under two different initiatives in order to promote the reconstruction of Eastern and Central Europe.

Small states' strategy in a multipolar world

In a multipolar world small powers should avoid being drawn into situations in which they can only work with and become totally dependent on a single great power. Great powers often seek to get small states totally on their side and under their control. During an official visit to Iceland in September 2019 then US Vice-President Mike Pence stated that

> [t]he United States is grateful for the stand Iceland took rejecting China's Belt and Road financial investment in Iceland. We truly believe that it is essential that we strengthen the ties that bind nations across this region of the world. And for Iceland to take that stand was an important step and one that we greatly welcome.[12]

This was an embarrassing statement given that the government of Iceland had not in fact declined to participate in the BRI.[13] However, it was a clear indication on the part of the US that Iceland would do well to reject participation in the BRI if it wanted to remain on good terms with the US government. The Chinese ambassador to Iceland, Jin Zhijian, said that Pence's statement was tantamount to 'fake news' and that the purpose of his comments was to damage the bilateral relationship between China and Iceland.[14] This reflects the extent of tensions between the US and China.

It is noteworthy that Iceland had already made the decision to join the China-led Asian Infrastructure Investment Bank together with all the other Nordic countries as well as Poland and Hungary against the wishes of the US government. Iceland had clearly decided that it would explore cooperation with China on its own terms without US interference.

Vice-President Pence was also critical of Russia's involvement in the Arctic during his visit. Iceland maintained important trade relations with both the Soviet Union at the height of the Cold War and with Russia prior to the imposition of sanctions following that country's invasion of Ukraine. As a small state, Iceland could continue to pursue good trade relations in addition to exploring further investment from China and Russia if only relations with Russia could be normalized through a negotiated peace settlement in Ukraine. In 2008, although NATO member states agreed that Ukraine should in the future join the alliance, it was arguably unwise to proceed at the time as the country was not yet ready to do so and indeed it might antagonize Russia (see, for example, Hilmarsson 2019). This decision contributed to the crisis that broke out in Ukraine in 2014. It would perhaps have been better for Ukraine to take smaller gradual steps towards EU integration and perhaps to have reached a partnership agreement with NATO.

Small states should try to maintain some neutrality in their dealings with great powers. Good relations with the US are important for the Nordic, Baltic and Visegrád countries since all the countries except Finland and Sweden participate in NATO. Finland and Sweden have participated in NATO military exercises and at the time of writing had applied for full membership of NATO. Furthermore, all the countries participate in European integration, albeit at different levels, and need to consider their commitment to the EU. But that does not mean that they cannot and should not cooperate with China and Russia in the future. Avoiding trade and investment with China if it continues to grow is also practically impossible because Chinese trade and investment will be such a large part of world trade and investment. Good relations with Russia are also important if a settlement can be reached following the conclusion of the war in Ukraine. In fact, given the potential growth of China into the largest economy in the world it is surprising that the US did not make greater efforts to resolve its disputes with Russia prior to the outbreak of war in Ukraine. The same could be said about Europe that needs stability. Further EU and especially NATO expansion should be reconsidered as it can result in confrontation with Russia as well as China. While the Nordic, Baltic and Visegrád countries should be open to doing business with China and Russia, they should avoid having overly close relations that create serious problems with the US and within the EU. This is a tricky balancing act, but relying on relations with one of the great powers would be a mistake. Given the ongoing conflict in Ukraine it is likely that it will take a long time for the West to normalize relations with Russia.

An Icelandic moment for Lithuania

It is noteworthy that while all three of the Baltic states have had bad relations with Russia, one of the countries, Lithuania, now has serious tensions with China. This was the result of Lithuania opening a Taiwanese representative office in its capital, Vilnius.[15] This act by Lithuania became a serious concern in China, which views Republic of China (Taiwan) as a breakaway province and claims Taiwan as part of its sovereign territory. China considers Lithuania's decision an act to undermine its sovereignty and territorial integrity as well as setting a bad precedent internationally. Most other countries have tried to avoid tensions with China by allowing Taiwan to open a representative office under the name of its capital, Taipei. In retaliation China has downgraded its diplomatic relations and restricted its trade with Lithuania. Lithuania is an EU member state and this means that the European Commission can file a complaint with the World Trade Organization if it is proved that China has imposed trade restrictions on Lithuania. Lithuania does not want its dispute with China to be treated merely as a bilateral issue. It would prefer the dispute to be treated as a European dispute against China and such a dispute needs a European solution. China's actions against Lithuania are regarded as the weaponization of trade.[16] Big businesses in Europe have sought to put pressure on Lithuania calling for immediate de-escalation of the Lithuania–China dispute.[17] As mentioned above Lithuania had already withdrawn from the China-led 17+1 initiative comprising Central and Eastern European states, citing disappointing economic benefits.

The Lithuanian initiative to support Taiwan has been compared to Iceland becoming the first country to recognize the restoration of independence of the Baltic states from the former Soviet Union. It was hailed as an 'Iceland moment' for Lithuania.[18] But one needs to keep in mind that at that time the Soviet Union was a declining power and was close to collapse. The move in Iceland was not without risks since Iceland had been engaged in trade with the Soviet Union for decades. Iceland, located some distance from the Soviet Union, also had a substantial military US presence stationed in the country at the time and felt secure.

Considering the Lithuanian case, China is not a falling state but a rising great power that could challenge the US in a foreseeable future. Lithuania already had serious tensions with Russia and has now added China to the list of great powers with which it is in conflict. And Lithuania counts on US-backed NATO for its security without having either a large NATO military presence or a large number of US troops permanently stationed in the country. Opposing two major powers such as China and Russia while relying on US is a gamble for a small state like Lithuania and the outcomes are uncertain. The Lithuanian move against China is, however, likely to be welcomed by the US, but that does not mean that the US will go to great lengths to support Lithuania in its dispute with China. It has even been suggested that Washington advised Lithuania to consider changing the name of its representative office in Taiwan in an effort to ease tensions between Lithuania and China.[19] The US closed its embassy in Taipei in 1979 and opened a US embassy in Beijing in the same year.[20] Taiwan currently has a Taipei Economic and Cultural Representative Office in the US[21] and the US has an American Institute in Taiwan which could be considered a de facto US embassy in Taiwan.[22]

The Lithuanian move could also become very difficult for EU countries that are engaged in extensive trade with China.[23] This includes countries such as Germany, the Visegrád country Slovakia and the Nordic countries, Denmark, Finland and Sweden. Lithuania could end up also having problems within the EU as some countries view Lithuania's move as unnecessary confrontation with China. And there is also controversy within Lithuania. The Lithuanian President Gitanas Nausėda expressed doubts about the wisdom of his country's principled stand while Minister of Foreign Affairs Gabrielius Landsbergis insisted that he had consulted the president about the naming of the Taiwanese office.[24] A survey, commissioned by the ministry of foreign affairs, conducted in December 2021, asked respondents how they viewed Lithuania's policy on China. Only 13% said they supported it, while 60% had a negative opinion.[25]

Lithuania is a small EU member state. However, it has little influence within the Union. Lithuania is in conflict with Russia and uses its EU membership to demand wider sanctions against Russia. The most powerful EU member state, Germany, sought good relations and expanding trade with Russia prior to the Russian invasion of Ukraine. A recent example of German-Russian cooperation, the Nord Stream 2 pipeline project, was fiercely opposed by Lithuania. However, it was placed on hold in mid-2022. Lithuania is hedging its bet on retaining US protection via the security guarantee enshrined in Article 5 at a time when the US is in the longer term likely to be increasingly occupied in East Asia owing to the economic and military rise of China and its own declining interest in Europe. Given the uncertainty of US support for Lithuania it seems like a high-risk scenario for the country to oppose both Russia and China and to irritate Germany. US military support for the Baltic states is untested but the fact that the US does not have a large military presence in these countries suggests that it is not very strong. Lithuania should avoid unnecessary confrontations with China and try to ease tensions with Russia in the long term. The US may be there for Lithuania when there is need, but it may choose not to become involved. Overall, in 2022 tensions with Russia were running very high owing to the ongoing conflict in Ukraine and it will take a long time to normalize those relations but in the long term better relations with Russia are in Lithuania's interest. It also remains to be seen if projects such as the Nord Stream 2 pipeline will ever be operational.

Notes

1 https://edition.cnn.com/2021/03/05/china/china-world-biggest-navy-intl-hnk-ml-dst/index.html.
2 www.nato.int/docu/review/articles/2020/06/08/nuclear-deterrence-today/index.html.
3 www.dw.com/en/nord-stream-2-pipeline-row-highlights-germanys-energy-dependence-on-russia/a-47344788.

4 www.cnbc.com/2019/11/15/china-wants-to-turn-greece-piraeus-port-into-europe-biggest.html.
5 www.nytimes.com/2019/03/18/world/europe/italy-trieste-china-belt-road.html.
6 https://thediplomat.com/2019/04/how-hungarys-path-leads-to-chinas-belt-and-road/.
7 www.reuters.com/article/us-finland-estonia-tunnel-idUSKCN1U70F3 and www.oboreurope.com/en/china-helsinki-tallinn-tunnel/.
8 www.lrt.lt/en/news-in-english/19/1098009/china-s-belt-and-road-grip-reaches-the-baltics-investigation.
9 www.china-ceec.org/eng/.
10 www.atlanticcouncil.org/blogs/new-atlanticist/will-nato-still-be-relevant-in-the-future/.
11 The TTIP negotiations were launched in 2013 and ended without conclusion at the end of 2016. A Council decision of 15 April 2019 states that the negotiating directives for the TTIP are obsolete and no longer relevant. See https://ec.europa.eu/trade/policy/in-focus/ttip/.
12 www.presidency.ucsb.edu/documents/remarks-the-vice-president-press-gaggle-reykjavik-iceland.
13 www.isdp.eu/pressure-in-the-arctic-china-iceland-relations/.
14 www.ruv.is/frett/segir-fullyrdingar-pence-meinfysinn-rogburd.
15 www.bbc.com/news/world-europe-59879762.
16 https://carnegieeurope.eu/strategiceurope/86208.
17 www.reuters.com/world/europe/german-big-business-piles-pressure-lithuania-china-row-2022-01-21/.
18 https://cepa.org/lithuanias-iceland-moment-for-taiwan/.
19 www.ft.com/content/e646155d-6d8c-482a-8dfb-e4ef7d081bd8.
20 On 1 January 1979 the US recognized the People's Republic of China and established diplomatic relations with it as the sole legitimate government of China. On the same day, the US withdrew its recognition of, and terminated diplomatic relations with, the Republic of China (Taiwan) as the government of China. See https://history.state.gov/countries/china.
21 www.roc-taiwan.org/us_en/index.html.
22 www.ait.org.tw/ait-celebrates-2021-international-education-week/.
23 www.bbc.com/news/world-europe-59879762.
24 www.bbc.com/news/world-europe-59879762.
25 www.lrt.lt/en/news-in-english/19/1586875/most-lithuanians-critical-of-vilnius-china-policy-survey?utm_campaign=wp_todays_worldview&utm_medium=email&utm_source=newsletter&wpisrc=nl_todayworld.

References

Hilmarsson, H. Þ. (2019). Drinking the Blood of Ukraine: East-West Competition for a Country in Crisis. *Social Europe*, 30 October. Available at: https://socialeurope.eu/drinking-the-blood-of-ukraine-east-west-competition-for-a-country-in-crisis (accessed 18 July 2022).

North Atlantic Treaty Organization (NATO) (2021). *Brussels Summit Communiqué: Issued by the Heads of State and Government Participating in the Meeting of the North Atlantic Council in Brussels on 14 June 2021*. Available at: www.nato.int/cps/en/natohq/news_185000.htm (accessed 18 July 2022).

Pendrakowska, P. (2018). Poland's Perspective on the Belt and Road Initiative. *Journal of Contemporary East Asia Studies*, 7(2), 190–206. Available at: www.tandfonline.com/doi/full/10.1080/24761028.2018.1552491 (accessed 18 July 2022).

6 The US and its role in Europe

Is the transatlantic alliance viable and feasible?

US leadership role after the Second World War

The end of the Second World War marked a turning point for the US in establishing itself as the most powerful country in the world. The role of the United Kingdom on the global stage was diminished and powers such as Germany and Japan were in ruins. During the Bretton Woods Conference, formally known as the United Nations Monetary and Financial Conference, that was convened in New Hampshire, US, in July 1944 the new international financial institutional architecture was established and put the US into a position of dominance (see, for example, Steil 2013).

As the most powerful country in the world the US was able to write the rules that governed the World Bank (then called the International Bank for Reconstruction and Development) and the International Monetary Fund (IMF), both of which became the leading financial institutions of the new world order. It was only normal to expect that a great power that had become dominant would want to write the rules of international organizations along with allied countries such as the UK, which took a leading role at the Bretton Woods conference but was less influential than the US. Not only did the US shape those institutions but it also ensured that they would be located in its back yard. The Bretton Woods institutions had their headquarters in Washington, DC, and the United Nations in New York. The US also had the resources to extend assistance to Europe that was in ruins through the Bretton Woods institutions and also through the Marshall Plan that was approved in 1948 to provide aid to Western Europe in the aftermath of the Second World War.

The US also took the lead in forming the North Atlantic Treaty Organization (NATO) in the aftermath of the Second World War to provide collective security against any military threat from the Soviet Union. Its purpose was to secure peace in Europe, to promote cooperation among its members and to guard their freedom. NATO's founding treaty was signed in Washington in 1949 by a dozen European and North American countries.[1] It commits member states to democracy, individual liberty and the rule of law, as well as to the peaceful resolution of disputes.[2] Importantly, the treaty sets

DOI: 10.4324/9781003212539-7

out the idea of collective defence, meaning that an attack against one or more member states is considered as an attack against all member states, the so-called Article 5 guarantee[3] (NATO 2019). The purpose of the NATO alliance is to ensure that the security of its European member countries is inseparably linked to that of its North American member countries. On the signing of the treaty the US became the security guarantor for Europe in the wake of the Second World War. Today NATO provides security for approximately one billion people in Europe and North America. Thus it can be argued that European NATO member states fall under the US security umbrella.

The fall of the Soviet Union and US influence on the former Soviet satellite states and republics

When the Soviet Union fell the US was influential in advising the former Soviet satellite states and republics in Central and Eastern Europe that had become fully independent, including on economic policy. Their economic and social policies tended to be more neoliberal than those of typical Western European countries. The Baltic states, all of which are former Soviet republics, are examples of this, with flat taxes, minimal government and weak welfare regimes. Their policies were closer to those of the US economist and University of Chicago Professor Milton Friedman than those adopted by the Western European welfare states; indeed, some observers refer to a social Europe. An example of this is Estonia.

Mart Laar became prime minister of Estonia in 1992 and served in that capacity until 1994 and again from 1999–2002. He decided to implement neoliberal policies in Estonia in the spirit of US economist Milton Friedman in a more orthodox way than any other country in the world had ever done, based on the assumption that this was common practice 'in the West' (Laar 2005).

The neoliberal era started in the 1980s as a revolt against the welfare state and was based on a belief in market infallibility. Markets self-corrected, and governments should get out of the way. The results of this policy became clear on a global scale in 2008, including in the Baltic states. The Baltics were radical in their neoliberal policies, and did not look to the Nordic welfare states as their mentors. The Nordic countries are well known for maintaining relatively generous welfare states and relatively strong social safety nets (Andersen et al. 2007).

Thus, after the Baltic states had regained their independence, reforms in those countries were characterized by the creation of an ultra-liberal, business-friendly environment that sought to attract foreign investment. The social system should, on the other hand, inspire 'people to assume responsibility for their own future' (Laar 2007, p. 9; see also Bohle and Greskovits 2012).

According to Bohle and Greskovits,

> Workers in the Baltic States suffered a dramatic loss of income in the early transformation period. Real wages fell as much as two-thirds in 1990–99, and even with the recovery thereafter, by the end of the millennium they only reached between 40 to 60 percent of their 1989 levels. Employment levels decreased sharply, leading to significantly lower labour participation and high unemployment.
>
> (2012, p. 123)

Solidarity, social inclusion and safety nets for the most vulnerable were not on the agenda. It was the survival of the fittest and the fittest had accumulated wealth that in some cases was based on the privatization of government property in a corrupt environment.

The Visegrád group is different, and despite having a similar per capita gross domestic product (GDP) as the Baltic states the Visegrád countries are very close to the Nordic countries on indicators for income equality and poverty (see, for example, Hilmarsson 2018).

In the 1990s the World Bank and the IMF preached neoliberal economic policies and the so-called Washington Consensus[4] (see Williamson 1990) that was popular around the time of the collapse of the Soviet Union and reflected the policies supported by both the Washington-based institutions and the US treasury. The term 'Washington Consensus' was coined by John Williamson and was widely used to describe the dramatic reforms that swept the world as many countries opted for less state control over their economies.[5] One version of the Washington Consensus indicated the general direction in which policy should move, away from a heavily statist approach while retaining an important regulatory role for government. Another version of the Washington Consensus came to represent an extreme market-fundamentalist neoliberal approach that simplified economic policy to 'stabilize, liberalize and privatize' with minimal government,[6] and this is the approach adopted by the Baltic states. Critics argued that the Washington Consensus ignored the problems associated with rising inequality and even encouraged the weakening of social safety nets. In some cases, hasty privatizations resulted in the emergence of billionaire oligarchs who enriched themselves through monopoly privileges rather than having to compete in the market for the benefit of consumers.[7]

Nonetheless, the former Soviet satellite states and republics became EU member states and joined a common labour market. All the Baltic and Visegrád countries became EU member states in 2004 and had to compete with wealthier EU member states for labour. The income difference was likely to result in outward migration, but the introduction of neoliberal policies would make the situation even worse. It is noteworthy that the Baltic states with their more extreme neoliberal policies lost many more people to outward migration than the Visegrád countries that are more welfare-oriented in their policies (see, for example, Hilmarsson 2018).

The rise of China and a stronger Russia

With the rise of China, the US has become increasingly preoccupied in East Asia and concerned about an unstable Russian Federation that also cooperates with the People's Republic of China. EU and European NATO member states have felt that they are increasingly under threat. One can argue that the rise of China poses the greatest threat to NATO as the US continues with is pivot to Asia, away from Europe. It is likely that the Russian Federation's military invasion of Ukraine may delay the US pivot to Asia. Furthermore, the US is expected to seek to protect its interests in the Persian Gulf and in East Asia owing to its concerns about energy supplies.

As a response to the rise of China and the emergence of a stronger Russia, Europe could establish its own European military and become more independent as a global power. But many European states fear that this will further weaken NATO and the guarantee of collective security enshrined in Article 5. The President of France, Emmanuel Macron, has openly expressed a desire to create a European army that would make Europe more independent in its defence and could help to turn Europe into a global power. Macron has warned European countries that they can no longer rely on the US to defend its NATO allies and described NATO as becoming brain-dead.[8] In contrast, the President of the US, Joe Biden, has reaffirmed the enduring transatlantic bond through NATO and underscored the 'ironclad' commitment of the US to upholding Article 5.[9]

Arguably in a multipolar world Europe should avoid being drawn into unnecessary conflict with Russia through the continued expansion of NATO to the east. The idea that NATO should expand to include Ukraine and Georgia has proved costly and an extended alliance beyond the current 30 NATO member states maybe unnecessary for European security. European NATO member states need to think about the need for a further NATO open-door policy and to balance the costs against the benefits. As the US progresses with its pivot to Asia, the European countries can build up their national armies and improve their military cooperation. European NATO member states should avoid being drawn into a conflict with China and into an East Asian security competition. At the same time, they can try to convince the US to maintain a military presence in Europe. European countries such as the Baltic states and Poland still look to the US for their security rather than to large European powers such as France and Germany.

NATO's common purpose is to secure lasting peace in Europe and North America, based on respect for democracy, individual liberty and the rule of law, as enshrined in the Washington Treaty. This stance may not meet with approval in Russia and China as talk about democracy may be understood as a NATO-led will to topple the regimes in Moscow and Beijing. This will increase tensions between NATO and the Russian and Chinese regimes.

How viable is the transatlantic link?

While attempting to maintain the transatlantic link in partnership with the US, Europe should try to maintain good trade and investment relations with China. Once the Ukraine war is over a new Cold War is likely to emerge in East Asia rather than in Europe and Europe does not need to be a direct participant in a US-Chinese security competition in Asia. In June 2021 the White House claimed that '[a]llies will enhance NATO's ability to strengthen the rules-based international order by increasing dialogue and practical cooperation with the Alliance's partners, including the European Union and those in the Indo-Pacific (Australia, Japan, New Zealand, and the Republic of Korea)'.[10]

For the Baltic states the guarantee of collective defence afforded by Article 5 is the cornerstone of their security. For the Visegrád countries, especially Poland that borders Russia (Kaliningrad), Belarus and Ukraine, NATO membership is also very important. NATO membership is also very important for the continental Nordic countries, Denmark and Norway. At the time of writing Finland and Sweden had applied for full membership of NATO.

NATO membership for Iceland is also important but the country is not faced by the same immediate threat from Russian military activity as are the continental Nordic countries. Iceland is also close to the Arctic, located between North America and Europe, and is thus of strategic importance for the US as well as the continental European countries. Europe should in the long term seek to resolve its dispute with Russia, but the transatlantic link and the security cooperation with the US will be important if tensions with Russia run high as there will be a risk of war, even a nuclear threat.

How should European small powers react to this change?

Should Europe prepare for a NATO without the US? One reason why the US might want to remain strong in Europe was if any European country was likely to dominate Europe regionally and then challenge US power on a global scale. But is there any such potential competitor? There are two major powers in Europe: Germany and Russia. Germany has the largest economy in Europe and is influential within the EU. In economic terms its role in the EU has not always been good. This is perhaps because Germany wants to be sure that other economically weaker members states, especially the new Eastern European member states and the southern EU member states, such as Greece, do not free ride on its wealth.

On the fiscal side Germany wants to enforce strict discipline among the economically weaker member states so as to ensure that the EU does not become a transfer union that redistributes resources from wealthier European countries to either the emerging Eastern European or southern European countries. This danger resulted in austerity in many EU countries during the 2008/09 global financial crisis when stimulus was needed. On the monetary side Germany is influential through the European Central Bank, an expanded Bundesbank, primarily concerned about inflation, but less about GDP growth and unemployment.

However, despite its wealth and industrial power, Germany does not have a sufficiently large population or economy to dominate Europe. Furthermore, EU integration means more shared power in Europe, thereby limiting German dominance. This was perhaps one of the key purposes behind the formation of the EU. The EU itself remains divided and despite its wealth several member countries, particularly Italy, have reached dangerous debt levels during the COVID-19 crisis and there is much uncertainty ahead threatening economic stability in the EU and especially the euro area. The ongoing conflict in Ukraine, the global energy crisis and higher inflation, have exacerbated the situation.

Russia, the other European power, cannot dominate Europe. It is powerful, especially considering its nuclear capabilities, but it is a declining power. It suffers from demographic decline and economic problems and is too dependent on exports of oil and gas. Its economy is smaller than that of Italy. Russia can threaten European countries at its borders, but not the rest of Europe.

While Europe might seek to keep the US engaged in Europe by all possible means via NATO European countries should avoid unnecessary tensions in distant regions, especially East Asia. Other wars that Europe has participated in have proved costly and without purpose. One example if the conflict in Afghanistan. According to the White House,

> As NATO winds down its military presence in Afghanistan after nearly 20 years, the United States and our NATO Allies and partners will continue supporting the people of Afghanistan through civilian and security assistance. The United States will also continue to stand shoulder to shoulder with our Allies and partners in NATO's non-combat advisory mission in Iraq.[11]

European countries should avoid participating in such conflicts to secure the NATO Article 5 guarantee for themselves.

Europe also needs to reconsider its commitment to NATO's 'open door policy', which provides a path to membership for any European country that shares its values and meets the necessary responsibilities and obligations. A commitment made to Ukraine and Georgia during the Bucharest 2008 NATO summit[12] (NATO 2008) has proved costly and European countries need to seriously consider if further NATO expansion to the east, including the former Soviet republics, will enhance its security.

The Baltic, Nordic and the Visegrád countries that fall under the US security umbrella should continue to maintain good relations with the US via NATO and encourage the US to retain its interest in Europe, but these countries should avoid being drawn into conflicts in East Asia and in the long term they should seek to normalize relations with Russia.

Notes

1 In 1949 there were 12 founding members of NATO, namely Belgium, Canada, Denmark, France, Iceland, Italy, Luxembourg, the Netherlands, Norway, Portugal, the United Kingdom and the US. See www.nato.int/cps/en/natolive/topics_52044.htm.
2 www.nato.int/wearenato/why-was-nato-founded.html.
3 Article 5 of the North Atlantic Treaty states that '[t]he Parties agree that an armed attack against one or more of them in Europe or North America shall be considered an attack against them all and consequently they agree that, if such an armed attack occurs, each of them, in exercise of the right of individual or collective self-defence recognised by Article 51 of the Charter of the United Nations, will assist the Party or Parties so attacked by taking forthwith, individually and in concert with the other Parties, such action as it deems necessary, including the use of armed force, to restore and maintain the security of the North Atlantic area. Any such armed attack and all measures taken as a result thereof shall immediately be reported to the Security Council. Such measures shall be terminated when the Security Council has taken the measures necessary to restore and maintain international peace and security.' See www.nato.int/cps/en/natolive/official_texts_17120.htm.
4 Washington Consensus policies included maintaining fiscal discipline, reordering public spending priorities (from subsidies to health and education expenditures), reforming tax policy, allowing the market to determine interest rates, maintaining a competitive exchange rate, liberalizing trade, permitting inward foreign investment, privatizing state enterprises, deregulating barriers to entry and exit, and securing property rights. See www.piie.com/commentary/speeches-papers/what-washington-means-policy-reform.
5 www.piie.com/blogs/realtime-economic-issues-watch/washington-consensus-stands-test-time-better-populist-policies.
6 Ibid.
7 Ibid.
8 www.economist.com/europe/2019/11/07/emmanuel-macron-warns-europe-nato-is-becoming-brain-dead.
9 www.whitehouse.gov/briefing-room/statements-releases/2021/06/13/fact-sheet-nato-summit-revitalizing-the-transatlantic-alliance/.
10 Ibid.
11 Ibid.
12 *Bucharest Summit Declaration issued by the Heads of State and Government Participating in the Meeting of the North Atlantic Council in Bucharest on 3 April 2008*. See www.nato.int/cps/en/natolive/official_texts_8443.htm.

References

Andersen, T. M., Holmström, B., Honkapohja, S., Korkman, S., Tson, S. H. and Vartiainen, J. (2007). The Nordic Model: Embracing Globalization and Sharing Risks. *ETLA*. Available at: http://websites.rcc.edu/biancardi/files/2010/03/The-Nordic-Model.pdf (accessed 19 July 2022).

Bohle, D. and Greskovits, B. (2012). *Capitalist Diversity on Europe's Periphery*. Cornell Studies in Political Economy.Ithaca, NY: Cornell University Press.

Hilmarsson, H.Þ. (2018). *The Economic Crisis and its Aftermath in the Nordic and Baltic Countries: Do As We Say and Not As We Do*. Abingdon: Routledge.

Laar, M. (2007). *The Estonian Economic Miracle*. The Heritage Foundation. Available at: www.heritage.org/report/the-estonian-economic-miracle (accessed 7 January 2021).

Laar, M. (2005). Walking on Water: How to Do It. *The Brussels Journal*. Available at: www.brusselsjournal.com/node/202 (accessed 23 October 2021).
North Atlantic Treaty Organization (NATO) (2019). *The North Atlantic Treaty*. Available at: www.nato.int/cps/en/natolive/official_texts_17120.htm (accessed 19 July 2022).
North Atlantic Treaty Organization (NATO) (2008). *Bucharest Summit Declaration Issued by the Heads of State and Government Participating in the Meeting of the North Atlantic Council in Bucharest on 3 April 2008*. Available at: www.nato.int/cps/en/natolive/official_texts_8443.htm (accessed 19 July 2022).
Steil, B. (2013). *The Battle of Bretton Woods*. Princeton, NJ: Princeton University Press.
Williamson, J. (1990). *What Washington Means by Policy Reform*. Available at: www.piie.com/commentary/speeches-papers/what-washington-means-policy-reform (accessed 19 July 2022).

7 The rise of China and its growing economic and political interest in Europe

The rise of China and the relative decline in US supremacy

The rise of the People's Republic of China poses the most serious threat to US global dominance that it has ever seen. If China were able to achieve the gross domestic product (GDP) per capita of the Republic of Korea (South Korea) it would become about twice as large as the US economy, with the GDP per capita of Hong Kong it would become about three times the size of the US economy, and with the per capita GDP of Singapore it would become about four times the size of the US economy.[1]

Where will China be in 20 to 30 years' time if it continues to grow economically even if its population does not expand? It will certainly be much larger than the US economy. It could even become bigger than the US and EU economies combined. Sooner or later this economic wealth is likely to be translated into military capabilities. As a result, the West is becoming increasingly nervous about the prospect of a country that does not embrace Western democratic values becoming dominant in the world. In fact, in the longer term the US economy will be the second – possibly the third – largest global economy. Should per capita incomes in India increase so that they are comparable to the average incomes of Indians living in the US, India will become a larger economy than that of the US. One fundamental difference between China and India is that India is a democracy, unlike China which has a single party government. Moreover, India is often seen as a US ally despite its close relations with the Russian Federation which supplies India with a large share of its military equipment.

China-Russia relations are now seen as a major threat to US supremacy and the rules-based international order. This was affirmed in the 2022 North Atlantic Treaty Organization (NATO) Strategic Concept: 'The deepening strategic partnership between the People's Republic of China and the Russian Federation and their mutually reinforcing attempts to undercut the rules-based international order run counter to our values and interests' (NATO 2022a, p. 5). Chinese-Russian cooperation has become a growing concern for the US, and the US-led NATO, since the military invasion of Ukraine, but once the war is over, China will in the long term pose the main threat to US dominance, not Russia, which is a declining great power.

DOI: 10.4324/9781003212539-8

Given this challenge the US is likely to focus more on Asia, and less on Europe. And a stronger China is already leading to growing tensions in Asia in the form of border disputes, disputes about islands and control over the oceans. Examples of these areas of potentially dangerous tension include the ongoing disputes with the breakaway Republic of China (Taiwan), which China considers part of its sovereign territory, disputes in the South China Sea, disputes about the Senkaku Islands (also known as the Diaoyu Islands) that lie between China and Japan, and disputes with South Korea owing to tensions with the Democratic Republic of Korea (North Korea).

Unlike the US, China is surrounded by hostile neighbours and the US can exploit this by building alliances within Asia. Furthermore, NATO is building alliances with countries in Asia that have issues with China. Thus, the NATO heads of state meeting in Madrid, Spain, in June 2022 was attended by leaders from Japan, South Korea, Australia and New Zealand, among others (NATO 2022b).

In addition to disputes with its neighbours, China's responses to protests within its own borders, including in Hong Kong, worry Western nations. These actions, and China's display of military power, already visible in trouble spots, hardly suggest that China will be soft in its dealings with its neighbours, nor does it provide assurances that China can rise peacefully in the world.

There is no single country in Europe that the US needs to worry about that could grow to dominate Europe and then challenge the US on a global scale. But there is an emerging regional hegemon in Asia. If China continues to grow it could dominate Asia and then challenge US authority worldwide. Given this situation it is natural that the US will become less interested in Europe and more interested in Asia. It will also become less interested in NATO and more interested in developing a strategic alliance in Asia. A balancing coalition is already taking shape between the US and its Asian allies such as India and Japan.[2] Countries such as South Korea, the Philippines, Viet Nam, Singapore may also join a balancing coalition against China in Asia.[3] Australia is also a US ally.

A stronger China thus means less US interest in Europe and a weaker NATO. If China manages to dominate Asia, thereby driving the US out of Asia, it is likely to seek more power in Europe as well as in other regions of the world just like the US did when it had sufficient resources to do so after the Second World War. In 20 to 30 years' time, we could be back to a unipolar world, but led by China. This would be the second unipolar moment the world has ever seen, and China could have the resources to make it happen. This transition would be a challenge for the US and the EU since both embrace democracy and values that are different to those embraced by the Chinese leadership.

China is already using its growing economic might to expand militarily. It is also forming its own international financial institutions to challenge the current global institutional architecture, the Bretton Woods institutions, established by the US following the Second World War. These include the

Asian Infrastructure Investment Bank (AIIB) based in Beijing, China, and the New Development Bank (NBD, also known as the BRICS Bank) based in Shanghai.

The AIIB supports the Chinese-led Belt and Road Initiative (BRI)[4] that China believes all participating countries could benefit from, but that can also be viewed as vital for China itself, a huge economy whose growth has primarily been based on exports. China needs to develop its infrastructure links to get its products to the end users worldwide. However, commentators view the BRI as constructing infrastructure links that could become an invaluable asset during a war. In Europe China is involved in the 16+1 Initiative (see European Parliament 2018) to forge better links with the Central and Eastern European countries that sometimes feel neglected by the EU and whose infrastructure is still linked to Russia 30 years after the dissolution of the Soviet Union. All the Visegrád countries, the Czech Republic (Czechia), Hungary, Poland and Slovakia, participate in the 16+1 Initiative as well as two Baltic states, Estonia and Latvia. Although the initiative predates the formal announcement of the BRI, the 16+1 Initiative is widely seen as an extension of the BRI. The three priority areas that China has identified for increasing cooperation under the 16+1 Initiative include infrastructure, advanced technologies and green technologies.[5]

The US in now supporting the Three Seas Initiative that was established to help Central and Eastern European countries to improve their infrastructure.

On 5 April 2015, when discussing the establishment of the AIIB, and the fact that major US allies had joined including the United Kingdom, former US Secretary of the Treasury Lawrence Summers[6] commented that '[t]his past month may be remembered as the moment the United States lost its role as the underwriter of the global economic system'.[7] He considered this event to be a global wake-up call for the US. Summers continued, 'I can think of no event since Bretton Woods comparable to the combination of China's effort to establish a major new institution and the failure of the United States to persuade dozens of its traditional allies, starting with Britain, to stay out'.[8] One can understand this frustration on the part of the US having opted to stay out of the AIIB.

The wide participation of US allies in the AIIB, which includes all the Nordic countries as well as two Visegrád countries, Poland and Hungary, can be understood as a signal that these allies are beginning to prepare themselves for a China that will play a bigger role in the world economy in the future than it did in the past. As Summers points out,

> This failure of strategy and tactics was a long time coming, and it should lead to a comprehensive review of the U.S. approach to global economics. With China's economic size rivaling that of the United States and emerging markets accounting for at least half of world output, the global economic architecture needs substantial adjustment. Political pressures from all sides in the United States have rendered the architecture increasingly dysfunctional.[9]

But one can ask if this development is really so bad for the world and for Europe specifically. Is it desirable, and even possible, that a country such as the US that represented about 40% of the world economy in 1944, when the Bretton Woods meeting took place, should occupy or indeed try to occupy the same dominating role after its economy has shrunk in relative terms to less than 20% of the total world economy?

It may be a psychological problem for the US leadership to become the world's second largest economy after China and potentially the third largest economy after India, but this seems inevitable. The growing role of emerging economies such as China, India, Brazil, Russia and South Africa (known as the BRICS countries), could be beneficial for the world and the European continent economically, but there are questions about security competition in the world and in different regions that can become dangerous. Then there are also questions about global values and democracy. The EU and NATO are clubs of nations that embrace Western values. The North Atlantic Treaty talks about safeguarding the freedom, common heritage and civilization of the peoples of the treaty that is founded on the principles of democracy, individual liberty and the rule of law.[10] The Chinese and Russian regimes are different, and this worries the West. These differences are also likely to worry China, and Russia even more as a weaker and declining power.

Alliances against China

The US is beginning to form alliances in Asia to respond to what they see as growing Chinese aggression and intimidation from China against its smaller and less powerful neighbours. The Quadrilateral Security Dialogue (known as the Quad) representing India, Japan and Australia along with the US is an example (see Panda and Gunasekara-Rockwell 2021). 'While not a formal military alliance like the North Atlantic Treaty Organization (NATO), it is seen by some as a potential counterweight to growing Chinese influence and alleged aggression in Asia-Pacific'.[11] The Quad was established in 2007 and lasted until 2008, but it was the rise of the Asian economic and military superpower, China, that led to the Quad's revival in 2017. The quadrilateral alliance seeks to counter China militarily and diplomatically in the Indo-Pacific region, particularly in South China Sea. Tensions between Quad members and China have led to fears of what could become a new Cold War in the region. The Quad seeks to promote a 'rules-based maritime order in the East and South China seas', which the Quad members state is needed to counter Chinese maritime claims. The Quad Plus also includes New Zealand, South Korea and Viet Nam. One can thus see the formation of a balancing coalition against growing Chinese power and dominance in Asia.

Admiral Philip Davidson, the former commander of the US Indo-Pacific Command, called the Quad grouping a 'diamond of democracies' in the Indo-Pacific.[12] 'China portrayed the organization as an attempt to encircle it and the possibility that Beijing could retaliate economically had the three US partners backing away from any strong positions.'[13] However, the Quad remains an informal gathering, with very little institutional backbone. In its present form the Quad cannot be viewed as an Asian NATO.

The Quad members may share concerns about China's growing military might and about the need to uphold the rules-based international order, but they also lack consensus on what to do about China. The priorities differ among Quad members, with India mostly focused on the Indian Ocean, while Australia and Japan are more concerned about the South China Sea.

If China steps up its military aggression against other countries, there is a possibility that the Quad could evolve into a more robust, institutionalized military alliance. 'Chinese diplomats and scholars regularly complain that U.S. alliances with Asian countries are relics of the Cold War that should be abandoned because they frustrate the desire and effort to create a regional security architecture that is appropriate for the twenty-first century'[14] (Bush 2016). Furthermore, if the US seeks to form alliances in Asia one must then draw the conclusion that there is a common enemy in the region. 'Chinese complaints also reflect an assumption that by definition alliances exist to counter an enemy, and so now China must be the new, not-so-secret adversary of the United States, now that the Soviet Union no longer exists'[15] (ibid.)

Although the Asian countries discussed above are forming an alliance with the US to address their security concerns, they depend on China for trade. The reality is that the Chinese economy is now so large that it is increasingly difficult to engage in international business without involving China. Economies in Asia are interlinked with specialization to exploit economics of scale (Gill et al. 2007). This has made Asian economies dependent on each other In fact,

> [i]n Asia, many U.S. allies are grappling with the reality of China's role as both their largest trading partner and most proximate security threat. Though most Asian allies are reluctant to publicly refer to China as a strategic threat, the increase in regional defense investments highlights the degree of concern China's military modernization has elicited in Asian capitals.[16]
>
> (Bush 2016)

Thus, in Asia, US allies look to the US for a security umbrella but economically they need its adversary, China, for trade. Economic and security concerns are at play here and Asian countries want both, not one at the cost of the other. While India sees China as a threat it also relies on Russia for the maintenance of its current military equipment and Russia is a close ally of China. The Russia-China relationship has grown stronger during the war in Ukraine that started in February 2022. The US may thus not be able to count on India as its interests are to avoid confrontation with Russia and China.

The China-Russia alliance

Currently China and Russia are forming an alliance. This became visible during the Ukraine crisis that has now turned into a war. China has joined Russia in opposing further NATO expansion to the east as the two countries move closer together in the face of Western pressure.[17] The Russian view is that Western powers are using the NATO defence alliance to undermine Russia. Russia and China are concerned about the AUKUS security pact between the US, the UK and Australia. AUKUS will see Australia build nuclear-powered submarines as part of efforts to boost security in the Asia-Pacific region.[18] It is largely seen as an effort to counter China.

While China supports Russia against further NATO expansion including Ukraine, Russia supports Beijing's 'One China' policy on the issue of Taiwan, namely that there is but one China and Taiwan is part of China. However, Taiwan refutes this stance and views itself as an independent country, with its own constitution and democratically elected leaders and is supported by the US.

According to a report published in 2020,[19] '[t]he scale of Chinese power and global reach poses acute challenges to open and democratic societies' (NATO 2020). Following the dissolution of the Soviet Union, Russia is not the main concern, but Russia and China together are seen as a threat to NATO and its democratic states (see also NATO 2022a, p. 5). The report continues,

> The rules-based international order, which underpins the security, freedom and prosperity of Allies, is under pressure from authoritarian countries, like Russia and China, that do not share our values. This has implications for our security, values, and democratic way of life. Through the NATO 2030 decisions, NATO will invest in increasing and deepening our partnerships in line with our values and interests to safeguard the rules-based international order.[20]
>
> (NATO 2020)

The rules-based international order was written by Western countries, primarily the US, and includes not only NATO, but also the Bretton Woods institutions, as well as the World Trade Organization (WTO, formerly the General Agreement on Tariffs and Trade). During its transition to a market economy China benefited by cooperating with the World Bank, the International Monetary Fund and the WTO, but it is unlikely to obey those institutions. Given the growing power of China, Europe and the US should rethink their communications with China and NATO should temper its language when referring to both Russia and China as enemies. A humiliated China is unlikely to obey the West and as US political scientist Joseph Nye famously warned, 'if you treat China as an enemy, you are certain to have an enemy'.[21]

Some other major alliances with and without China

A number of forums have been established, such as the Group of Seven (G7), the Group of Twenty (G20) and a new Democracies Ten (D-10), all of which have an impact on the economic and security competition between the superpowers, including the US and China.

The G7 is an informal forum that seeks to bring together the leaders of the world's leading industrial nations. The annual G7 summits have over the years developed into a platform for determining the course of multilateral discourse and shaping political responses to global challenges. The G7 summit brings together leaders from the EU as well as from Canada, France, Germany, Italy, Japan, the UK and the US. It is noteworthy that China and Russia are not currently members of this grouping. In fact, Russia joined the G7 in 1997, which in the following year became known as the Group of Eight (G8). However, in 2014 Russia was suspended indefinitely following the annexation of the Crimean Peninsula.

To some degree the G7 is capable of setting the global agenda because decisions taken by these major economic powers have a real impact. The political direction set by these leaders on a policy issue also affect across many other international institutions.[22] One can expect that institutions such as the Bretton Woods institutions, the Asian Development Bank, the Inter-American Development Bank, the European Bank for Reconstruction and Development and the African Development Bank are heavily influenced by the G7. China, which has been excluded from the G7, has established its own international organizations, the AIIB and the NDB. The latter was established in partnership with the BRICS countries, that feel left out and are mobilizing under Chinese leadership. This is not to say that China, along with the other BRICS, has not participated in the institutions such as the Bretton Woods institutions and the regional banks mentioned above. In fact, one can argue that the Bretton Woods institutions played a major role in helping China to make the transition from a Soviet-style centrally planned economy to a market economy.

The G7 complements the role of the G20, which is widely regarded as the framework for ongoing global economic coordination. The G20 is a strategic multilateral platform connecting the world's major developed and emerging economies. The G20 holds a strategic role in securing future global economic growth and prosperity. Together, the G20 members represent more than 80% of global GDP, 75% of international trade and 60% of the global population. Starting in 1999 as a meeting of finance ministers and central bank governors, the G20 has evolved into an annual summit involving the heads of state and of government.[23] The G20 can be viewed as challenging the G7 as it also includes the major emerging market economies that are assuming a greater role in world affairs.

The US and its democratic allies and partners in Europe and Asia view themselves as playing a central role in promoting and defending the rules-based international order by serving as the core of regional and bilateral security alliances, leading global economic institutions that promote free trade and financial flows and championing the expansion of democratic values. In their view the challenges posed by China and Russia are setting the terms for a new era of strategic competition between democracies and autocracies that is likely to play out in the foreseeable future.

The D-10 can serve to drive a common approach to counter the wide range of autocratic threats posed by Russia and China. At the top of the D-10's agenda should be the challenge of autocratic coercion posed by China and Russia.[24] The D-10 core members include the US, the UK, Germany, France, Italy, Japan and Canada, plus Australia, South Korea and the EU. Given its size in terms of population and economy, China is viewed as the main threat to the D-10 and one can wonder if it is wise to play democracies against a single-party government such as China as this can damage world peace and prosperity. In the 1980s there was an emphasis to engage China by integrating it into the global system. Now that China has become a major power capable of challenging the US we can see a growing trend from the West, especially the US, to try to exclude China and to slow its growth so the US can contain China.

United Nations Security Council, NATO and the great power rivalry

The United Nations (UN) Security Council first met in 1946. Today it is composed of 15 members, including five permanent members, China, France, Russia, the UK and the US, and 10 non-permanent members elected for two-year terms by the General Assembly[25] (United Nations 2022a). The functions and powers under the UN Charter are as follows:

- to maintain international peace and security in accordance with the principles and purposes of the UN;
- to investigate any dispute or situation which might lead to international friction;
- to recommend methods of adjusting such disputes or the terms of settlement;
- to formulate plans for the establishment of a system to regulate armaments;
- to determine the existence of a threat to the peace or act of aggression and to recommend what action should be taken;
- to call on members to apply economic sanctions and other measures not involving the use of force to prevent or stop aggression;
- to take military action against an aggressor;
- to recommend the admission of new members; to exercise the trusteeship functions of the UN in 'strategic areas';
- to recommend to the General Assembly the appointment of the Secretary-General and, together with the Assembly, to elect the judges of the International Court of Justice.

Among the key problems that limits the power and usefulness of the Security Council is the veto power of the five permanent members[26] (United Nations 2022b). The Security Council is thus only useful in the event that the permanent members agree. If one or more disagree, which often happens in international relations, the Security Council becomes useless and no decision can be made.

The Security Council has changed little since its inception in 1946. There is no permanent member from Latin America or Africa and there is no Muslim country represented among the permanent members. India is not among the permanent members, nor is the largest economy in Europe, Germany.

Owing to the limitations posed by the right to veto, the Security Council cannot be viewed as a higher authority that nation states can turn to and rely on. There is a high probability that the Security Council will not reach a conclusion due to the veto power of one or more of the permanent member states.

Furthermore, the whole UN system is weak financially. In the General Assembly one country has one vote which larger states like the US dislike. This is in contrast with the Bretton Woods institutions that vote according to shares which are related to the size of a member country's economy. This means that powers such as the US have much more power in the Bretton Woods institutions than in the UN. Thus, the US has often starved the UN by putting its financial contributions on hold.

If China continues to grow economically, and if it succeeds in dominating Asia and becoming a regional hegemon, it could subsequently seek further influence in Europe and other regions.

It is well known that the US dominates the Americas and does not have any peer competitors in the region. Canada is not a threat, neither is Mexico, nor any other country in Central or South America. The same cannot be said about China that borders many countries, including countries that have military capabilities such as India, Russia and Viet Nam. Japan, South Korea, the Philippines, Taiwan and Thailand are not far away. All these countries threaten Chinese dominance in the region.

In addition to this the US has a large and growing military presence in Asia, precisely because of China's rising power. India, Viet Nam, South Korea and Japan are either US allies or potential US allies. NATO was founded because of the threat posed by the Soviet Union. When the Soviet Union fell, Russia became NATO's main problem. But now NATO is beginning to see China as a problem. Although Russia poses a threat to Europe, China is now perceived as posing a growing threat to the US and its allies.

According to a report published in 2020,

> NATO allies feel China's influence more and more in every domain. Its Belt and Road, Polar Silk Road, and Cyber Silk Road have extended rapidly, and it is acquiring infrastructure across Europe with a potential bearing upon communications and interoperability … because of its

> scale and economic trajectory, China is a driver of global growth, trade and investment, and a significant investor in many NATO countries. It has begun to develop a strategic-commercial presence in the Euro-Atlantic Area via the Belt and Road Initiative, the 17+1 format, numerous bilateral agreements, and its MCF [military-civil fusion] strategy.
>
> (NATO 2020)

According to the Strategic Concept launched at NATO's Madrid Summit held in June 2022,

> The PRC [People's Republic of China] seeks to control key technological and industrial sectors, critical infrastructure, and strategic materials and supply chains. It uses its economic leverage to create strategic dependencies and enhance its influence. It strives to subvert the rules-based international order, including in the space, cyber and maritime domains.
>
> (NATO 2022a, p. 5)

In the same report concerns are expressed over 'the deepening strategic partnership between the People's Republic of China and the Russian Federation' (ibid.). For the US, China is the main threat, not Russia.

There are concerns in Europe regarding China's real intentions. Could they be to increasingly drive the US out of Asia and then increase its influence in Europe just as the US did after the Second World War? China is already increasing its influence in Europe via the 16+1 Initiative and one can find the Baltic and Visegrád countries among the 16 countries cooperating with China. US concerns about the growing influence of China are not only seen in NATO reports but also within US-led alliances in Asia including the Quad and AUKUS (see above).

Kishore Mahbubani, a distinguished fellow at the Asia Research Institute at the National University of Singapore has argued that

> it is not the Quad per se that is destabilizing Asia, but rather the lack of a comprehensive, long-term U.S. strategy for managing the arrival of China as a great power and the simultaneous decline in America's relative power … [The Quad] ignores the reality that the nature of competition in Asia is not military but economic in nature. The real danger of the Quad, therefore, is that it risks becoming oriented around the old Cold War-era notion that building a strong countervailing military alliance or security partnership will lead China's power to collapse as the Soviet Union's did. The focus on the Quad also distracts the United States from the 'real game' of economic integration, as embodied in the Regional Comprehensive Economic Partnership (RCEP), a free trade agreement signed by 15 Asia-Pacific nations in November 2020.[27]

Thus, according to Mahbubani, China's intentions are more economic than military. The US is using old Cold War tactics but at the same time it is losing out on trade. Mahbubani's views may reflect the fact that Singapore wishes to compete economically with China without the fear of military reprisals. However, China's relations with its smaller neighbours are not particularly peaceful which is one important reason why they are forming alliances with the US. Singapore is more likely to ally with the US than with China. Mahbubani's argument that China's power is unlikely to collapse under pressure from the US and its allies seems credible. The Soviet Union had a centrally planned economy and was always much poorer than the US. While China has a single-party government it has adopted principles of market economy resulting in an economy that rivals the US economy and could, if it continues to grow, become a much larger economy than that of the US. At current prices the US economy measured by GDP is larger than the Chinese economy, but if one corrects GDP for the price differences within those economies, i.e. on a purchasing-power parity basis, the Chinese economy is already larger than the US economy.

The threat from China has now been added to NATO's expanding agenda, already providing a surprising point of agreement at the December 2019 NATO summit, at which NATO members committed the alliance for the first time to deal with China's growing influence and international policies.[28] In April 2020 NATO Secretary-General Jens Stoltenberg charged an independent 'Reflection Group' with preparing a report that looked to the future; released in November 2020 the 'NATO 2030' document put the challenge in stark terms: 'China is … best understood as a full-spectrum systemic rival, rather than a purely economic player or an only Asia-focused security actor'[29] (NATO 2020). Both China and Russia are viewed as a threat to NATO and that threat extends beyond Asia. China is thus not only a threat to US dominance in Asia but also in Europe, and a stronger China could potentially also threaten North America. This is exactly what the US does not want. A stronger China could dominate Asia, thereby driving the US out of the region. It appears that the US is using NATO, and its European allies, to counter China.

How can Europe deal with this challenge? How should Europe manage its relations with China vs the US?

There are clouds hanging over many EU and euro area countries as a result of the COVID-19 pandemic due to growing public expenditure, fiscal deficits and high and rising public debt. The conflict in Ukraine has only made matters worse. It has resulted in increased uncertainty, an energy crisis and higher inflation. Nevertheless, the EU remains an economic powerhouse. So far, the EU has not sought to become a military power on its own account compared to that of the US. In fact, the EU depends on the US for its defence via NATO. The EU is the only economic superpower in the world to rely on another power for its own defence and EU expansion has resulted in increased dependency on the US via NATO a parallel expansion. The other powers in the world, notably China and Russia, take full responsibility for their own defence.

Considering the future of European defence there are divisions within the EU. The President of France, Emmanuel Macron, has talked about Europe becoming a global power with its own army and in his view NATO is becoming 'brain-dead'.[30] According to Macron, Europe needs to start thinking of itself strategically as a geopolitical power, one that is not dependent on other countries for its defence.

Countries located on the eastern flank of the EU such as Poland and the Baltic states still give priority to NATO and some EU countries fear that a European army would weaken NATO. The Eastern European countries do not trust Germany on defence matters and many countries, especially Poland and the Baltics, have criticized the extent of Germany's economic ties with Russia during the Ukraine war as well as its dependency on Russia for its energy requirements. France does not seem to be a credible ally to many European countries, again especially the eastern flank that relies on US-backed NATO. The eastern flank countries trust the authorities in Washington, not those in Berlin or Paris.

NATO was established in 1949 due to the threat that the Western countries saw in the Soviet Union. When the Soviet Union fell in 1991 Russia was seen as posing a threat to NATO member states. There are certain vulnerabilities that the EU and Europe is faced with in their relations with Russia. One of these is energy dependency. And the EU's largest economy, Germany, is not only dependent on Russia for gas. It also has close trade ties with China.

During the Ukraine crisis Russia has allied with China and China is the US's main adversary in Asia. The fact that in 2019 more than 50% of European exports to China originated in Germany made the Merkel government more hesitant than some of its European neighbours to openly criticize Beijing.[31] It is also noteworthy that Germany contributes generously to Chinese development cooperation (see Chapter 2 in this volume). It remains to be seen how Germany's new chancellor, Olaf Scholz, will deal with China and Russia but while the EU countries, including Germany, depend on the US for their security, they depend on Russia for energy and on China for trade. This dependency on superpowers makes the EU vulnerable.

Meanwhile, China is showing a keen interest in investing in Europe via the BRI (EBRD n.d.) and notably in Eastern and Central Europe via the 16 + 1 format[32] (European Parliament 2018). Some of the eastern flank countries in Europe that are generally supportive of NATO feel neglected by the EU in terms of investment, including infrastructure connections. Furthermore, Italy and Greece's decisions to sign wide-ranging BRI investment agreements sparked concern in other European capitals, which have been more circumspect about Chinese infrastructure investments on the continent.[33] One could ask if growing trade and investment from China can become a security threat for Europe and the EU. Furthermore, conflict with Russia has pushed Russia more and more into the arms of China.

Despite Europe's continued dependency on the US for its security, it is time for a reconceptualization of the trans-Atlantic relationship. NATO's continuation after the end of the Cold War was a way of keeping the US in charge of European security during an uncertain period after the dissolution of the Soviet Union.[34] One can argue that the purpose of NATO has been to keep the US in Europe, to keep Russia out, and to keep Germany down.

As China grows, the US will become increasingly preoccupied with East Asia, and with China in particular, and will have less interest or the capacity to defend Europe. At the same time European allies cannot help the US much in East Asia and would hardly be eager to be drawn into a conflict in Taiwan or the South China Sea. Also, given that Article 5 of the 1949 Washington Treaty refers to 'an armed attack against one or more [NATO members] in Europe or North America shall be considered an attack against them all',[35] an East Asian conflict, involving US forces, would technically fall outside NATO's scope.[36]

If the US is going to succeed in rebalancing its defence posture toward Asia, it needs a stronger Europe able to take the lead in its broader neighbourhood. But there are fears that European efforts to build greater capacity will undermine NATO.[37] Europe is faced with dilemma. It depends on the US for its security and needs China for economic growth. The US may need European support in East Asia but that will aggravate China. If China becomes a much bigger economy than that of the US, it will first seek to drive the US out of East Asia and then out of Europe. Western democracy and Western values are then in danger unless China transforms into a democracy which at this moment seems unlikely. A single-party government and an export-driven market economy has so far worked for China.

As regards the Nordic, Baltic and Visegrád countries they all fall under the US security umbrella, either through formal NATO membership, or by cooperating with NATO as Finland and Sweden have done in the past. At the time of writing Finland and Sweden had applied for full NATO membership. Countries in the Baltic, Nordic and Visegrád groups also work with China, some via the AIIB and others via the 16+1 Initiative, for example. They want to take advantage of trade with China and investment from China via the 16+1 Initiative and some also seek to invest in China via the AIIB. Although they maintain good relations with the US they appear to be preparing for China to assume a larger role in the world economy. The challenge now is how to take full advantage of trade with China while maintaining good cooperation with the US in terms of security.

Notes

1 See the IMF *World Economic Outlook Database*, www.imf.org/en/publications/weo/weo-database/2020/october/weo-report?c=924,532,542,576,111,&s=ngdpdpc,

lp,&sy=2019&ey=2025&ssm=0&scsm=1&scc=0&ssd=1&ssc=0&sic=0&sort=country&ds=.&br=1.

2 https://edition.cnn.com/2020/10/20/asia/australia-india-malabar-naval-exercises-int-hnk-ml/index.html.

3 The US likes to count India among its allies, but India's reliance on Russian military equipment is a challenge for India and the fact that Russia and China are allies makes India's situation even more complicated.

4 China's Belt and Road Initiative is a strategy initiated by China that seeks to connect Asia with Africa and Europe via land and maritime networks with the aim of improving regional integration, increasing trade and stimulating economic growth. See www.ebrd.com/what-we-do/belt-and-road/overview.html.

5 www.csis.org/analysis/will-chinas-161-format-divide-europe.

6 Lawrence Summers is a professor at and former president of Harvard University. He was Secretary to the Treasury from 1999–2001 and economic adviser to President Obama from 2009–10.

7 www.washingtonpost.com/opinions/a-global-wake-up-call-for-the-us/2015/04/05/6f847ca4-da34-11e4-b3f2-607bd612aeac_story.html.

8 Ibid.

9 Ibid.

10 www.nato.int/cps/en/natolive/official_texts_17120.htm.

11 The Quad alliance comprising the US, Japan, India and Australia forms part of President Biden's plan to contain China. However, some experts are not so sure. See https://edition.cnn.com/2021/03/11/asia/quad-us-india-japan-australia-intl-hnk/index.html.

12 https://edition.cnn.com/2021/03/10/asia/us-pacific-commander-china-threat-intl-hnk-ml/index.html.

13 https://edition.cnn.com/2021/03/11/asia/quad-us-india-japan-australia-intl-hnk/index.html.

14 www.brookings.edu/wp-content/uploads/2016/11/fp_20160713_alliances_introduction.pdf.

15 Ibid.

16 Ibid.

17 www.bbc.com/news/world-asia-60257080.

18 Joint Leaders' Statement on AUKUS: 'As the first initiative under AUKUS, recognizing our common tradition as maritime democracies, we commit to a shared ambition to support Australia in acquiring nuclear-powered submarines for the Royal Australian Navy. Today, we embark on a trilateral effort of 18 months to seek an optimal pathway to deliver this capability. We will leverage expertise from the United States and the United Kingdom, building on the two countries' submarine programs to bring an Australian capability into service at the earliest achievable date'. See www.whitehouse.gov/briefing-room/statements-unreleases/2021/09/15/joint-leaders-statement-on-aukus/.

19 www.nato.int/nato_static_fl2014/assets/pdf/2020/12/pdf/201201-Reflection-Group-Final-Report-Uni.pdf.

20 www.nato.int/nato_static_fl2014/assets/pdf/2021/6/pdf/2106-factsheet-nato2030-en.pdf.

21 www.huffingtonpost.com/joseph-nye/china-contain-china_b_6845588.html.

22 https://ec.europa.eu/info/food-farming-fisheries/farming/international-cooperation/international-organisations/g7_en.

23 https://g20.org/about-the-g20/.

24 www.atlanticcouncil.org/wp-content/uploads/2021/06/From-the-G7-to-a-D10-Strengthening-Democratic-Cooperation-for-Todays-Challenges.pdf.

25 www.un.org/securitycouncil/content/current-members.

26 The creators of the UN Charter conceived that five countries – China, France, the USSR, the UK and the US – because of their key roles in the establishment of the

UN, would continue to play important roles in the maintenance of international peace and security. They were granted the special status of Permanent Member States at the Security Council, along with a special voting power known as the 'right to veto'. It was agreed by the drafters that if any one of the five permanent members cast a negative vote in the 15-member Security Council, the resolution or decision would not be approved. All five permanent members have exercised the right of veto at one time or another. If a permanent member does not fully agree with a proposed resolution but does not wish to cast a veto, it may choose to abstain, thus allowing the resolution to be adopted if it obtains the required number of nine favourable votes. See www.un.org/securitycouncil/content/voting-system.

27 https://quincyinst.org/2021/04/27/experts-debate-the-role-of-the-quad-in-a-changing-asia/.
28 www.brookings.edu/wp-content/uploads/2016/11/fp_20160713_alliances_introduction.pdf.
29 www.nato.int/nato_static_fl2014/assets/pdf/2020/12/pdf/201201-Reflection-Group-Final-Report-Uni.pdf.
30 www.economist.com/europe/2019/11/07/emmanuel-macron-warns-europe-nato-is-becoming-brain-dead.
31 www.brookings.edu/research/retooling-americas-alliances-to-manage-the-china-challenge/.
32 Since 2012 China has engaged 16 Central and Eastern European countries, including 11 EU member states and five Western Balkan countries, under the 16+1 cooperation format, which it has portrayed as an innovative approach to regional cooperation. Although framed as multilateralism, in practice this format has remained largely bilateral and highly competitive in nature. See www.europarl.europa.eu/RegData/etudes/BRIE/2018/625173/EPRS_BRI(2018)625173_EN.pdf.
33 www.brookings.edu/research/retooling-americas-alliances-to-manage-the-china-challenge/.
34 www.brookings.edu/wp-content/uploads/2016/11/fp_20160713_alliances_introduction.pdf.
35 www.nato.int/cps/en/natolive/official_texts_17120.htm.
36 www.brookings.edu/wp-content/uploads/2016/11/fp_20160713_alliances_introduction.pdf.
37 Ibid.

References

Bush, R. (2016). *America's Alliances and Security Partnerships in East Asia: Introduction*. Washington, DC: Brookings Institution. Available at: www.brookings.edu/wp-content/uploads/2016/11/fp_20160713_alliances_introduction.pdf (accessed 20 July 2022).

European Bank for Reconstruction and Development (EBRD) (n.d.). *Belt and Road Initiative (BRI)*. Available at: www.ebrd.com/what-we-do/belt-and-road/overview.html (accessed 20 July 2022).

European Parliament (2018). *China, the 16+1 Format and the EU*. Available at: www.europarl.europa.eu/RegData/etudes/BRIE/2018/625173/EPRS_BRI(2018)625173_EN.pdf (accessed 20 July 2022).

Gill, I. S., Kharas, H. J. and Bhattasali, D. (2007). *An East Asian Renaissance: Ideas for Economic Growth*. Washington, DC: World Bank. Available at: https://openknowledge.worldbank.org/handle/10986/6798 (accessed 21 February 2022).

Mahbubani, K. (2021). Why Attempts to Build a New Anti-China Alliance Will Fail. *Foreign Policy.* Available at: https://foreignpolicy.com/2021/01/27/anti-china-alliance-quad-australia-india-japan-u-s/ (accessed 21 February 2022).

North Atlantic Treaty Organization (NATO) (2022a). *NATO 2022 Strategic Concept. Adopted by Heads of State and Government at the NATO Summit in Madrid, 29 June 2022*. Available at: www.nato.int/nato_static_fl2014/assets/pdf/2022/6/pdf/290622-strategic-concept.pdf (accessed 20 July 2022).

North Atlantic Treaty Organization (NATO) (2022b). *Madrid Summit Declaration: Issued by NATO Heads of State and Government Participating in the Meeting of the North Atlantic Council in Madrid on 29 June 2022*. Available at: www.nato.int/cps/en/natohq/official_texts_196951.htm (accessed 20 July 2022).

North Atlantic Treaty Organization (NATO) (2020). *NATO 2030: United for a New Era. Analysis and Recommendations of the Reflection Group Appointed by the NATO Secretary General.* Available at: www.nato.int/nato_static_fl2014/assets/pdf/2020/12/pdf/201201-Reflection-Group-Final-Report-Uni.pdf (accessed 27 February 2022).

North Atlantic Treaty Organization (NATO) (2019). *The North Atlantic Treaty.* Available at: www.nato.int/cps/en/natolive/official_texts_17120.htm (accessed 19 July 2022).

Panda, J. P. and Gunasekara-Rockwell, E. (Eds) (2021). *Quad Plus and Indo-Pacific: The Changing Profile of International Relations.* London: Routledge.

United Nations (UN) (2022a). *United Nations Security Council. Current Members.* Available at: www.un.org/securitycouncil/content/current-members (accessed 27 February 2022).

United Nations (UN) (2022b). *United Nations Security Council. Voting System.* Available at: www.un.org/securitycouncil/content/voting-system (accessed 27 February 2022).

8 Sharing a border with Russia

Ukraine and the challenge of EU and NATO expansion

Introduction

The build-up of Russian military forces close to the border of Ukraine in late 2021 was of great concern not only for Ukraine but also for the European Union (EU) and North Atlantic Treaty Organization (NATO) member states in Europe that either border Russia or are close to the Russian Federation. This includes many of the the Baltic, Nordic and Visegrád countries. Few expected the all-out Russian military invasion of Ukraine that started on 24 February 2022. Arguably Russia is putting the EU and especially NATO to the test.

The Baltic states are all members of the EU, the euro area and NATO. All the Baltics border Russia and are concerned about their security and rely on the principle of collective defence that is enshrined in Article 5 of the Washington Treaty – or North Atlantic Treaty – that forms the basis of NATO. The Visegrád countries are also concerned. They are all members of the EU and NATO, but Slovakia is the sole member of the euro area. Three of the Nordic countries, Denmark, Finland and Sweden, are EU member states and three of them, Denmark, Norway and Iceland are NATO member states. Finland is also a member of the euro area. Finland has a long eastern border with Russia and Norway has a northern border.

Like Lithuania, Poland has a border with the Russian exclave of Kaliningrad. Poland, Slovakia and Hungary have borders to the east with Ukraine. In addition to tensions at the Ukrainian border there have been tensions with Belarus owing to an influx of refugees at the Polish border. This has been of concern not only to Poland, but also to Lithuania and Latvia which also share a border with Belarus. Belarus is seen as a Russian ally by NATO member states.

The Nordic countries are also affected by these tensions, especially Finland which borders Russia and Sweden which has, similarly to Finland, long pursued a policy of neutrality. Finland and Sweden are the only Nordic countries that are not NATO member states and thus they cannot rely on the security guarantee afforded by Article 5 of the Washington Treaty. At the time of writing both Finland and Sweden had applied for membership of NATO owing to the threat posed by growing tensions with Russia.

DOI: 10.4324/9781003212539-9

Thus all the countries in the Baltic, Nordic and Visegrád groups are affected by these tensions with Russia and by the conflict in Ukraine. There are also tensions and divisions within NATO over Ukraine. Prior to the conflict Germany and Russia agreed on the construction of the Nord Stream 2 gas pipeline that runs beneath the Baltic Sea and links the two countries without crossing a third country. Once operational, it was envisaged that Nord Stream 2 would result in the reduced transit of gas from Russia to Europe via Ukraine. In the longer term Nord Stream 2 could mean that no Russian gas would be transmitted via Ukraine weakening Ukraine vis-à-vis Russia and result in large revenue losses for Ukraine. The Baltic states and Poland fiercely opposed the Nord Stream 2 project, which was completed in 2021. Prior to the Russian invasion of Ukraine both Russia and Germany wanted to go ahead but as a consequence of the war the project has been put on hold.

The US objected to the Nord Stream 2 project during the presidency of Donald Trump but prior to the war Joe Biden accepted the project on the grounds that it was almost completed when he took office as president of the US. Russia strongly objects to Ukraine's proposed membership of NATO and this was one of the main reasons for the Russian military build-up at Ukraine's borders and subsequent military invasion.

This chapter will focus on Ukraine and the challenges of further EU and NATO expansion. First, we will assess Ukraine's position, including its post-Soviet economic performance and productivity, integration with the West with support from the EU, NATO and the US, and the consequent conflict with Russia, the effect of weak governance and corruption, and finally outward migration from Ukraine and unemployment. Other academic papers and reports tend to analyse the challenges facing Ukraine from an economic, political or security view. This chapter seeks to consider those challenges simultaneously and more holistically.

Ukraine

Ukraine is a middle-income country with significant potential for economic growth. The country is endowed with key assets, such as fertile land, considerable natural resources, a geographic location at the crossroads of Europe and Asia, and an industrialized base with a skilled labour force.

The dissolution of the Soviet Union in 1991 resulted in the collapse of gross domestic product (GDP) in Ukraine (see Figures 8.1 and 8.2). This was to a large extent due to the disintegration of the Soviet economy and its central planning system.

From 2000–08 Ukraine's GDP grew by more than 7% per annum. However, the pattern of that growth was based on international capital inflows and credit expansion that proved unsustainable. Prior to the current war with Russia, Ukraine was still paying the consequences, most noticeably in the high non-performing loans in the banking sector and difficulties in accessing new credit.

From 2014–16 Ukraine experienced acute political, security and economic challenges. Public discontent over fundamental governance failures, capture of the state by vested interests, and corruption resulted in the Maidan uprising[1] triggering new elections and changes in government. These changes also led to the rupture of economic and political relationships and the realignment of commercial relationships with the rest of the world. In addition to Russian occupation of the Crimean Peninsula, the government effectively lost control of parts of Ukraine and military conflict began in the east of the country.

It should be noted that the Crimean Peninsula was a gift to Ukraine in 1954 but remained part of the Soviet Union as Ukraine also was part of the Soviet Union.[2] Boris Yeltsin, the first president of post-Soviet Russia, did not propose the acquisition of Crimea during negotiations to dissolve the Soviet republics.[3] Crimea thus remained Ukrainian territory. Tensions grew between Ukraine and Russia when in 2008 NATO announced its plan that Ukraine should become a member of the alliance (NATO 2008). The Crimean Peninsula was annexed by Russia and Russia took control over Donbass in the eastern part of Ukraine.

In 2021 and early 2022 there was a large Russian military build-up close to the Ukrainian border and growing concern over possible Russian invasion into Ukraine. Russia demanded a guarantee that Ukraine would never join NATO, a demand that NATO was not willing to accept. These tensions resulted in meetings between the presidents of Russia and the US with Russia demanding guarantees that Ukraine would stay out of NATO and the US president threatening economic sanctions should Russia invade Ukraine. On 24 February 2022 Russia invaded Ukraine and the conflict between Russia and Ukraine was still ongoing at the time of writing. In April 2022 the World Bank predicted that Ukraine's economy would shrink by 45% in that year as a result of the Russian invasion (World Bank 2022).[4]

Post-Soviet Union economic performance and productivity

At the beginning of its transition from a centrally planned to a market economy in 1991, Ukraine's GDP per capita at constant prices (in purchasing power parity – PPP – terms), was about 37% higher than that of neighbouring Poland. By 2021 Ukraine's GDP per capita at constant prices (in PPP terms) was only about 38% of that of Poland (see Figure 8.1). This occurred despite the fact that Ukraine has a better climate and soil and more mineral deposits than Poland; moreover, in 1991 it also had a stronger industrial base and lower public debt.

The only period of high growth in Ukraine post-Soviet Union was short-lived and was supported by favourable external conditions. As noted above between 1999 and the beginning of the global financial crisis in 2008 GDP in Ukraine grew by an annual average rate of 7% (see Figure 8.2). With this growth rate, Ukraine managed to almost double its GDP per capita in about the space of one decade (see Figure 8.1).

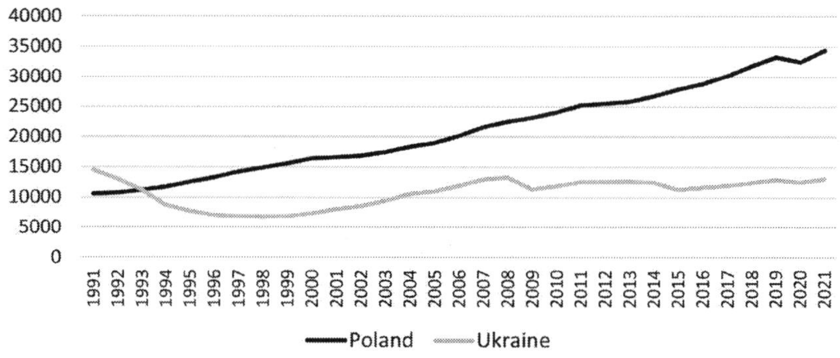

Figure 8.1 GDP per capita in US $ in constant prices (PPP terms) in Poland and Ukraine, 1991–2021
Source: IMF (2022).

According to the World Bank about half of the accumulated income gap between Ukraine and Poland is explained by divergent growth trajectories during the first decade of the transition (World Bank 2019b). But the 2000s and 2010s were also challenging, particularly the global financial crisis in 2008/09 and the Crimean Peninsula crisis in 2014/15. This was followed by the outbreak of the COVID-19 pandemic in 2020.

Poland and Ukraine are large countries geographically, in close proximity and with similar size of population, but their economic fates have been very different. Ukraine experienced a severe crisis in 2008/09 with GDP in constant prices declining by 15% in 2009, while Poland did not experience negative growth. In 2014/15, when the Crimean Peninsula was annexed to Russia, Ukraine recorded another period of negative growth. During the COVID-19 crisis both countries experienced a recession.

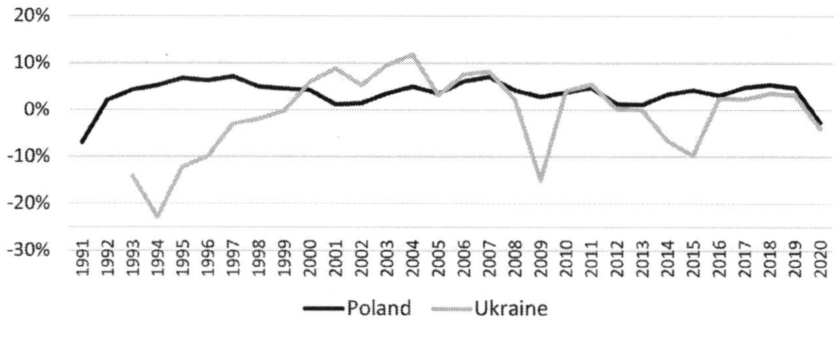

Figure 8.2 GDP in Poland and Ukraine in constant prices (% change), 1991–2020
Source: IMF (2021).

In summary the decrease in Ukraine's GDP in the 1990s was to a large extent due to the disruption of commercial and production networks associated with the disintegration of the Soviet Union. This was followed by a period of recovery from 2000–08. Following the 2008/09 global financial crisis Ukraine experienced a sharp recession in 2009, with GDP falling by about 15%. A weak and short-lived recovery gave way to an even sharper recession in 2014–15, triggered by the Maidan uprising (see above) and a conflict in the east of Ukraine. As a result, from 2014–15 Ukraine's GDP declined by a cumulative 16% (see Figure 8.2).

In 2019, prior to the outbreak of the COVID-19 pandemic, the World Bank estimated that at the current GDP growth rate of just about 3% per annum it would take Ukraine almost 100 years to reach the current levels of income of Germany and about 50 years to reach the income levels of Poland (World Bank 2019a, 2019b). Clearly, this would increase pressure on outward migration as the young and most talented Ukrainians are unlikely to want to wait for the country to catch up with its neighbours, and may choose to leave the country for wealthier Western countries; indeed, some may move to Russia.

Aggregate productivity in Ukraine remains low. According to the World Bank, an average worker in Germany can in 17 days produces as much as an average worker in Ukraine in one year (World Bank 2019b). Differences in output per worker in Ukraine and Germany are due to efficiency gaps[5] and capital gaps.[6] Increasing productivity of the aggregate economy will among other things require improved public investment and infrastructure to reduce costs and equip firms to be able to produce more competitively (ibid.).

In Chapter 4 in this volume it was noted that after 30 years of independence the Baltic states were behind the Nordic countries when measured by GDP per capita. This is true both for GDP per capita measured at current prices in US dollars and for GDP per capita in US dollars on a purchasing-power parity basis. In comparison to Finland and Iceland, both Latvia (a former Soviet republic) and Poland (a former Soviet satellite state) remain behind in terms of GDP per capita at current prices in US dollars. However, in comparison to Ukraine (a former Soviet republic), both Latvia and Poland have made good progress according to this indicator (see Figure 8.3).

All the countries take part in European integration. Finland and Latvia are EU and euro area member states, Iceland is a European Free Trade Association (EFTA) and European Economic Area member state, and Ukraine has an Association Agreement with the EU and is now an EU candidate country. Tensions with Russia from 2014 onwards severely damaged the Ukrainian economy and Ukraine could hardly be considered a feasible destination for foreign direct investment given the security threat it is faced with and high political risks. The Russian invasion is projected to have catastrophic effects on Ukraine.

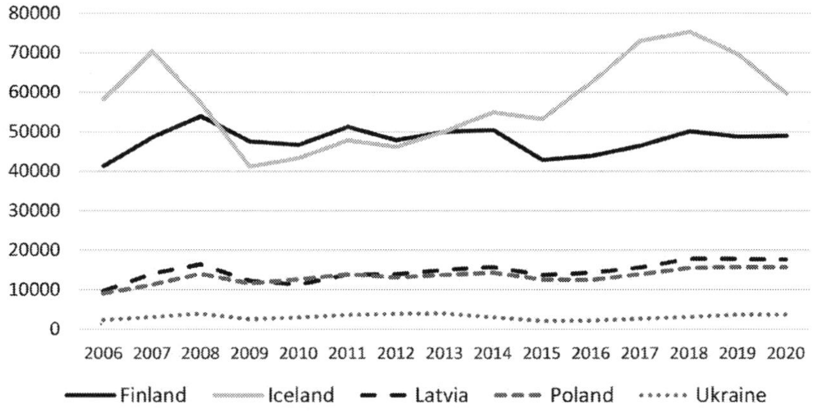

Figure 8.3 GDP per capita at current prices in US $ in Finland, Iceland, Latvia, Poland and Ukraine, 2006–20
Source: IMF (2021).

Internal and external (im)balances in Ukraine and Poland

The general government debt-to-GDP ratio in Ukraine was low in 2007 at around 12% of GDP, but it then increased from 2007–10 and again from 2013–16. Thereafter the debt-to-GDP ratio declined from 2016–19 until the COVID-19 crisis hit. Remarkably, in 2020 the Ukrainian debt-to-GDP ratio was close to 60%; thus, it fulfils the EU criteria for membership on this indicator (see Figure 8.4). Meanwhile, since 2006 Poland's general government debt-to-GDP ratio has remained under the maximum 60% of GDP rule of the EU, and also during COVID-19 crisis.

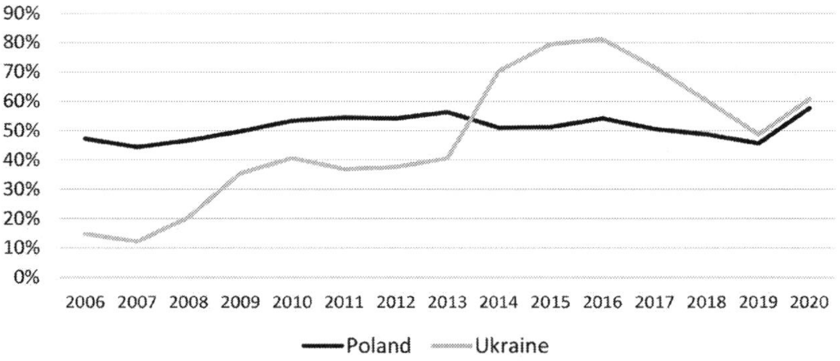

Figure 8.4 General government gross debt in Poland and Ukraine (% of GDP), 2006–20
Source: IMF (2021).

Poland ran current account deficits from 2006–14. Thereafter, its current account has was close to balance and it enjoyed a sizeable surplus in 2020. From 2006 to 2014 and again from 2016 to 2019 Ukraine was running current account deficits that were exceptionally large in 2012 and 2013. Only in 2015 and 2020 did Ukraine enjoy current account surpluses (see Figure 8.5).

From 2006–08, prior to the 2008/09 global financial crisis, the government headline deficit (also known as general government net lending/borrowing) in both Ukraine and Poland was under or close to the EU fiscal rule that states that member states must not run public deficits higher than 3% of GDP. After the 2008/09 crisis, both countries ran headline deficits well above the 3% of GDP limit, Poland from 2009–14 and Ukraine from 2009–10 and again from 2012–14. From 2015–19 both countries were within the 3% of GDP fiscal rule until the COVID-19 crisis hit and both countries ran large headline deficits (see Figure 8.6).

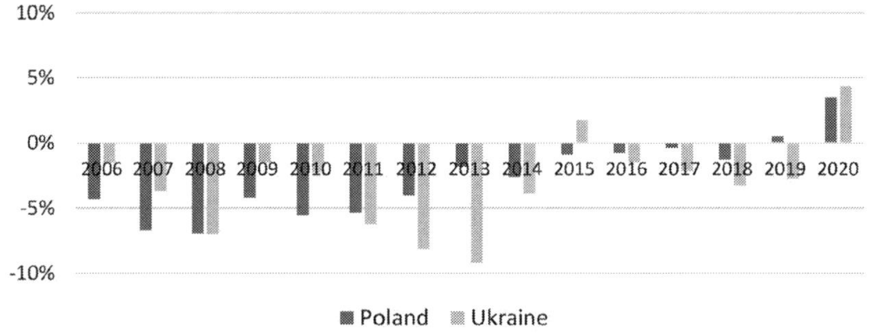

Figure 8.5 Current account balance in Poland and Ukraine (% of GDP), 2006–20
Source: IMF (2021).

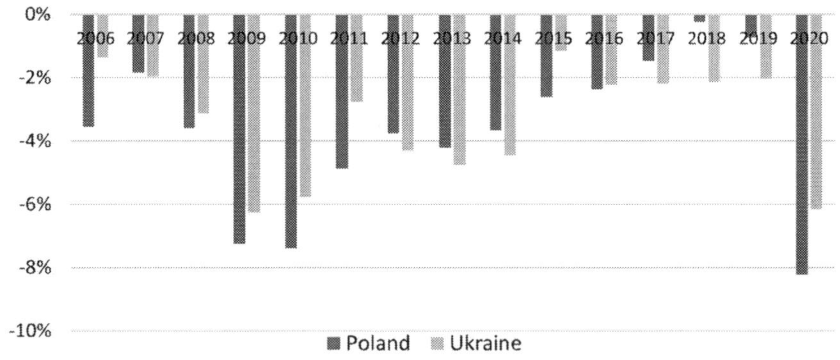

Figure 8.6 Government headline deficit in Poland and Ukraine (% of GDP), 2006–20
Source: IMF (2021).

From 2006–20 government debt grew from 15% to 61% of GDP in Ukraine, while in Poland it grew from 47% to 58% of GDP (see Figure 8.4). The debt level as a percentage of GDP will only worsen as the conflict in Ukraine goes on, both because of the collapse of GDP and also because of growing government debt. There is also great uncertainty about the future of the country, including how its reconstruction will be financed.

Integration with the West with the support of the EU, NATO and the US, and the subsequent conflict with Russia and full-scale war

The absence of a clear path to EU accession after the fall of the Soviet Union limited the resources available to transform Ukraine's economy anywhere close to the transformation that took place in neighbouring Poland that had a shared vision for EU membership and successfully accessed EU investment grants.

Prior to the Russian invasion, Ukraine was a politically divided country, with the western part tending to support EU and NATO accession, while the eastern part tended to favour stronger relations with Russia. Thus it would never be easy to seek full EU membership if the goal was to keep the country together. Russia perceived Ukraine's aspiration to join the EU, and NATO in particular, as a security threat. Russia continues to demand a guarantee that Ukraine will not join NATO. As the EU and NATO have moved closer to Russia proper, the blowback from Moscow has increased (Howarth 2017). Nevertheless, Ukraine's access to the EU common market is critical. Ukraine has now formally applied for EU membership, but full membership is not likely to materialize any time soon. Nevertheless, Ukraine could benefit from pre-accession assistance form the EU, especially grants for reconstruction of infrastructure and to strengthen its institutions.

Prior to the Russian invasion in 2022 Ukraine was taking steps towards European integration. The Association Agreement between the EU and Ukraine entered into force in September 2017 and it commenced its application to join the Deep and Comprehensive Free Trade Area in January 2016 (EEAS 2019; see also EU 2014). Furthermore, the EFTA states signed a free trade agreement with Ukraine in Iceland in 2010. That agreement entered into force in 2012 (EFTA 2019).

According to the World Bank, the free trade agreement with the EU could provide an institutional umbrella that would facilitate the modernization of the Ukrainian economy. According to the Bank, introducing laws and regulatory procedures and reforming non-transparent practices could certainly become easier with the support of this Agreement than has previously been the case (World Bank 2019b).

In addition, Ukraine was affected by the US prior to the 2022 invasion, as was highlighted by a telephone conversation in 2019 between the Ukrainian President, Volodymyr Zelensky, and the former President of the US, Donald Trump. During the call Trump requested an investigation into the former US

Vice-President, Joe Biden, at the time a nominee for the Democratic presidential candidacy, and his son. The presidents agreed during their conversation that the EU was not doing much to help Ukraine. In Trump's view, 'Angela Merkel [the former German chancellor] she talks Ukraine, but she doesn't do anything' (CNN 2019). Joe Biden became president of the US in 2020 and Angela Merkel was replaced by Olaf Scholz in 2021.

President Biden met Vladimir Putin, president of Russia, prior to the invasion of Ukraine and discussed the situation in Ukraine with him in online meetings. The US was prepared to impose severe economic sanctions should Russia invade Ukraine but did not plan to send military forces to Ukraine. Owing to tensions between the US and Russia, the US sent weapons to Ukraine, strengthened its military presence along the eastern European flank and several NATO members have purchased weapons from the US, including fighter jets. Finland, a non-NATO member state, purchased new fighter jets from the US owing to growing tensions in Europe. These tensions thus resulted in significant sales of military equipment from the US to Europe.

Prior to the 2022 invasion Ukraine was in a vulnerable position because it needed not only continued bilateral financial and military support from the US, but also support from international organizations such as the International Monetary Fund (IMF) and the World Bank, headquartered in Washington, in which the US is very influential. Currently Ukraine receives support in the form of military equipment, training and probably intelligence information primarily from the US but also from its NATO allies.

Ukraine's interactions with external forces have often been complicated and have taken unexpected turns. With the Budapest Memorandum in 1994, it agreed to eliminate all its nuclear weapons in exchange for respect of its independence and sovereignty and its existing borders. Russia, the US and the United Kingdom were all signatories to the agreement (Budapest Memorandum 1994). The trouble with Russia began with the declaration issued by the heads of state and of governments after the North Atlantic Council held in Bucharest in 2008: 'NATO welcomes Ukraine's and Georgia's Euro-Atlantic aspirations for membership in NATO. We agreed today that these countries will become members of NATO. Both nations have made valuable contributions to Alliance operations' (NATO 2008). It was clear that this would not be acceptable to Russia, and it eventually resulted in military conflict in Georgia in 2008 and in Ukraine in 2014 and then contributed to an all-out invasion of Ukraine in 2022. It has been argued that US and European leaders blundered in attempting to turn Ukraine into a Western stronghold on Russia's border (Mearsheimer 2014). Russia knows well that NATO and the EU are not likely to admit countries as members if their borders are disputed. Russia acted accordingly and initiated military conflict in both Georgia and Ukraine. The massive Russian invasion in February 2022 came as a surprise to many but it shows how far Russia is willing to go to secure its influence over Ukraine.

Ukraine is not of strategic importance to the US and the EU has few obvious interests in Ukraine except cheap labour flowing from Ukraine to

Western Europe. If Ukraine was of strategic importance to the EU or the US, there would also be willingness to sacrifice lives, if necessary, in order to defend their interests. It is clear that neither the US nor the EU are willing to send troops to fight alongside the Ukrainian military against Russia. Nevertheless, the military assistance that the US and its allies have provided during 2022 has been important and the strength of the Ukrainian military has surprised many nations, particularly Russia, which has suffered a large number of casualties and the loss of military equipment. The Ukrainian army has also shown strong determination to defend the country.

It has been argued that Russia knows what it wants from Ukraine, while Ukraine clearly knows what it wants from the EU, but the EU has no clear policy goal towards Ukraine (Getmanchuk 2014). And one can add that the US may not care much about the fate of Ukraine. The US does not appear to consider Ukraine a vital interest. Although Ukraine has applied for EU membership, full membership is unlikely to materialize any time soon, and could even take decades. Wealthier EU countries are unlikely to be willing to carry the financial burden of Ukraine's reconstruction. It is also not clear whether the US is willing to accept Ukraine into NATO. The 2022 invasion looks in many ways like a proxy war between the US and Russia. Ukrainians are fighting Russia using weapons supplied by the US and other Western countries. Ukraine is a victim of geopolitical tensions between the West and Russia. The latter has allied with China which also opposes further NATO expansion. As the war goes on, Ukraine is getting destroyed.

The effect of weak governance and corruption

The 2022 invasion has seriously damaged Ukraine, but prior to the war many internal problems contributed to Ukraine's decline, including misguided economic policies, corruption and failed privatization. In 2017 the total net worth of Ukraine's three richest individuals comprised more than 6% of Ukraine's total GDP, more than three times the proportion in Poland (World Bank 2019b). The influence of vested interests on the economy undermined the effectiveness of Ukraine's economic institutions and delayed much-needed industrial restructuring towards developing high value-added, export-oriented industries. Achieving a better balance between vested interests/oligarchs and the government is one of the key arguments in favour of Ukraine's EU membership as it could result in more shared power and responsibility between Kiev and Brussels. It is not clear whether Ukraine will be able to handle the challenge of corruption on its own when the war is over.

Policies that would distribute economic growth dividends more fairly across society in Ukraine by creating access to opportunities for all could make growth more inclusive. Economic growth is only sustainable if it does not leave vulnerable groups behind. But one can ask whether the EU can assist Ukraine with that in an effective and efficient way. Given the EU's strict fiscal and monetary policies during and after the 2008/09 global financial crisis in former Soviet republics, such as the Baltic states, one could question the benefits of EU membership for a country that needs more flexible fiscal and monetary policies that the EU demands. Such policies are more suitable for the wealthy EU member states than emerging countries such as Ukraine. Furthermore, the former Soviet republics that have already joined the EU do not have a very impressive record when it comes to income and wealth equality, inclusiveness and social justice (Hilmarsson 2018; Eurostat 2019). The Baltic states shifted from a Soviet-style, centrally planned economy to neoliberalism, which emphasizes flat taxes and minimal government, but this system was too weak to support anything approaching the Scandinavian welfare states with their progressive tax systems and systems for redistribution to the most vulnerable members of their societies. Outward migration (discussed in the next section) has also weakened the tax base in the Baltics and in Ukraine younger segments of the population tend to migrate to other countries. Nevertheless, government institutions need to be strengthened in Ukraine after the war and the government needs to fight corruption. Both the EU and the World Bank can help the government in this respect; nevertheless, it will be difficult and will take a long time.

Outward migration and unemployment

There are limited economic opportunities for a large share of Ukraine's human capital. In 1992 Ukraine had a population of approximately 52 million people (IMF 2022). In 2021 the size of the population had dwindled to approximately 41 million. In contrast, Poland's population has remained stable at about 38 million during the same period.[7] Since 2000 Ukraine has lost about 15% of its population (see Figure 8.7). Following the Russian invasion that started in February 2022 many people have left Ukraine for Poland and other neighbouring countries. It remains to be seen how many people will return once things normalize.

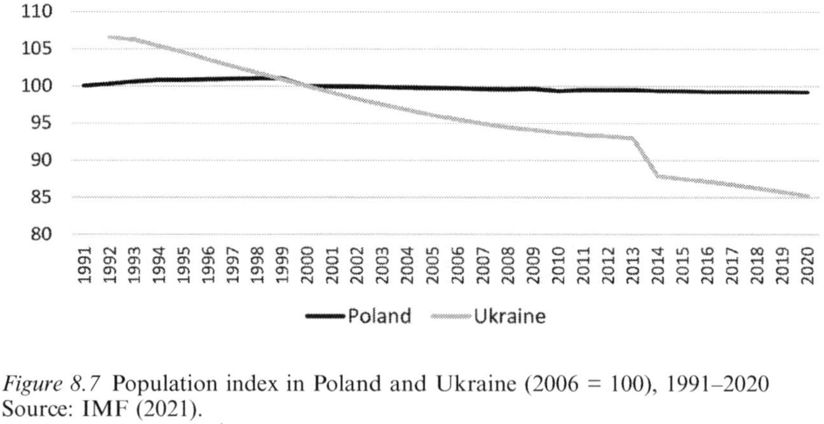

Figure 8.7 Population index in Poland and Ukraine (2006 = 100), 1991–2020
Source: IMF (2021).

Prior to the 2022 invasion many young Ukrainians opted to emigrate, attracted by higher expected earnings in EU countries such as Poland and Germany. The majority of those leaving Ukraine were highly skilled/tertiary educated (Atoyan et al. 2016). Given the demographic characteristics of the country and outward migration, there will be a significant decline in the labour force in Ukraine in the next decade. Without the necessary human capital Ukraine cannot sustain economic growth, will not have a workforce prepared for highly skilled jobs and will not compete efficiently.

On the one hand the burden on investment and productivity growth are particularly high in Ukraine given that its labour force is projected to decline due to demographic factors and migration. On the other hand, the contribution of capital to support growth is also constrained by a low domestic savings rate and low foreign direct investment. Furthermore, in order to be productive a workforce requires physical capital (i.e. infrastructure) and a well-governed economy.

For the wealthier EU member states, outward migration from Ukraine to the EU has not necessarily been viewed negatively. Countries such as Germany are facing competition from Asia, particularly China. An influx of skilled workers from Ukraine, an industrial country, who are willing to work for low pay helps in this competition.

Since 2006 unemployment as a percentage of the total labour force in Ukraine has ranged from approximately 6% to approximately 10%; from 2014–20 it averaged 9%. Unemployment was much higher in Poland than in Ukraine in 2006, at 14%, when it started to decline. Prior to the 2008/09 global financial crisis relatively high unemployment had been declining in Poland, but was rather stable in Ukraine. From 2008 unemployment increased in both countries. From 2013 unemployment in Poland declined from 10% to 3% in 2020, a much lower rate than in Ukraine, which recorded an unemployment rate of 9% in 2020 (see Figure 8.8). Unemployment

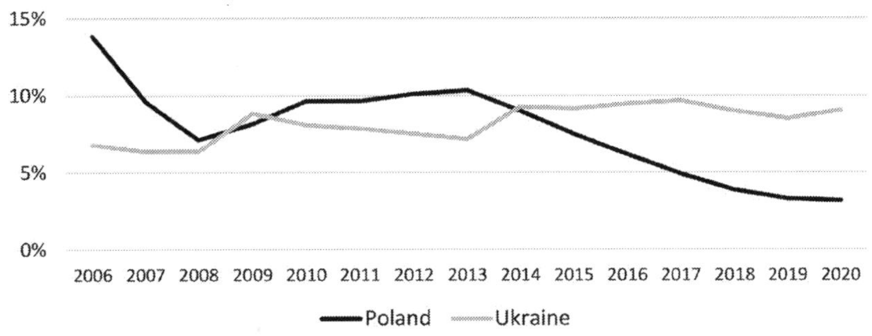

Figure 8.8 The unemployment rate in Poland and Ukraine (% of the total labour force), 2006–20
Source: IMF (2021).

increased slightly in Ukraine when the COVID-19 crisis broke out, but not in Poland. One of the key reasons for the level of unemployment in Ukraine can be attributed to the country's transition to a market economy whereby part of the labour force, especially the older generation, lacks the necessary skills to fully participate in the reformed economy.

Given the loss of population, especially the young skilled people emigrating mainly to richer European states, the tax base in Ukraine, like that of the Baltic states, is now weaker than it was and this in turn weakens the state, its revenues and its ability not only to assist the most vulnerable members of society, but also young families. This can contribute to continued outward migration of the youngest and most productive members of society to countries offering more opportunities.

Discussion

As mentioned in the beginning of this chapter many questions come to mind when assessing the current situation in Ukraine and the concomitant international tensions. Those discussed below are as follows:

1 Is it wise for the West to seek further EU and NATO expansion given Russia's response to NATO efforts to include Ukraine and Georgia in the alliance?
2 Is it wise for the EU to aggravate Russia during times of reduced US interest in NATO and Europe, and growing Chinese power?
3 Does Russia pose a real threat to Europe?
4 How should Europe and the US manage their relations with China?

The Soviet Union that fell in 1991 stretched from the Baltic and Black Seas to the Pacific Ocean and, in its final years, consisted of 15 Soviet socialist republics: Armenia, Azerbaijan, Belorussia (Belarus), Estonia, Georgia, Kazakhstan, Kirgiziya (now Kyrgyzstan), Latvia, Lithuania, Moldavia (now Moldova), Russia, Tajikistan, Turkmenistan, Ukraine and Uzbekistan.[8] Three of those republics, Estonia, Latvia and Lithuania, have now been firmly integrated into Western structures and are members of the EU, the euro area and NATO.

The idea to integrate Georgia and especially a large country like Ukraine into those same structures (EU and especially NATO) was very sensitive in Russia. All the Soviet satellite states that were parties to the Warsaw Pact are now members of NATO. Three former Soviet socialist republics, namely the three Baltic states Estonia, Latvia and Lithuania, are also members of NATO. It is only natural for Russia to be concerned about what will happen to the remaining former Soviet socialist republics. Will they also end up in NATO? This also raises questions about the motives of NATO to continue expanding to the east closer and closer to Russia and Moscow.

If both Georgia and Ukraine join NATO, five out of 15 former Soviet socialist republics will have joined NATO. Some NATO member states will undoubtably be more comfortable with an expanded NATO and will feel less threatened by bordering another NATO member state. The US may also become more powerful at the head of a larger NATO alliance. For Russia, continued expansion of NATO is considered unnecessary and threatening if it results in a more powerful West and a more isolated Russia. Russia is likely to respond to an enlarged NATO with a greater military build-up, including nuclear weapons, so European member states of NATO may not be safer following NATO enlargement.

In 2008 Russia launched a full-scale invasion of Georgia. Then, in 2014, it annexed the Crimean Peninsula. In the same year Russia began an armed conflict in Donbas and in early 2022 it invaded Ukraine resulting in a large-scale war that was still ongoing at the time of writing and is ravaging Ukraine. The idea of increasing security by having Ukraine join NATO has not produced peace and it seems unlikely that having other former Soviet socialist republics join NATO will produce peace. Expanding the EU may have proved to be more prescient as the EU is not a military alliance, but it is unlikely that EU member states, especially the wealthier countries, will accept Ukraine as a member any time soon. The level of destruction caused by the conflict in Ukraine will only make Ukraine less attractive to the current members of the EU.

The US is pushing Russia into the arms of China when it might need Russian support, for example in the Middle East. Russia will probably be harder pressed economically with continued and increased EU and US sanctions and rising military costs. Great economic hardship could result in political instability in a country that has a vast nuclear arsenal. It might become dangerous for the West to attempt to destabilize a major nuclear power not knowing when those weapons may be used or it could become unsure into what hands those weapons might fall, including outside Russia. Aggravating Russia might thus not be the best strategy for the West also when the rise of China puts more military pressure on the US in East Asia. The US is likely to become increasingly occupied in East Asia due to the rise of China and less able or interested in supporting EU defence. The US is also likely to ask Europe to get involved in the security competition in Asia against China. It is probably in the long-term interest of Europe to make a settlement with Russia after the Ukraine war to promote stability in Europe and avoid getting drawn into a conflict in Asia and continue benefiting from growing trade with China. However, a settlement with Russia will be more and more difficult as the war in Ukraine drags on.

Then there is the question whether Russia poses a real threat to Europe given its demographic and economic problems and its dependency on oil and gas exports that point to a declining great power. Europe is dependent on Russian gas as the disputes about Nord Steam 2 show. Tensions between the West and Russia will create problems in Europe, including with Germany, a great European power and a leading country within the EU. Like many countries in Europe, Germany needs cheap gas from Russia. For Europe it might thus make more sense to normalize relations with Russia as much as possible. This could be done after the Ukraine war which at the time of writing had made Russia weaker due to the relatively strong performance of the Ukrainian army that has been supported with military equipment from the West and the performance of the Russian army has been weaker than many military experts expected.

Regarding China, the interests of Europe and the US may not be the same. While the US is engaged in a serious security competition with China owing to the ongoing disputes with the Republic of China (Taiwan), which China considers part of its sovereign territory, disputes in the South China Sea, and disputes about the Senkaku Islands (also known as the Diaoyu Islands) that lie between China and Japan, Europe and the EU might still have good trade and investment relations with China. Tensions between the US and Russia over Ukraine have now resulted in an alliance between China and Russia with both countries opposing further NATO expansion. In both countries NATO is primarily seen as a US threatening military instrument. Opposing both China and Russia could mean that the US needs to engage in conflict in Europe and Asian simultaneously. This could become a nightmare scenario for the US making it difficult to support its allies on two very distant fronts.

Concluding remarks

What are the options for Ukraine now? How can the country move forward?

Prior to the Russian military invasion there was little pressure from outside forces to help Ukraine. The EU benefited from the flow of mostly young and skilled people from Ukraine, numbering approximately 10 million since 1991 until the start of the war in 2022. The populations of the Western European countries are ageing. Many Ukrainians left for Poland, others to Germany which needs skilled workers for its industry and where the pay is good. Others migrated to Russia whose per capita income is higher than that of Ukraine. The ongoing conflict in Ukraine has witnessed a serious refugee crisis, with many women and children fleeing the country, while the men are required to stay behind and join the armed forces.

Ukraine is not of strategic importance to the US, which is increasingly preoccupied with Asia, because of the rise of China, and with the Persian Gulf countries, and because of the competition for oil, including with China. Tougher EU and US sanctions are hurting Russia, but Russia has been unwilling to accept the further integration of Ukraine into the West and opposes Ukraine's proposed membership of NATO as well as its full EU membership. Geographically Ukraine is perhaps as strategically important to Russia as Canada or Mexico are to the US. What would the US do if Russia or China formed a military alliance with either of those countries? We saw how the US reacted to the Soviet presence in Cuba during the Cuban missile crisis of 1962 when a confrontation between the US and the Soviet Union escalated into an international crisis. This confrontation is often considered the closest the Cold War came to escalating into a full-scale nuclear war. Arguably the current Ukraine crisis is more serious than the Cuban missile crisis because US President Kennedy made attempts to deescalate the crisis, while President Biden seems to be escalating the crisis in the hope that Ukraine will win the war.

Prior to the ongoing conflict Ukraine was stuck in a crisis. It was a low-growth country and many people in eastern Ukraine wanted the country to have closer ties with Russia, which has a higher per capita income, while an increasing number of people in western Ukraine wanted to migrate to the EU. The risk was that an already divided country could formally split into two.

Prior to the ongoing war Ukraine had the option to become an independent and neutral buffer state between the EU and Russia, rather than to seek formal membership of the EU and NATO. It could have co-operated with and receive increased financial assistance from the EU, the US, the IMF and the World Bank on the condition that Russia would respect its territorial integrity. Institutions such as the World Bank, the EBRD and the European Investment Bank could have become more involved in Ukraine with grants and loans that might also have resulted in increased foreign investment flows. In that scenario, Ukraine could possibly have achieved the necessary peace to grow and reach its economic potential.

Following the Russian invasion on 24 February 2022, all trust between the Ukrainian and Russian authorities has disappeared. Ukraine now needs massive assistance from the West for its reconstruction. This could involve further integration with the EU with full membership as a long-term goal. It is less clear if NATO membership is feasible, not only because Russia opposes it, but also because China also opposes further NATO enlargement to the east. Whatever scenario is chosen it needs to have the ownership of the Ukrainian people, not only outside forces. Despite their differences, most Ukrainians want to keep the country together. Nevertheless, EU, NATO and US leaders need to start tabling options that could be acceptable once the ongoing war is over.

What can be said about conditions for favourable inclusive growth dynamics for Ukraine when the war is over? The first condition is political commitment. Fast and sustained growth sufficient for Ukraine to catch up requires long-term commitment by its political leaders. There is a need to adjust the role of the state, giving everyone an equal opportunity and strengthening the rule of law to make economic institutions more resilient. Second, economic growth and development depend on human and physical capital, and on the factors affecting their productivity. The speed of growth is to a large extent driven by Ukraine's ability to keep its highly skilled labour force within its borders by offering attractive job opportunities, but also by the pace of investment, public and private. This investment requires increased domestic savings and external capital flow into Ukraine. Facilitating foreign direct investment and integration into global value chains, improving logistics and connectivity to fully leverage external opportunities is also important. Third, more integration into the world economy, especially the EU common market, is critical. Markets for exports and opportunities to import ideas, technology and know-how is vital for Ukraine. Fourth, Ukraine needs to develop coordination capacity to manage the international assistance, bilateral and multilateral, that the country will be receive when the war is over. This will be a challenge given the extensive damage undergone by the country. Many Ukrainians who will return after the war will not be able to return to their homes immediately and assisting them will be a challenge for the government even with the external assistance that will be forthcoming for Ukraine's reconstruction.

To achieve much-needed economic growth and reconstruction Ukraine also needs to maintain stable macroeconomic policies and above all it needs peace and stability, not the deadlock that has to a large extent been caused by the East–West competition for this country in crisis that eventually resulted in an all-out invasion by Russia. Ukraine needs help from the West to build a healthy, sustainable and enabling environment for growth and prosperity.

Notes

1 www.britannica.com/place/Ukraine/The-Maidan-protest-movement.
2 The transfer merited only a paragraph in *Pravda*, the official Soviet newspaper, on 27 February 1954. The story was one long sentence and dense with detail. This is what it said: 'Decree of the Presidium of the USSR Supreme Soviet transferring Crimea Province from the Russian Republic to the Ukraine Republic, taking into account the integral character of the economy, the territorial proximity and the close economic ties between Crimea Province and the Ukraine Republic, and approving the joint presentation of the Presidium of the Russian Republic Supreme Soviet and the Presidium of the Ukraine Republic Supreme Soviet on the transfer of Crimea Province from the Russian Republic to the Ukraine Republic'. See www.npr.org/sections/parallels/2014/02/27/283481587/crimea-a-gift-to-ukraine-becomes-a-political-flash-point?t=1619270786559 See also http://soviethistory.msu.edu/1954-2/the-gift-of-crimea/.
3 Crimea was given to Ukraine by premier Nikita Khrushchev (himself born at the border with Ukraine) to mark the 300th anniversary of Ukraine's inclusion in the Russian Empire, a 'donation' many in Russia still see as illegitimate. Surprisingly, Boris Yeltsin, the first president of post-Soviet Russia, did not propose an acquisition of Crimea during negotiations to dissolve the Soviet republics. Thus, a region that had been part of Russia for centuries was 'gifted' to Ukraine. See www.theguardian.com/world/2014/mar/07/ukraine-russia-crimea-naval-base-tatars-explainer#why.
4 www.worldbank.org/en/news/press-release/2022/04/10/russian-invasion-to-shrink-ukraine-economy-by-45-percent-this-year.
5 For example, learning better ways how to use machinery and tools to produce more vehicles in the same amount of time.
6 For example, increased access to machinery and tools to produce more vehicles in the same amount of time.
7 www.imf.org/en/Publications/WEO/weo-database/2022/April/weo-report?c=964,926,&s=LP,&sy=1991&ey=2021&ssm=0&scsm=1&scc=0&ssd=1&ssc=0&sic=0&sort=country&ds=.&br=1.
8 www.britannica.com/place/Soviet-Union.

References

Atoyan, R., Christiansen, L., Dizioli, A., Ebeke, C., Ilahi, N., Ilyina, A., Mehrez, G., Qu, H., Raei, F., Rhee, A. and Zakharova, D. (2016). *Emigration and Its Economic Impact on Eastern Europe*. IMF Staff Discussion Note, July 2016. SDN/16/07. Available at: www.imf.org/external/pubs/ft/sdn/2016/sdn1607.pdf (accessed 20 March 2021).

Budapest Memorandum (1994). *Memorandum on Security Assurances in Connection with Ukraine's Accession to the Treaty on the Non-Proliferation of Nuclear Weapons*. Available at: www.pircenter.org/media/content/files/12/13943175580.pdf (accessed 3 December 2021).

CNN (2019). *Read Trump's Phone Conversation with Volodymyr Zelensky*. CNN, 26 September. Available at: https://edition.cnn.com/2019/09/25/politics/donald-trump-ukraine-transcript-call/index.html (accessed 3 December 2019).

European External Action Service (EEAS) (2019). *Advancing Mutual Commitment: Joint Statement Following the 21st EU-Ukraine Summit*. Available at: https://eeas.europa.eu/delegations/ukraine/65219/advancing-mutual-commitment-joint-statement-following-21st-eu-ukraine-summit_en (accessed 30 January 2020).

European Free Trade Association (EFTA) (2019). *Free Trade Agreement between the EFTA States and Ukraine*. Available at: www.efta.int/free-trade/free-trade-agreements/ukraine (accessed 14 January 2020).

Eurostat (2019). Available at: http://ec.europa.eu/eurostat/data/database.

European Union (EU) (2014). Association Agreement between the European Union and Ukraine. *Official Journal of the European Union*. Available at: https://trade.ec.europa.eu/doclib/docs/2016/november/tradoc_155103.pdf (accessed 14 January 2021).

Getmanchuk, A. (2014). Tracing the Origins of the Ukraine Crisis: Should the EU Share the Blame? *Europe's World*, 15 June. Available at: www.friendsofeurope.org/insights/tracing-the-origins-of-the-ukraine-crisis-should-the-eu-share-the-blame/ (accessed 15 December 2021).

Hilmarsson, H. Þ.. (2018). *The Economic Crisis and its Aftermath in the Nordic and Baltic Countries: Do as We Say and Not as We Do*. Europa Economic Perspectives. Abingdon: Routledge.

Howarth, J. (2017). 'Stability on the Borders': The Ukraine Crisis and the EU's Constrained Policy Towards the Eastern Neighbourhood, *JCMS*, 55(1), 121–136. Available at: http://onlinelibrary.wiley.com/doi/10.1111/jcms.12448/pdf (accessed 15 May 2020).

International Monetary Fund (IMF) (2022). *World Economic Outlook Database*. Available at: www.imf.org/en/Publications/WEO/weo-database/2022/April.

International Monetary Fund (IMF) (2021). *World Economic Outlook Database*. Available at: www.imf.org/en/Publications/WEO/weo-database/2021/October.

Mearsheimer, J. J. (2014). Why the Ukraine Crisis Is the West's Fault. *Foreign Affairs*, 93(5), 1–12.

North Atlantic Treaty Organization (NATO) (2008). *Bucharest Summit Declaration Issued by the Heads of State and Government Participating in the Meeting of the North Atlantic Council in Bucharest on 3 April 2008*. Available at: www.nato.int/cps/en/natolive/official_texts_8443.htm (accessed 21 April 2021).

World Bank (2022). *Russian Invasion to Shrink Ukraine Economy by 45 Percent this Year*. Available at: www.worldbank.org/en/news/press-release/2022/04/10/russian-invasion-to-shrink-ukraine-economy-by-45-percent-this-year (accessed 21 June 2022).

World Bank (2019a). *Financial Inclusion. Europe and Central Asia Economic Update.* Washington, DC: Office of the Chief Economist. Available at: www.sipotra.it/wp-content/uploads/2019/04/World-Bank-ECA-Economic-Update-Spring-2019.pdf (Accessed 15 December 2021).

World Bank (2019b). *Ukraine Growth Study Final Document: Faster, Lasting and Kinder.* Washington, DC: World Bank. Available at: http://documents.worldbank.org/curated/en/543041554211825812/Ukraine-Growth-Study-Final-Document-Faster-Lasting-and-Kinder (accessed 11 December 2021).

9 How can Europe move forward post-COVID-19 and Brexit?

Challenges ahead for the European Union

European integration has been under way for over 60 years. The European Union (EU) has been credited for being successful in maintaining peace for decades and peace has been credited for bringing about ever closer integration. The international relations theories discussed in Chapter 2 in this volume are relevant here. Following the dissolution of the Soviet Union, the EU sought to expand and by doing so helped to turn new member states into democracies. With closer integration the EU countries were made more interdependent. By becoming EU member states the countries were also integrated into a multilateral institution. This is in line with the international relations theories mentioned above. The *democratic peace theory* is the idea that democracies do not fight other democracies and therefore it is important to spread democracy. The *economic interdependence theory* stipulates that if countries depend on one another for trade and investment, peace will follow. The EU common market guarantees the free movement of goods, services, capital and people. Finally, *liberal institutionalism* stipulates that international organizations generate rules that nations obey. The EU's 'acquis' is the body of common rights and obligations that are binding on all EU member states.

The conflict in Ukraine has cast a shadow on this process. The expansion of both the EU and the North Atlantic Treaty Organization (NATO) is at least partially responsible for growing tensions in the Russian Federation that contributed to that country's military invasion of Ukraine. The plan to integrate Ukraine into the EU and by doing so to promote democracy and create greater interdependence by integrating Ukraine into EU systems and institutions did not produce the peace Europe was hoping for. The announcement at the Bucharest Summit in 2008 that Ukraine should become a member of NATO only made things worse. It is noteworthy that when Russia invaded Ukraine the country was nowhere near achieving membership of the EU and NATO. There was never consensus among the EU or NATO member states to admit Ukraine into those institutions. Prior to the war in Ukraine, the COVID-19 crisis had devastated Europe following the

DOI: 10.4324/9781003212539-10

imposition of national lockdowns intended to curb the spread of the pandemic as well as high death tolls in many countries. The COVID-19 pandemic had serious economic consequences. The COVID-19 crisis and the Russian invasion of Ukraine have already been discussed in Chapters 4 and 8 in this volume. This chapter will primarily focus on several important challenges which face the EU, and which will shape or determine its future. They include the euro and the fragility of the several European economies, including Italy, the United Kingdom's decision to leave the EU (known as Brexit), and the possibility of the further disintegration of the Union. It will also discuss some underlying problems including migration and the rise of populism. The migration crisis has put a strain on EU finances and the tolerance of many people in Europe. Populism has grown in the EU with political groups demanding priorities be given to national rather than European needs.

The euro and the fragility of some euro area economies

The euro area is a common currency area, i.e. a geographic area in which a single currency circulates as the medium of exchange (see, for example, Mankiw and Taylor 2020). The costs and benefits of a common currency were discussed in Chapter 1 in this volume.

In 1992 the EU member states signed the Maastricht Treaty, paving the way for the creation of the euro as the common currency of the EU. The treaty limited government/fiscal deficits to 3% of gross domestic product (GDP) and public debt levels to 60% of GDP (European Commission 2022a). The euro was launched in 1999, and euro notes and coins entered into circulation in 2002. The euro is thus a relatively new currency that has sometimes been under threat particularly during the 2008/09 global financial crisis (see, for example, Hilmarsson 2018, 2016 and 2013).

When discussing a common currency as a monetary arrangement Nobel Prize-winner Milton Friedman commented that

> [w]hether it is good or bad depends primarily on the adjustment mechanisms that are available to absorb the economic shocks and dislocations that impinge on the various entities that are considering a common currency. Flexible exchange rates are a powerful adjustment mechanism for managing shocks that affect the entities differently.
>
> (1997, p. 1)

Friedman was thus concerned about asymmetric shocks, i.e. any situation whereby changes in aggregate demand and/or supply differ from one country to another in the currency union. By joining a common currency area, a country gives up its national currency and thereby its freedom to set its own monetary policy and the possibility of macroeconomic adjustment coming through movements in the external value of its currency. In the euro area, monetary policy is decided by the European Central Bank (ECB). If countries maintain their own currencies and a flexible foreign exchange rate, then short-term fluctuations in aggregated demand would be alleviated by a movement in the exchange rate of the national currency. In a currency union this automatic adjustment mechanism is not available since countries have the same currency and the best they can do is to wait for wages and prices to adjust.

An optimum currency area is a group of countries for which it is optimal to adopt a common currency and form a currency union (Mankiw and Taylor 2020, p. 760). Friedman (1997) considered the US an example of a situation favourable to a common currency, referring to wage and price flexibility, labour mobility across states, as well as goods and capital mobility. According to Friedman,

> By contrast, Europe's common market exemplifies a situation that is unfavorable to a common currency. It is composed of separate nation states, whose residents speak different languages, have different customs, and have far greater loyalty and attachment to their own country than to the common market or to the idea of 'Europe'.
>
> (1997, p. 1)

In 2004 Friedman commented that 'there is a strong possibility that the euro zone could collapse in the next few years because differences are accumulating between countries ... I'm not saying it is a certainty, just that it is a strong possibility'.[1]

Friedman's comments are still to a large extent valid but at the time of writing, in 2022, the euro is still in existence but there are challenges. Tensions remain within the euro area and the northern euro area countries are suspicious of their southern neighbours, who they view as being more undisciplined and enjoying free-rider status. Southern euro area member states buy into the notion of price stability but are not showing sufficient financial discipline There still needs to be greater reform of labour and capital, both of which should be allowed to flow more freely if there are asymmetric shocks in the euro area.

When commenting on financial integration in the euro area the Vice-President of the ECB, Vítor Constâncio, stated:

> The degree of financial integration in the euro area is currently insufficient. Indeed, in the recent crisis, the degree of financial integration fell, as interbank markets fragmented along national lines. This fragmentation exacerbated the overall impact of the shocks on the euro area, deepening the recession, lengthening the recovery and increasing the need for unconventional monetary policy measures. The single currency area provides fertile conditions for deeper financial integration and that deeper integration in turn helps build resilience to shocks and

> strengthens the effectiveness of monetary policy by means of a more homogenous transmission. Monetary policy and Capital Markets Union (CMU) are thus linked.
>
> (Constâncio 2017)

This lack of integration is an issue that could affect the future viability of the euro area particularly in the event of another financial crisis.

Moreover, as Friedman (1997) noted, the motivation for the EU to form a monetary union was not only prompted by economics. Two of the leading European economies, Germany and France, had fought against each other in two world wars. This relates to the economic interdependence theory (see Chapter 2 in this volume) that stipulates that if countries depend on one another for trade and investment, peace will follow. Thus, according to this theory, extensive economic interdependence networks help to maintain peace between countries. As Friedman argued,

> [t]he drive for the euro has been motivated by politics, not economics. The aim has been to link Germany and France so closely as to make a future European war impossible, and to set the stage for a federal United States of Europe. I believe that adoption of the euro would have the opposite effect. It would exacerbate political tensions by converting divergent shocks that could have been readily accommodated by exchange rate changes into divisive political issues. Political unity can pave the way for monetary unity. Monetary unity imposed under unfavorable conditions will prove a barrier to the achievement of political unity.
>
> (1997, p. 2)

France and Germany have not gone to war against each other since the EU and the euro area came into existence and many in Europe credit this fact to successful European integration. But there have been tensions within the euro area because some countries have greater difficulty than others following the fiscal rules stipulated by the Maastricht Treaty (see above). All the euro area countries ran fiscal/headline deficits above 3% of GDP in 2020. Many countries were under pressure due to COVID-19. Now these same countries will be under pressure to increase their military expenditure due to the war in Ukraine (see Figure 9.1). This is to be expected during a crisis, but even during normal times many euro area countries have had difficulties.

In 2020 10 out of 19 euro area countries exceeded the government debt ratio of 60% of GDP (see Figure 9.2). Many countries became more indebted as a consequence of the COVID-19 pandemic. The southern European countries tended to be more indebted than the countries in the north. The debt-to-GDP ratios of Greece (212%), Portugal (135%) and Spain (120%) were all well above the 60% benchmark. The status of the largest euro area member states was of particular concern. The debt-to-GDP ratio of Italy, the

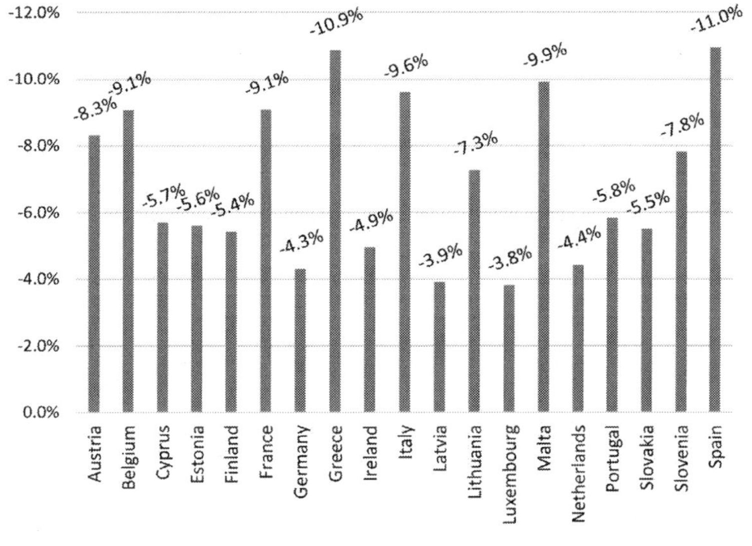

Figure 9.1 Fiscal (headline) deficit or general government net lending/borrowing in the euro area countries (% of GDP), 2020
Source: IMF (2022).

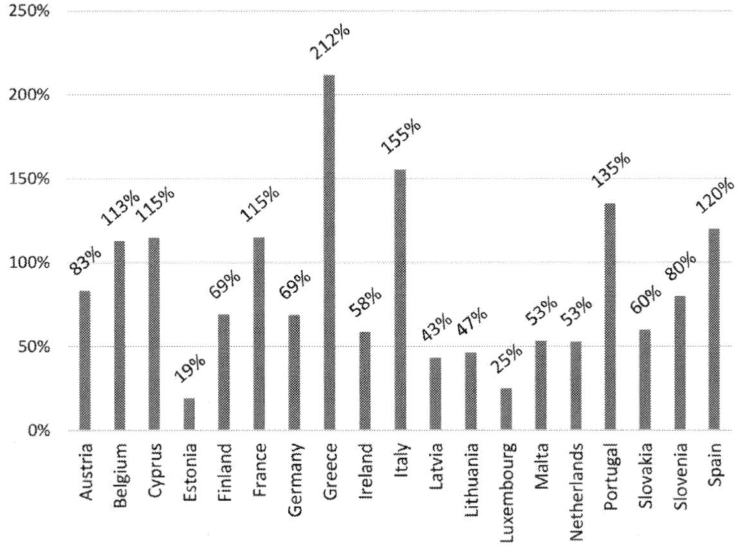

Figure 9.2 General government gross debt among the euro area member states (% of GDP), 2020
Source: IMF (2022).

third largest economy in the euro area stood at 155%, and that of France, the second largest economy in the euro area, was 115%. Germany, the largest economy in the euro area, was also above the limit (69%). These ratios are expected to go down once economic growth resumes, but the ongoing conflict in Ukraine will make progress more uncertain in the short term. Meanwhile, the debt-to-GDP ratios of the Baltic states were well below the 60% benchmark, while that of Slovakia had reached 60% and Finland was above the limit at 69%.

When discussing the participation of Italy, Spain and Portugal in the monetary union, Eichengreen notes that

> [t]he participation of these last three countries was a source of concern for Germany, which had doubts about their commitment to price stability. It encouraged skepticism among academics, who questioned the wisdom of consigning such a diverse group in a single monetary policy. (2008, p. 370)

Given the high debt-to-GDP levels reached in 2020 by France, Italy, Greece, Portugal and Spain one cannot help wondering about the viability of the EU fiscal criteria (see Figures 9.1 and 9.2). Moreover, as countries in Europe continue to recover from the COVID-19 crisis, they must also contend with the conflict in Ukraine. European countries, including the euro area countries, most of whom are members of NATO, are required by the alliance to increase their military expenditure. This will put pressure on their fiscal deficits and increase their government debt levels. Countries such as Italy could have problems in servicing their debt. Should their national banks fail, there is risk of this failure spreading to other euro area countries and therefore exerting pressure on the euro.

The euro continues to be controversial, but it did survive its first real test during the 2008/09 economic and financial crisis and the resulting sovereign debt crisis that almost brought it to its knees. Nevertheless, many economists remain sceptical. US economist Joseph Stiglitz stated that the euro 'is a case study of how, even with the best intensions, when new institutions and policies are created on the basis of oversimplified views on how economies function, the result can be not only disappointing, but even disastrous' (2016, p. 7).

If we look at the Baltic, Nordic and Visegrád countries that are in the euro area it can be argued that they have been disciplined. In 2020 the government debt-to-GDP ratio in Estonia stood at 19%, that of Latvia at 43%, Lithuania at 47%, Slovakia at 60% and Finland at 69%. These countries, especially the Baltic states, have performed particularly well, but this achievement was partly due to the strict austerity programmes that the Baltics implemented during the 2008/09 global financial crisis. Moreover, the five euro area countries in these country groups are relatively small in comparison with the larger European countries, France, Italy, Spain, Portugal and Greece, whose debt-to-GDP ratios are well above the recommended limit. Their status could lead to a sovereign debt crisis that would destabilize the euro area and jeopardize the existence of the euro.

Fiscal discipline in the euro area

When the 2008/09 global financial crisis hit all the Baltic states had their own currency but sought to become euro area member states as soon as they could. This required fiscal austerity during difficult times. Åslund and Dombrovskis discuss how Latvia came through the 2008/09 financial crisis:

> The gross disregard of the fiscal Maastricht criteria or the Stability and Growth Pact by most euro area countries is not likely to be repeated. The cost of fiscal laxity is probably so evident that most nations will discipline themselves, and if not other EMU [economic and monetary union] members are likely to impose their will. This crisis has changed the economic policy mindset for a long time. Moreover, when countries with strong fiscal discipline, such as Estonia and Latvia, enter the board of the ECB, monetary discipline will be further reassured.
>
> (2011, p. 123)

All the Baltic states eventually entered the euro area: Estonia in 2011, Latvia in 2014 and Lithuania in 2015. However, the implementation of austerity programmes during a recession resulted in, among other things, large outward migration to wealthier European countries. Having gained their independence the Baltic states adopted neoliberal policies with minimal governments and very small social programmes. This is different from the Nordic countries which have strong welfare states and thus strong automatic stabilizers. According to De Grauwe,

> The automatic stabilizers in the government budget constitute an important social achievement in the developed world, as for many people they soften the pain created by boom and bust in capitalist societies. If monetary union has the implications of destroying these automatic stabilizers, it is unclear whether the social and political basis for such a union can be maintained. It is therefore important to design a governance structure that maintains these automatic stabilizers.
>
> (2016, p. 118)

However, experience shows that the treatment of large and small countries differs when it comes to fiscal discipline in the euro area. As the euro area experienced sluggish growth in the early years of EMU, several member countries – and France and Germany in particular – found themselves in breach of the Stability and Growth Pact (SGP) excessive deficit criteria. However, both France and Germany managed to persuade other EMU members not to impose fines and, in 2004, the European Commission drew up guidelines for softening the SGP (Mankiw and Taylor 2020, p. 769; see also Eichengreen 2008, p. 373). As Eichengreen pointed out, the response might have been different if it involved a country such as Portugal (ibid.). It is questionable whether such flexibility would be applied to smaller states such as the Baltics. Greece, for example, was obliged to conform with the fiscal criteria because the Maastricht Treaty has no provisions for an exit.

Populist movements and the migration crisis

The EU is an is an elite project. EU institutions are run by experts, bureaucrats and technocrats. The ECB, arguably EU's most powerful institution, is based in Frankfurt, Germany. Monetary policy is determined there for all the euro area member states. The EU fiscal rules require that governments balance their budgets. This means that monetary policy does not take place at the national level and within the euro area and fiscal policy is severely restricted. During the 2008/09 global financial crisis the EU advocated austerity which was very unpopular, and the EU was blamed. Furthermore, the EU is vulnerable because in the eyes of the citizens of the member states the EU institutions are mostly run by foreigners. The large EU member states, especially France and Germany, are more powerful than smaller member states such as Greece and Portugal.

During the 2008/09 global financial crisis many Greeks believed that outside forces, the German government in particular, were responsible for the austerity policies that were implemented in their country. In the meantime, the German taxpayers were unhappy about bailing out a Greek government with poor fiscal discipline.

Populism can be defined as an attempt by groups to appeal to the 'ordinary' people who are cast aside by the political elite and marginalized in society (Mankiw and Taylor 2020, p. 775). Often it is right-wing politicians who claim to champion the people. Economic insecurity is often at the heart of the problem. People feel the loss of control over their lives. The less educated are often the most vulnerable. The question arises whether the political mainstream is able respond properly to their demands. If not, populist governments are likely to thrive during elections.

Populism in Europe has grown partly due to the migrant crisis which the EU has had to cope with, but it is by no means restricted to that problem. Migrants have been fleeing persecution and political instability in Libya, parts of Africa, Afghanistan, Pakistan, the Syrian Arab Republic and more recently Ukraine. There also are economic migrants who travel to Southern or Eastern Europe with the goal of reaching the wealthier EU member states such as Germany or one of the Nordic countries. A large number of migrants puts pressure on host countries' resources with costs related to policing and accommodating migrants, for example. Greece and Italy have faced the most immediate challenges of migrants arriving on their shores. These countries felt that they were not getting enough EU assistance. Germany did receive a large number of migrants and in response there was an upswing in support for populist parties that exploited fear, mistrust and anger among the citizenry.

The migrant crisis could result in the collapse of the Schengen area, which would be a blow to one of the fundamental tenets of the EU internal market (also known as the single market). The Schengen agreement allows the free movement of people between the countries without passport controls. The free movement of workers is one of the fundamental tenets of the single market, but this has contributed to a rise in right-wing populism, and in some countries governments are taking steps to prevent migrants crossing their borders despite being in the Schengen area.

Some countries strongly feel that they have the right to control the flow of people into the Schengen area. Hungary, which is located on the Schengen area's southernmost border, has taken action to prevent the unlimited flow of refugees across its borders and into other Schengen countries. When Belarus directed refugees from the Middle East to its Polish border the government of Poland refused to accept them. Two of the Baltic states, Latvia and Lithuania, were also affected as both countries share borders with Belarus.

When Russia invaded Ukraine there was a concerted effort to help refugees by allowing them to pass into the EU and the Schengen area. Three of the Visegrád countries, Poland, Hungary and Slovakia, border Russia and accepted large numbers of refugees.

Brexit

The United Kingdom was always a reluctant partner in European integration. Nevertheless, it has been noted that Winston Churchill, the former British prime minister, was committed to the idea of European integration and was one of the first to call for a 'United States of Europe' (EU 2022). As Churchill urged a Franco-German partnership to lead his vision of a new Europe, he declared that Great Britain and the British Commonwealth, along with the US and the Union of the Socialist Soviet Republics, should be 'friends and sponsors' of the project. He did not talk of the UK becoming a member itself.[2] He saw the UK as a leader in the Commonwealth.

The UK had a leadership role in establishing the European Free Trade Association (EFTA) that became operative in 1960 (Hilmarsson 2018). The EFTA was a free trade area that did not go as far on integration as the European Economic Community (EEC – later the EU). In January 1973, however, the UK and Denmark became members of the EEC and left the EFTA (Britannica 2022). With full membership in the EEC, the UK would become one of the largest member states of EEC and could because of its economic size exercise influence there.

But the UK's membership of the EEC was always controversial, and in June 2016 a national referendum on whether to stay or leave the EU saw

51.9% in favour of leaving the EU and 48.1% wanting to remain (Mankiw and Taylor 2020, p. 778). The country was thus divided. In Wales and England the majority voted to leave the EU, while in Scotland and Northern Ireland the majority voted to remain. In March 2017 the British government triggered Article 50 of the Treaty of Lisbon, which provides the right of an EU member state to unilaterally declare its intention to leave the Union.

The process of leaving the EU was complex and Brexit created tensions across the EU. There were many problems that needed to be solved between the UK and the EU. The backstop in Ireland was one of the major points of contention, and it proved difficult to find a resolution that would satisfy the British Parliament and the 27 member states of the EU.

As a member of the EU, the UK had its own laws but was also subject to EU laws, the EU law having supremacy over British law. The UK could not, for example, restrict the free movement of workers within the EU. The UK was part of the EU customs union, and was bound by the EU's agricultural and fisheries policies and targets to cut greenhouse emissions, etc.

The creation of a free market within the EU allowing for the free movement of capital, goods, services and people resulted in the expansion of trade between the UK and other members of the EU. On leaving the EU without a deal, the UK, in theory, would be subject to the common external tariff and have border customs checks. Leaving with a deal on a new trading relationship presented a challenge in that the UK could not be seen to have the same benefits of free trade without fulfilling the responsibilities and obligations that go with membership.

Remaining part of the customs unions would mean free trade within the EU, at the expense of limiting the UK to negotiate free deals with countries outside the EU. A rise in immigration increases the labour supply and reduces the wage rate, keeps inflation under control and lowers firms' costs. Skilled immigrants, such as health care professionals, can benefit society as a whole. Low-skilled immigrants might be prepared to work for less wages and this has an impact on local populations.

With the UK now relegated to third country status outside the EU, what was once a relatively seamless process at the border has been swapped for a significant processing burden with the potential for major hold-ups. At the time of writing, in 2022, things looked very different. Brexit is far from being done, if the constant arguments over the Irish border and the chaos at Dover are anything to go by.[3]

The effects of Brexit will unravel over many years. For businesses, the biggest problem is uncertainty especially over the nature of the trading relationship between the UK and the EU. Multinationals might move their operations away from the UK and this has a knock-on effect on suppliers. The Baltic, Visegrád and the Nordic countries are all affected by Brexit as many of their citizens live and work in the UK and many companies have business relations with the UK.

Can Brexit result in further disintegration?

The departure of the UK from the EU has proved to be time-consuming and complex. This is likely to discourage other EU member states from leaving, especially those who also are in the euro area. The conflict in Ukraine has also united the EU against Russia. Some countries such as the Baltic states and Finland that border Russia feel more secure being part of the EU in addition to having euro area membership. The Visegrád countries, three of which border Ukraine, may feel that their security is enhanced by being within the EU, rather than being outside of the EU. Although the EU and the euro area are facing challenges, at present there does not appear to be the prospect of further disintegration.

What about EU enlargement? Currently there are seven recognized candidates for membership of the EU: Türkiye (Turkey, since 1999), North Macedonia (2005), Montenegro (2010), Albania (2014), Serbia (2012), Ukraine (2022) and Moldova (2022). Potential candidate countries include both Bosnia and Herzegovina and Kosovo.[4] None of these countries seems likely to become member in the near future and the decision to accept Ukraine as a candidate country must be viewed primarily as a symbolic gesture due to the war with Russia. The EU's financial conditions would not allow for the reconstruction of such a large country at present.

There are issues within Europe about the European project and some citizens are unsure about the benefits of the EU project. Some feel that the EU is too interfering. Views of the role of the EU range from concentrating only on the single market, to doing much more together including having a common currency. Many voters are unhappy about the prospect of further integration. Moreover, the rise of populism in Europe shows that many are questioning the value of the EU.

In future the EU member states need to decide what should be done at the Union level and what at the national level. Climate policy is an example of something that could or perhaps should be done at the Union level. Arguably, fiscal policy should be done at the national level and where there could be more flexibility than the current EU fiscal rules discussed above allow.

More flexible fiscal rules in the euro area?

As Figure 9.1 shows, in 2020 all the euro area countries breached the fiscal rule that member states must not run fiscal deficits higher than 3% of GDP. Unexpected events can and do happen, such as the global financial crisis that occurred in 2008/09. Meanwhile, unpredictable events do occur such as the outbreak of the COVID-19 pandemic in 2020 that is still ongoing, and the Russian invasion of Ukraine in February 2022. This means that national governments need more scope to react to such crises. Furthermore, when the fiscal deficit goes out of control it takes governments time to fully recover and repay the government debt that has accumulated. Shrinking the government-debt-to-GDP ratio to 60% can be quite challenging especially when it has reached very high levels (See Figure 9.2) Still the EU and the euro area needs to stay financially sound, and this is quite a challenge with different countries that need different responses when crisis occur. Also, since the euro area countries have given up their options to exercise independent monetary policy, this puts more demands on fiscal policy with more need for flexibility. As Kamps and Leiner-Killinger (2019) have stated, '[r]eportedly, the 3% of GDP deficit reference value that was later to become a cornerstone of the EU fiscal framework was not derived from in-depth economic analysis but was born from political considerations in France in the early 1980s'. The authors also noted that '[a]t the time the Treaty's government debt reference value was agreed, a level of 60% of GDP did not seem overly ambitious when compared to the average debt ratio in the EU at that time' (ibid.). It can be argued that there was no clear economic analysis to support these criteria.

During the 2008/09 global financial crisis the EU emphasized austerity. But austerity often does not work as proved to be the case during the 2008/09 global financial crisis. During the COVID-19 crisis €700 billion was made available under EU recovery plans for member states to adapt to new social and economic realities.[5] The European pillar of social rights that seeks to deliver better rights for citizens is also of interest.[6] Furthermore, the NextGenerationEU was conceived as a temporary instrument designed to boost recovery. It will be the largest stimulus package ever financed in Europe (European Commission 2022b).[7] Thus, it appears that the EU is learning some lessons on fiscal policy. That in itself does not change the fact that

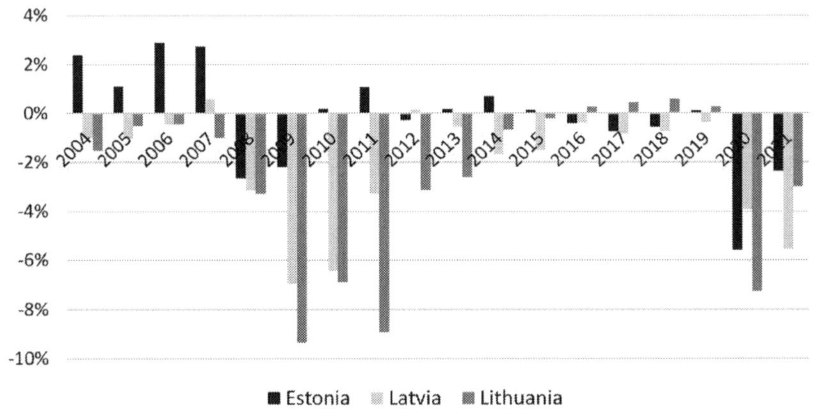

Figure 9.3 Fiscal (headline) deficit or general government net lending/borrowing in the Baltic states (% of GDP), 2004–21
Source: IMF (2022).

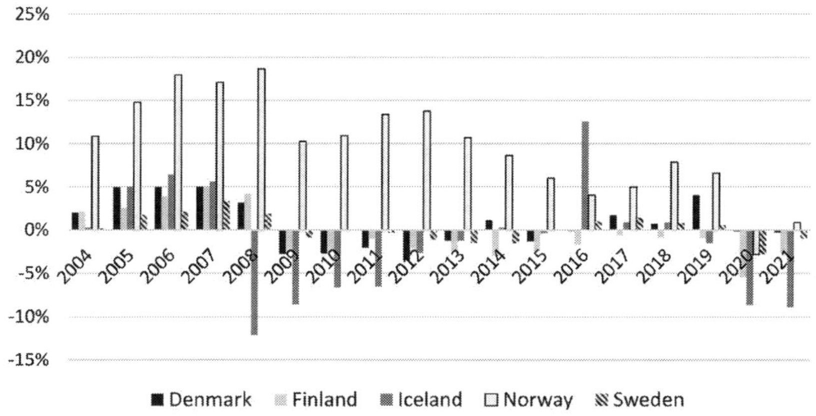

Figure 9.4 Fiscal (headline) deficit or general government net lending/borrowing in the Nordic countries (% of GDP), 2004–21
Source: IMF (2021).

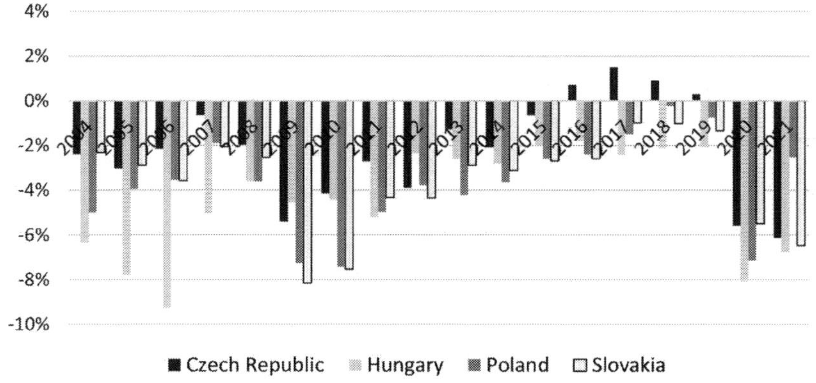

Figure 9.5 Fiscal (headline) deficit or general government net lending/borrowing in the Visegrád countries (% of GDP), 2004–21
Source: IMF (2021).

Table 9.1 Fiscal (headline) deficit or general government net lending/borrowing in the Baltic, Nordic and Visegrád countries (% of GDP), 2004–21

Country	*2004*	*2005*	*2006*	*2007*	*2008*	*2009*	*2010*	*2011*	*2012*	*2013*	*2014*	*2015*	*2016*	*2017*	*2018*	*2019*	*2020*	*2021*	*Fiscal deficit more than 3% of GDP*
Czech Republic	−2.4	−3.0	−2.2	−0.6	−2.0	**−5.4**	**−4.2**	−2.7	**−3.9**	−1.3	−2.1	−0.6	0.7	1.5	0.9	0.3	**−5.6**	**−6.1**	**5**
Denmark	2.1	5.0	5.0	5.0	3.2	−2.8	−2.7	−2.1	**−3.5**	−1.2	1.1	−1.3	−0.1	1.8	0.8	4.1	−0.2	−0.3	**1**
Estonia	2.4	1.1	2.9	2.7	−2.6	−2.2	0.2	1.1	−0.3	0.2	0.7	0.1	−0.4	−0.7	−0.6	0.1	**−5.6**	−2.4	**1**
Finland	2.2	2.6	3.9	5.1	4.2	−2.5	−2.5	−1.0	−2.2	−2.5	−3.0	−2.4	−1.7	−0.7	−0.9	−0.9	**−5.4**	−2.8	**1**
Hungary	**−6.3**	**−7.8**	**−9.3**	**−5.0**	**−3.6**	**−4.6**	**−4.4**	**−5.2**	−2.3	−2.6	−2.8	−2.0	−1.8	−2.4	−2.1	−2.1	**−8.1**	**−6.8**	**10**
Iceland	0.3	5.0	6.4	5.6	**−12.1**	**−8.6**	**−6.7**	**−6.5**	−2.6	−1.2	0.3	−0.4	12.5	1.0	0.9	−1.5	**−8.7**	**−8.9**	**6**
Latvia	−1.0	−1.0	−0.5	0.6	**−3.1**	**−6.9**	**−6.4**	**−3.3**	0.2	−0.6	−1.7	−1.5	−0.4	−0.8	−0.7	−0.4	**−3.9**	**−5.5**	**6**
Lithuania	−1.5	−0.5	−0.4	−1.0	**−3.3**	**−9.3**	**−6.9**	**−8.9**	**−3.1**	−2.6	−0.7	−0.2	0.3	0.5	0.6	0.3	**−7.3**	**−3.0**	**7**
Norway	10.9	14.8	18.0	17.1	18.6	10.2	10.9	13.4	13.8	10.7	8.6	6.0	4.1	5.0	7.9	6.6	−2.8	0.9	0
Poland	**−5.0**	**−3.9**	**−3.5**	−1.9	**−3.6**	**−7.3**	**−7.4**	**−5.0**	**−3.8**	**−4.2**	**−3.6**	−2.6	−2.4	−1.5	−0.2	−0.7	**−7.1**	−2.5	**11**
Slovakia	−2.3	−2.9	**−3.6**	−2.1	−2.5	**−8.1**	**−7.5**	**−4.3**	**−4.4**	−2.9	**−3.1**	−2.7	−2.6	−1.0	−1.0	−1.3	**−5.5**	**−6.5**	**8**
Sweden	0.2	1.8	2.1	3.3	1.9	−0.8	−0.1	−0.3	−1.1	−1.5	−1.5	0.0	1.0	1.4	0.8	0.6	−2.8	−1.0	0

Source: IMF (2022).

Note: Figures in bold show that the fiscal deficit has exceeded 3% of GDP.

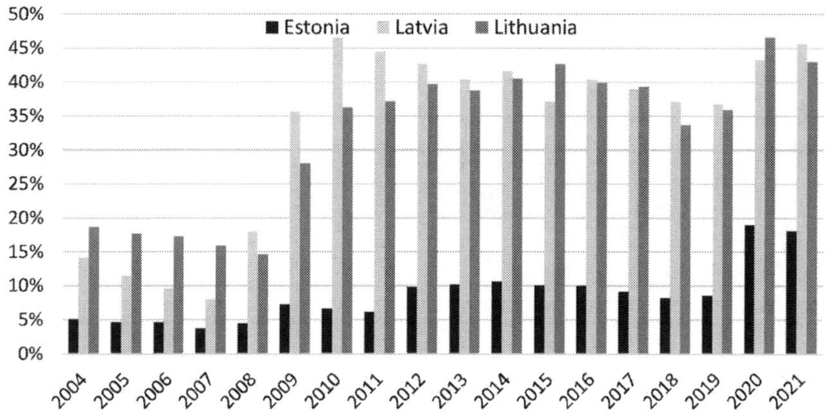

Figure 9.6 General government gross debt in the Baltic states (% of GDP), 2004–21
Source: IMF (2022).

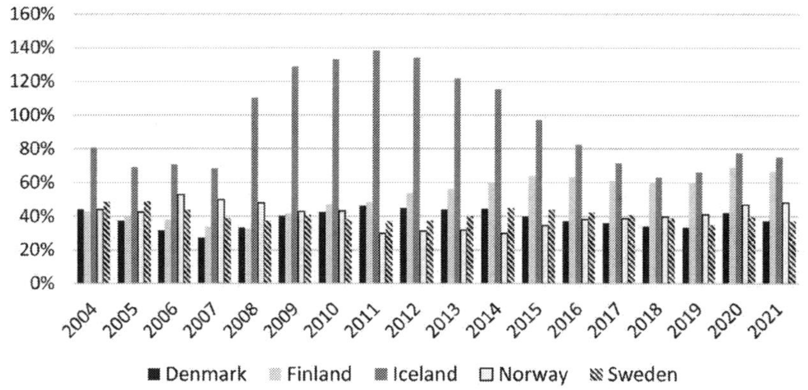

Figure 9.7 General government gross debt in the Nordic countries (% of GDP), 2004–21
Source: IMF (2022).

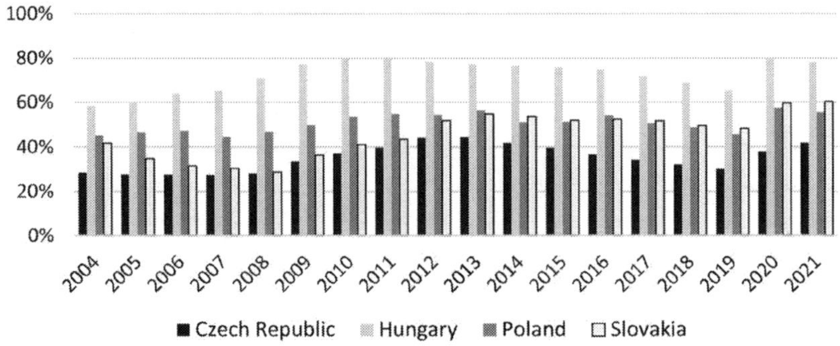

Figure 9.8 General government gross debt in the Visegrád countries (% of GDP), 2004–21
Source: IMF (2022).

many euro area member states are very heavily indebted, and it will take a very long time to adjust to the total government debt-to-GDP criteria.

Below is an overview on how the Baltic, Nordic and the Visegrád countries stand regarding their fiscal/headline deficits (see Figures 9.3–9.5 and Table 9.1) and their government debt-to-GDP levels (see Figures 9.6–9.8 and Table 9.2). Five of the countries are already in the euro area and seven are not. Among the countries discussed in this volume that are not in the euro area, Iceland (also a non-EU member state), and Hungary and Poland in particular, frequently run fiscal deficits in excess of 3% of GDP. Hungary and Iceland have also exceeded the 60% government debt-to-GDP criteria. Given how many countries in the euro area are heavily indebted, especially large countries such as Italy and France, there are risks for candidate countries in the event of another euro crisis when less indebted countries are asked to help those who are more indebted. For example, it was difficult for the governments of the Baltic countries to explain why they should help Greece during its crisis in 2008/09.

Fiscal deficit or general government net lending/borrowing

The Baltic states have shown greater fiscal discipline than the Visegrád countries, but the Nordics have showed the greatest fiscal discipline, with the exception of Iceland. Among the Baltic states, from 2004–21 Estonia has only once had a fiscal/headline deficit in excess of 3% of GDP, Latvia six times and Lithuania seven times (see Table 9.1). All the Baltic states are in the euro area. From 2004–21 Denmark and Finland have only once had a fiscal/headline deficit in excess of 3% of GDP, Iceland six times and Norway and Sweden never (see Table 9.1). Among the Nordic countries only Finland is in the euro area. Denmark has opted out and therefore does not have to adopt the euro, while

Table 9.2 General government gross debt in the Baltic, Nordic and Visegrád countries (% of GDP), 2004–21

Country	*2004*	*2005*	*2006*	*2007*	*2008*	*2009*	*2010*	*2011*	*2012*	*2013*	*2014*	*2015*	*2016*	*2017*	*2018*	*2019*	*2020*	*2021*	*Government debt more than 60% of GDP*
Czech Republic	28,4	27,7	27,6	27,3	28,1	33,4	37,1	39,7	44,2	44,4	41,9	39,7	36,6	34,2	32,1	30,0	37,7	41,8	0
Denmark	44,2	37,4	31,5	27,3	33,3	40,2	42,6	46,1	44,9	44,0	44,3	39,8	37,2	35,9	34,0	33,6	42,1	37,3	0
Estonia	5,1	4,7	4,6	3,8	4,5	7,2	6,7	6,2	9,8	10,2	10,6	10,1	10,0	9,1	8,2	8,6	19,0	18,1	0
Finland	42,6	39,9	38,0	33,9	32,6	41,5	46,9	48,3	53,6	56,2	59,8	**63,6**	**63,2**	**61,2**	59,8	59,6	**69,0**	**66,7**	**5**
Hungary	58,3	**60,2**	**64,2**	**65,2**	**71,2**	**77,4**	**80,2**	**80,4**	**78,4**	**77,4**	**76,7**	**75,8**	**74,8**	**72,1**	**69,1**	**65,5**	**80,0**	**78,1**	**17**
Iceland	**80,9**	**68,9**	**70,7**	**68,4**	**110,4**	**128,8**	**133,1**	**138,2**	**133,9**	**122,0**	**115,2**	**97,2**	**82,4**	**71,6**	**63,1**	**66,2**	**77,4**	**75,0**	**18**
Latvia	14,1	11,5	9,6	8,1	17,9	35,6	46,5	44,5	42,7	40,4	41,6	37,1	40,4	39,0	37,1	36,7	43,3	45,6	0
Lithuania	18,7	17,6	17,3	15,9	14,6	28,0	36,2	37,1	39,7	38,7	40,5	42,7	39,9	39,3	33,7	35,9	46,6	43,0	0
Norway	44,0	42,5	52,8	49,7	47,8	42,7	43,2	29,8	31,1	31,6	29,9	34,5	38,1	38,6	39,7	40,9	46,8	48,1	0
Poland	45,1	46,6	47,3	44,5	46,7	49,8	53,5	54,7	54,4	56,5	51,1	51,3	54,2	50,6	48,8	45,6	57,4	55,5	0
Slovakia	41,7	34,7	31,4	30,3	28,6	36,4	41,0	43,4	51,8	54,7	53,6	51,9	52,4	51,6	49,6	48,1	59,7	**60,4**	**1**
Sweden	48,5	48,8	43,7	39,0	37,5	40,7	38,1	37,1	37,5	40,2	44,9	43,7	42,3	40,7	38,9	34,9	39,6	37,3	0

Source: IMF (2022).

Note: Figures in bold show that general government gross debt has exceededs 60% of GDP.

Sweden must in theory at some point adopt the euro. Norway and Iceland are not in the EU and cannot adopt the euro. Among the Visegrád countries from 2004–21 the Czech Republic has had a fiscal/headline deficit in excess of 3% of GDP five times, Hungary 10 times, Poland 11 times and Slovakia eight times (see Table 9.1). Among the Visegrád countries only Slovakia is in the euro area. At some point the Czech Republic (Czechia), Hungary and Poland must adopt the euro and those countries could have difficulty following the fiscal criteria of the euro area (see Figures 9.3–9.5 and Table 9.1).

General government gross debt

Currently (in 2021) the Baltic states all meet the criterion that government debt should not exceed 60% of GDP. Government debt grew rapidly in Latvia and Lithuania during the 2008/09 global financial crisis. Both countries could reach the 60% limit if they continue to run fiscal deficits as they did during the COVID-19 crisis. (see Figures 9.3 and 9.6 and Table 9.2). The Nordic countries meet the criterion that government debt should not exceed 60% of GDP with the exception of Finland and Iceland. Iceland was severely affected by the 2008/09 global financial crisis, but its government debt-to-GDP ratio was declining from 2011 until the COVID-19 crisis hit (see Table 9.2). Among the Visegrád countries the Czech Republic and Poland meet the criterion that government debt should not exceed 60% of GDP, but Hungary does not. Slovakia is only slightly above the 60% of GDP government debt limit (see Figures 9.6–9.8 and Table 9.2).

Notes

1 https://euobserver.com/green-economy/16030.
2 www.ft.com/content/3d6-bbabc-7122-11e6-a0c9-1365ce54b926.
3 https://edition.cnn.com/2022/07/29/uk/brexit-absent-from-uk-political-debate-intl-gbr-cmd/index.html.
4 https://ec.europa.eu/environment/enlarg/candidates.htm.
5 www.europarl.europa.eu/news/en/headlines/priorities/covid-19-recovery.
6 https://ec.europa.eu/info/strategy/priorities-2019-2024/economy-works-people/jobs-growth-and-investment/european-pillar-social-rights_en.
7 https://ec.europa.eu/info/strategy/recovery-plan-europe_en.

References

Åslund, A. and Dombrovskis, V. (2011). *How Latvia Came through the Financial Crisis* (Vol. 17). Washington, DC: Peterson Institute.

Britannica (2022). *European Free Trade Association*. Available at: www.britannica.com/topic/European-Free-Trade-Association (accessed 30 July 2022).

Constâncio, V. (2017). *Effectiveness of Monetary Union and the Capital Markets Union*. Frankfurt am Main: European Central Bank. Available at: www.ecb.europa.eu/press/key/date/2017/html/sp170406_2.en.html (accessed 26 July 2022).

De Grauwe, P. (2016). *Economics of the Monetary Union*. New York: Oxford University Press.

Eichengreen, B. (2008). *The European Economy since 1945: Coordinated Capitalism and Beyond*. Princeton, NJ: Princeton University Press.

European Commission (2022a). *History of the Stability and Growth Pact*. Available at: https://economy-finance.ec.europa.eu/economic-and-fiscal-governance/stability-and-growth-pact/history-stability-and-growth-pact_en (accessed 30 July 2022).

European Commission (2022b). *Next Generation EU Investment Plan: NextGenerationEU*. Available at: https://ec.europa.eu/info/strategy/recovery-plan-europe_en (accessed 26 July 2022).

European Union (EU) (2022). *Winston Churchill: Calling for a United States of Europe*. Available at: https://european-union.europa.eu/principles-countries-history/history-eu/eu-pioneers/winston-churchill_en (accessed 29 July 2022).

Friedman, M. (1997). The Euro: Monetary Unity to Political Disunity? *Project Syndicate*. Available at: www.project-syndicate.org/commentary/the-euro-monetary-unity-to-political-disunity?barrier=accesspaylog (accessed 26 July 2022).

Hilmarsson, H. Þ. (2018). *The Economic Crisis and its Aftermath in the Nordic and Baltic Countries: Do as We Say and Not as We Do*. Europa Economic Perspectives. Abingdon: Routledge.

Hilmarsson, H. Þ. (2016). Iceland and the Challenge of European Integration: Is European Union Membership Feasible? In Lino Briguglio (Ed.), *Small States and the European Union*. Europa Economic Perspectives. Abingdon: Routledge.

Hilmarsson. H. Þ. (2013). Small States and Big Banks: The Case of Iceland. *Baltic Journal of Economics*, 13(1), 31–48.

International Monetary Fund (IMF) (2022). *The World Economic Outlook Database*. Available at: www.imf.org/en/Publications/WEO/weo-database/2022/April.

Kamps, C. and Leiner-Killinger, N. (2019). *Taking Stock of the Functioning of the EU Fiscal Rules and Options for Reform*. ECB Occasional Paper (231). Available at: www.ecb.europa.eu/pub/pdf/scpops/ecb.op231~c1ccf67bb3.en.pdf (accessed 30 July 2022).

Mankiw, N. G. and Taylor, M. P. (2020). *Economics* (5th edn). Boston, MA: Cengage.

Stiglitz, J. E. (2016). *The Euro: How a Common Currency Threatens the Future of Europe*. New York: W. W. Norton & Company.

10 Dancing with giants

What can small powers do to maintain their economic and political sovereignty in a multipolar world?

Great powers in a multipolar world

Currently we live in a multipolar world comprising at least three great powers, the People's Republic of China, the Russian Federation and the US. It is possible to measure the size of their economies in different ways. Following the dissolution of the Soviet Union in 1991 the economies of Russia, the largest former Soviet republic, and China were far smaller than that of the US. Since then, if measured by gross domestic product (GDP) at current prices in US dollars China has grown tremendously and is fast approaching the US economy in size (see Figure 10.1). If measured by GDP at current prices on a purchasing-power parity (PPP) basis China has already overtaken the US economy (see Figure 10.2). Since 1991 Russia has emerged as a third great power, but economically it is a distant third power.

The US economy has grown steadily since the collapse of the Soviet Union, as have its military capabilities. Geographically it occupies a safe environment and does not have a border with any other great power that could challenge its authority in the Americas. Since 1991 and until recently

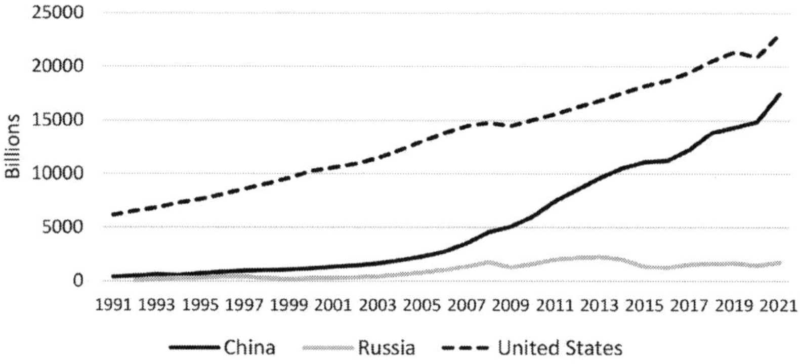

Figure 10.1 GDP at current prices in US $ in China, Russia and the US, 1991–2021
Source: IMF (2022).

DOI: 10.4324/9781003212539-11

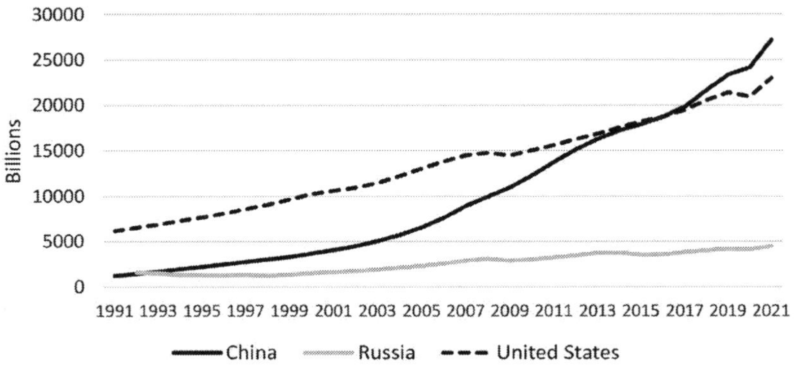

Figure 10.2 GDP at current prices (PPP terms) in international dollars, in China, Russia and the US, 1991–2021
Source: IMF (2022).

the US has been considered a global hegemon. Despite its economic growth its economic size has diminished in relative terms worldwide, including as a result of the rise of China. In other words, the US's share of the world economy is smaller now than it was decades ago. Now the US is struggling to maintain its power in Asia, where it is forming alliances such as the Quadrilateral Security Dialogue (known as the Quad) and the trilateral security pact between Australia, the United Kingdom and the US (AUKUS), while in Europe it leads the most powerful defence alliance in the word, the North Atlantic Treaty Organization (NATO). The latter views Russia as a major threat but is increasingly concerned about the rise of China and its military build-up.

Ironically, China has benefited from economic reforms that were supported by international financial institutions created under the leadership of the US and its allies, most notably the Bretton Woods Institutions, the International Monetary Fund (IMF) and the World Bank, as well as the World Trade Organization (formerly the General Agreement on Tariffs and Trade). China has also benefited from the West with its elite often attending Western universities, particularly top US universities. Unlike the US, China either has a border with or is located close to nations that can become hostile. Tensions exist with neighbouring countries over border disputes and disputes in the South China Sea and the East China Sea. The South China Sea disputes involve island and maritime claims within the region by several states, including Brunei, the Republic of China (Taiwan), Indonesia, Malaysia, the Philippines and Viet Nam. China also has unresolved territorial disputes with Japan over the Senkaku Islands (also known as the Diaoyu Islands) that lie between China and Japan. China also has border disputes with several countries in Asia, particularly with India. It also does not always have friendly relations with the Republic of Korea (South Korea). The US also has strong military presence in Asia which China views as a threat and it wants to get the US military out of Asia.

Russia is not a superpower if measured by the size of its economy only, but if one considers its natural resources, geographical size and nuclear capabilities it can be considered a distant third great power after the US and China. Among Russia's weaknesses are disputes in Europe with the EU and NATO, both of which have expanded since the collapse of the Soviet Union. These disputes have been greatly aggravated by the Russian invasion of Ukraine in February 2022. Russia also has a declining population and an economy that is heavily dependent on oil and gas exports. Russian influence in Europe has been diminished by the US military presence in Europe via NATO as well as the US alliance with the EU. Russia also has disputes in Asia, for example with Japan. The Ukraine war has pushed Russia closer to China, which now sees China as its main ally, and Russia has recently sought to divert its trade to Asia, mainly to China, as a consequence of trade sanctions imposed by the EU and the US following Russia's invasion of Ukraine. The US and its allies in the EU, NATO, the Quad and AUKUS are considered democracies and are now seen as competing with China and Russia, which are seen as non-democracies or even autocracies. The conflict in Ukraine has deepened these tensions and groupings such as the Democracies 10 (D-10) have suggested that democracies should unite against autocracies or authoritarian regimes.

Small states and small state alliances in a multipolar world

Given the tensions in this multipolar world, how should small states and small state alliances behave in a world of great powers seeking regional and even ultimately global dominance? Should they present themselves as neutral, strengthen alliances among themselves, seek alliances with one of the great powers, or seek alliances with multiple large powers?

All the countries in the Baltic, Nordic and Visegrád groups participate in European integration either as EU member states or as European Free Trade Association member states with access to the EU common market via the European economic area agreement. All the states are members of the Schengen area. All the states are either members of NATO or have participated in NATO military exercises. Finland and Sweden are currently seeking full membership of NATO. Thus, the Baltic, Nordic and Visegrád countries are strongly allied via European integration, as well as via the NATO. All the countries subscribe to Western values including democracy.

Within the EU and NATO, the Baltic, Nordic and Visegrád countries can as like-minded sub-groups further their interests by cooperating on issues of common interest. The Baltics have a common approach to European integration and NATO, while the Nordics have had different approaches which complicates their cooperation. All the Baltics are in the euro area but among the Nordics only Finland uses the common currency, the euro. The Visegrád group has a common approach to the EU and NATO, despite the fact that only one member state, Slovakia, is in the euro area. All three country groups fall under the US security umbrella. These countries and country groups are too small to stand alone. In addition to association with the EU they rely on the US for their security. In fact, the EU is the only economic superpower in the world that relies on another superpower for its defence. The US does not want to see the emergence of a regional hegemon in Europe like Germany became before the Second World War and the Soviet Union threatened to become during the Cold War. During the Cold War it seemed that the purpose of NATO was to keep the US in Western Europe, the Soviet Union out and Germany down.

All the countries are in some way affected by the ongoing conflict in Ukraine. Most of them either share a border with Russia or are located close to Russia. Three of the Visegrád countries share a border with Ukraine. None of the countries in the Baltic, Nordic or Visegrád groups have sought close economic integration or a military alliance with Russia since the collapse of the Soviet Union. In fact many fear Russia and this is especially true of the Baltic states. Russia nevertheless remained an important trading partner for the EU, particularly in terms of its energy requirements, and hitherto has been a leading supplier of natural gas to Europe.

All the countries in the three different groups benefit from trade with China and some participate in its Belt and Road and 17+1 (now 16+1 following the departure of Lithuania) Initiatives. China's economic growth since its transition to a market economy has largely been export-driven relying on trade with wealthy countries in the West. Given the size of the Chinese economy it is increasingly hard to participate in world trade without China. International product networks, including in East Asia, have become very specialized utilizing economies of scale to reduce costs and increase competitiveness. Components for high-technology products are often produced in many countries but assembled in just one, frequently China. The 'Made in China' label has become ubiquitous so that it is now neither feasible nor possible to bypass China without seriously hurting the European economy or indeed the entire global economy, including the US.

Small European countries are not the only countries caught in the dilemma as to how to manage their dealings with great powers, particularly the US and China. East Asian powers such as Japan and South Korea depend on a security alliance with the US. At the same time, they depend on trade with China. Having to deal with competing powers, namely the US as a security guarantor and China as an important trading partner, poses a complex dilemma for them. Australia is also faced with serious challenges as it relies on China for trade but on the US for security.

Tensions between the US and China have put the countries in the Baltic, Nordic and Visegrád groups into a difficult situation. Can these countries continue to strengthen their trade and investment relations with China while maintaining constructive security cooperation with the US? Currently NATO appears to look at the world as competition between countries that embrace democracy and those that have autocratic forms of government, such as China and Russia. This is reflected in reports and communiques released by NATO (see, for example, NATO 2020, 2022a, 2022b).

Given this great power economic and security competition other questions come to mind. Do European NATO member states want to be drawn into a conflict in Asia because of US-China tensions? Do they want to be part of a global conflict between democracies and autocracies? Is it feasible to play democracies and non-democracies against one another?

It can be difficult for small powers to find themselves caught between two great powers. Great powers focus on their own interests and survival. Countries such as Ukraine and Taiwan are examples of relatively small powers that have been caught up in great power rivalry. The war in Ukraine could be viewed as a proxy war between Russia and NATO. Ukraine has already suffered significant damage to its infrastructure following the invasion. It is unlikely that Ukraine will become a member of either the EU or NATO in the near future.

Taiwan has for a long time been caught up between China and the US. Higher political risks owing to an uncertain security environment can reduce foreign investment and thereby dampen potential economic growth and the quality of life for the people of Taiwan.

Finland and Sweden, both of which are EU member states, have hitherto sought to maintain their military neutrality, but are now applying for full NATO membership following Russia's invasion of Ukraine. Both countries have participated in NATO military exercises. Once they become members of NATO more tensions can be expected given Finland's long border with Russia and more tensions can be expected in the Baltic Sea region when surrounded by NATO members states, except at the coasts of St Petersburg and the exclave of Kaliningrad. It is questionable whether Finland and Sweden will be safer as members of NATO than remaining neutral; however, the Baltic states are likely to feel safer being in close proximity to other NATO member states that would formally be required to come to their aid if necessary. The Visegrád countries, especially Poland because of its geographic location, are likely to welcome Finland and Sweden as members of NATO.

Why are great powers opportunistic and unreliable?

Great powers are primarily concerned about their own interests and their behaviour is often regarded as opportunistic. Great powers are likely to interpret bilateral and international agreements and international law in line with their own interests. A good example of this is the Budapest Memorandum from 1994 when Ukraine gave up all its nuclear weapons in exchange for Russia respecting its existing borders and sovereignty (United Nations

2014). In addition to Ukraine and Russia, both the US and the UK were signatories of this agreement that has since then been violated multiple times. First with the annexation of the Crimean Peninsula in 2014 and the ensuing conflict in Donbass, and then with the invasion of Ukraine in 2022. Having the US and the UK as signatories of the agreement was presumably to provide assurances for Ukraine but in effect it proved useless. Russia as a great power did what it considered in its own interest regardless of any agreement.

Overall, Iceland has maintained good relations with the US since the end of the Second World War, but as a great power the US can be said to have shown opportunistic behaviour towards Iceland. Iceland was supported informally by the US in resolving the so-called cod wars with the UK. At the time the Cold War between the US and the Soviet Union was at its peak and the US needed the Keflavík air base in Iceland owing to its security competition with the Soviet Union. Thus, it was in the best interest of the US to support Iceland in its dispute with the UK.

Iceland has been a founding member of NATO since 1949 (NATO 2019) and has a bilateral defence agreement with the US since 1951 (Government of Iceland 1974). Despite this the US unilaterally withdraw its forces from Iceland in 2006 when the Cold War was over. No permanent military US forces are currently stationed in Iceland, and Iceland has no standing army. The US interpreted the defence agreement in a way that suited US interests only, ignoring the views of the Icelandic government. Nevertheless, Iceland still falls under the US security umbrella, but during the 2008/09 global financial crisis Iceland sought support from the US to resolve the difficulties experienced by its financial sector (Hilmarsson 2015, p. 28). As the US no longer needed to station its troops at the military base in Keflavík the US government showed little interest is assisting Iceland as it might have done during the Cold War. Consequently, the government of Iceland sought support from Russia and China. This shows that although US-Iceland relations have been good overall, the US considers its own self-interest and Icelandic interests have little weight in Washington's calculations if the interests of the two countries are different.

Such opportunistic behaviour can be seen in alliances of small states like the Nordic and Baltic group. The Nordic countries supported the Baltic states when they sought membership of the EU and NATO. The continental Nordic countries invested heavily in the Baltic financial sectors and ultimately began to dominate their banking sectors. This was especially the case with the Swedish banks. During the 2008/09 global financial crisis Sweden and the other Scandinavian countries obliged the Baltic states to carry the cost of banking mismanagement in the Baltics through the introduction of fixed exchange rate policies and austerity programmes designed to rescue their banking portfolios there. In effect Sweden, as a much more powerful state than the three Baltic states, caused the less powerful and at the time vulnerable countries to bear the brunt of the costs of the financial crisis (see Hilmarsson 2018a, 2018b).

There can also be questions about the commitment of great powers to guaranteeing the security of small states. For example, NATO has been reluctant to station large military forces in the Baltic states, although this stance has changed somewhat following the Russian invasion of Ukraine. The US has also generally avoided stationing its military along Russia's borders. This raises questions about the credibility of NATO and its small military force especially when military reinforcements are far away. In the case of the Baltic states, were Russia to close the Suwałki Gap between Belarus and Kaliningrad (Russia) the Baltics would be completely isolated from assistance from NATO-affiliated land forces.

The only country in the country groups discussed in this book that is not classified as small state was Poland. Poland is vulnerable owing to its difficult geographic location, with Germany to the west and the former Soviet Union to the east of its borders. During the Second World War Poland was partitioned by its more powerful neighbours, Germany and the Soviet Union. Even today Poland has vulnerabilities with Belarus and Ukraine to the east. However, Poland today is mainly threatened by Russia via its exclave, Kaliningrad, which borders Poland from the north. Russia also exercises control over Belarus and caused great instability in the region by invading Ukraine.

If the US pivots to Asia, its reduced military presence in Europe will make NATO less credible as a defence/military alliance. The war in Ukraine will delay the US pivot to Asia process, but it is uncertain if the US will continue to support NATO in the future as it has done in the past. Furthermore, any changes in the US political leadership can dramatically change US policy towards NATO.

The risk of relying on great powers

It is risky for small states to be caught between great powers. They need if possible to maintain balance and good relations with all the great powers while at the same time preserving their sovereignty. If small powers, such as the countries discussed in this volume, lean towards one great power, in this case the US, they should nevertheless seek good relations with other great powers. In other words, they should seek US support but maintain good relations with China and normalize their relations with Russia if and when possible. The US is largely responsible for which countries become NATO member states and thereby benefit from Article 5 that guarantees that the resources of the whole alliance can be used to protect any single member nation. However, the Article 5 guarantee has not been tested in any serious way in Europe. And Article 5 may not mean the same under US President Biden or even President Trump should he win re-election.

The enlargement of the EU and NATO is one of the main reasons for the Russian military invasion of Ukraine, which in turn is having a devastating effect on Europe and harming the global economy. Germany and France, the two largest and most influential powers in Europe, determine largely which countries obtain EU membership and how the EU is run. They have a say in its future security, particularly over a possible European army. Ultimately, the US and the large countries in Europe do act in their own best interests. Small states do not have much weight in their calculations.

Among the main arguments for the formation of the EU and especially the euro area was to make countries interdependent of one another so that it would not make sense for any of them to start a war against their neighbours. But interdependence does not necessarily promote peace, as the recent tensions with Russia have shown. When the EU and NATO seek to enlarge, Russia uses Europe's dependency on its supplies of natural gas as a threat and as a weapon against Europe. Furthermore, when one considers tensions in the world, US and EU interests vis-à-vis China may not be the same. While the US engages in security competition with China, Europe's interests may primarily be to benefit from trade with China. While some interests in the US benefit from selling military equipment to Europe, Europe may benefit in the long term from normalizing its relations with Russia and spending more on social programmes that contribute to social stability, rather than on stocking on state-of-the-art US weapons.

Thus, while there is no simple formula for the behaviour for small states for ensuring their survival in the future, they can enhance their security by participating in European integration, joining alliances such as NATO and forming like-minded sub-groups within alliances such as the Baltic, Nordic and Viesgrád groups. Nevertheless, small powers should avoid confrontation with great powers in a multipolar world, even if they tend to lean towards just one great power such as the US.

References

Government of Iceland (1974). *Defence Agreement – pursuant to the North Atlantic Treaty between the United States of America and the Republic of Iceland*. Available at: Avalon Project - Defense of Iceland: Agreement Between the United States and the Republic of Iceland, May 5, 1951 (yale.edu) (accessed 14 November 2022).

Hilmarsson, H. Þ. (2018a). *The Economic Crisis and Its Aftermath in the Nordic and Baltic Countries: Do as We Say and Not as We Do*. Abingdon: Routledge.

Hilmarsson, H. Þ. (2018b). Iceland Alone and Latvia Captured. *Social Europe*. Available at: https://socialeurope.eu/iceland-alone-latvia-captured (accessed 20 July 2022).

Hilmarsson, H. Þ. (2015). The Collapse of the Icelandic Banking System and the (Dis)honest and/or (In)competent Response of the International Community. *Regional Formation & Development Studies*, 2(16). Available at: https://e-journals.ku.lt/journal/RFDS/article/1586/file/pdf (accessed 20 July 2022).

International Monetary Fund (IMF) (2022). *World Economic Outlook Database*.

North Atlantic Treaty Organization (NATO) (2022a). *NATO 2022 Strategic Concept: Adopted by Heads of State and Government at the NATO Summit in Madrid on 29 June 2022*. Available at: www.nato.int/nato_static_fl2014/assets/pdf/2022/6/pdf/290622-strategic-concept.pdf (accessed 20 July 2022).

North Atlantic Treaty Organization (NATO) (2022b). *Madrid Summit Declaration: Issued by NATO Heads of State and Government Participating in the Meeting of the North Atlantic Council in Madrid on 29 June 2022*. Available at: www.nato.int/cps/en/natohq/official_texts_196951.htm (accessed 20 July 2022).

North Atlantic Treaty Organization (NATO) (2020). *NATO 2030: United for a New Era. Analysis and Recommendations of the Reflection Group Appointed by the NATO Secretary General.* Available at: www.nato.int/nato_static_fl2014/assets/pdf/2020/12/pdf/201201-Reflection-Group-Final-Report-Uni.pdf (accessed 27 February 2022).

North Atlantic Treaty Organization (NATO) (2019). *The North Atlantic Treaty.* Available at: www.nato.int/cps/en/natolive/official_texts_17120.htm (accessed 19 July 2022).

United Nations (UN) (1994). *Memorandum on Security Assurances in Connection with Ukraine's Accession to the Treaty on the Non-Proliferation of Nuclear Weapons. Budapest, 5 December 1994*. Available at: https://treaties.un.org/doc/Publication/UNTS/Volume%203007/Part/volume-3007-I-52241.pdf (accessed 20 July 2022).

11 Conclusion and policy implications

The five Nordic countries, three Baltic states and the four Visegrád countries discussed in this volume are all participants in European integration. They are all in the European Economic Area (EEA) and in the Schengen Area. Furthermore, they are all member states of the North Atlantic Treaty Organization (NATO),[1] except Finland and Sweden, which are not full member states but do cooperate with NATO and take part in NATO military exercises. At the time of writing both countries had applied to become full members of NATO. Finland and Sweden no longer see neutrality as a viable option. The level of European integration among the countries discussed in this volume differs. Of the 12 countries 10 are EU member states, but only five are in the euro area and have adopted a common currency, the euro, as their legal tender. Two of these countries are European Free Trade Association (EFTA) member states and have access to the EU common market via the EEA Agreement. This shows that all these countries want to participate in European integration and take advantage of the common EU market. All the countries have accepted the free flow of people within the Schengen Area. The difference here is that some countries want more integration with the European Union (EU) and some less.

Only the Baltic states have a unified approach to EU integration as both EU and euro area member states. The two other groups have a diverse approach with Denmark, Finland and Sweden within the EU, Iceland and Norway out of EU but within the EFTA, and only Finland is both a EU member state and is in the euro area. The Visegrád countries are all EU member states, with only Slovakia in the euro area.

The close EU integration of the Baltic states may have to do with their turbulent past as former Soviet republics; they now seek stability and security and wish to distance themselves as much as possible from the Russian Federation. The former Soviet satellite states in the Visegrád group also want strong ties with Europe but three of them have not taken steps to join the monetary union. The Nordic countries have the most diverse European integration, perhaps because they feel less threatened by Russia. The two Nordic EU outsiders are Iceland and Norway. Iceland has history of political ties with the US since the Second World War, including a bilateral defence

DOI: 10.4324/9781003212539-12

agreement. Norway has a border with Russia but in the far north, far away from major cities, and not comparable to Finland's long eastern border with Russia. All the countries discussed are small states, with the exception of Poland which has the largest population among the country groups, but does not yet have the necessary wealth to be considered a big power. In fact, as noted at the beginning of this book the Polish economy in terms of its gross domestic product (GDP) at current prices in US dollars is similar to that of Sweden. Poland nevertheless plays an important role in Europe because of its geographic size and location and because of the size of its population.

All the countries in the three groups discussed participate in global institutions such as the World Trade Organization, the World Bank, the International Monetary Fund (IMF), the United Nations and the Organisation for Economic Co-operation and Development and embrace globalization, democracy and the market economy. They participate less in regional institutions such as the regional development banks, the Asian Development Bank, the African Development Bank, the Asia Infrastructure Investment Bank (AIIB), and the Inter-American Development Bank. Only four Nordic countries, Denmark, Finland, Norway and Sweden, participate in all these banks and are also more ambitious in their bilateral development cooperation. The continental Nordic countries are wealthier than the other countries and are more visible on the global stage.

All the countries are members of the European Bank for Reconstruction and Development. All the Baltic and the Nordic countries are members of the Nordic Investment Bank. It is also noteworthy that Hungary, Iceland and Poland have become members of the People's Republic of China-led AIIB that can be viewed as challenging the Bretton Woods institutions established by the US. With AIIB membership these countries may be preparing themselves for the growing role of China in a new world order. It can be assumed that the US government would prefer these countries to stay out of the AIIB.

As regards bilateral development cooperation the Baltic states, which are former Soviet republics, and the Visegrád group, which are former Soviet satellite states, keep a low profile possibly because they are preoccupied with their own transition and development. It is interesting that the Baltic states tend to provide bilateral development assistance to other less advanced transition countries, rather than to the poorest development countries, which are often recipients of Nordic countries' aid (see, for example, Hilmarsson 2011). This may be because they want to share their recent transition experience but have limited funds as they are still dealing with their own development including upgrading their infrastructure. As explained by Sadecki,

> Moreover, the V4 countries focused on the Eastern neighborhood in terms of their emerging development assistance. They directed their Official Development Assistance (ODA) mostly towards the Eastern European countries (Belarus, Moldova, and Ukraine), while from the

> three South Caucasus countries Georgia also figured high on their agenda. Moreover, the V4 countries engaged in sharing their transition experience with these countries.
>
> (2018, pp. 264–65)

The countries within the three country groups under study have formed alliances not only due to their geographical proximity, but also because of their shared histories, cultures and areas of common interest. They can often be viewed as like-minded groups. Such alliances can be useful to share views and to formulate a common policy and agendas but are less effective when there are diverse views within the alliances.

Alliances between the continental Nordic countries and Iceland had limited value during the so-called Cod Wars, a series of disputes between the United Kingdom and Iceland from the 1950s to the 1970s over the right to fish in Icelandic waters when Iceland expanded its exclusive economic zone from 12 miles to 50 miles out to sea and then eventually to 200 miles, and this caused disputes with several other countries, the UK in particular. An alliance with the Nordic countries was of limited value during the 2008/09 global financial crisis when countries such as Poland and the Faroe Islands were more willing to assist Iceland than the Nordics, which were only prepared to offer assistance under the auspices of the IMF.

Some countries may have different allies outside the Visegrád group; the relationship between Hungary and Russia being a good example. Recently, Hungary has cooperated more closely with Russia than neighbouring Poland whose relations with Russia have been tense. According to Havelka,

> [a]ll four member states agree on a common position towards the Eastern Partnership, Enlargement, and Western Balkans. One might argue that these areas are the only where the V4 can positively influence the European discourse, and even manage to set the agenda. It must be stressed, though that in other issues – such as EU policy towards Russia – the Visegrád states fail to agree. In this sense, relations with Russia break the otherwise strong tandem of Poland and Hungary. Whereas Polish policy on Russia has always been cautious, Hungary tends to position itself as a 'bridge' between Russia and the rest of the EU. Czechia and Slovakia somehow oscillate between these rather extreme positions.
>
> (2021, p. 112)

The Visegrád group incorporates Soviet satellite states that sought to increase their chance to become members of the EU and NATO. The alliance had a common goal which was to form stronger links with the West. Within the EU the countries also share a common agenda and interests; migration policies are a pertinent example of this. As Havelka states, '[i]n … areas such as migration there is a strong consensus on a common policy and thus the V4 creates a solid block of four EU member states' (2021, p. 110). These countries are vulnerable owing to the flows of migrants from Africa and Asia, many of which enter the EU from the southern border of Hungary.

The Baltic states and the Nordic countries have formed a separate alliances with their own institutions such as the Baltic Alliance and the Nordic Council. However, another grouping, the Nordic-Baltic Eight (NB8) includes all the Nordics and the Baltics also sometimes meets with the Visegrád countries. The NB8 sometimes meets as a subgroup such as the Nordic-Baltic Six (NB6) which includes the six Nordic and Baltic countries that are EU member states. The Baltic group formed an alliance using the Nordic alliance as model. Instead of the Nordic Council there is the Baltic Alliance, as mentioned above, and instead of the Nordic Council of Ministers there is the Baltic Council of Ministers. These subgroups can help their member states to be more influential within the larger EU and NATO. The subgroups on their own have limited effectiveness unless they can be used to influence the larger groups and that is only possible when the states in the subgroup have a common interest and approach the larger groups with united front.

All the countries were negatively affected by the 2008/09 global financial crisis and again by the outbreak of the COVID-19 pandemic. During the 2008/09 crisis the Nordic countries, with the exception of Finland and Iceland in particular, only experienced a recession. All the Baltic states were hard hit, especially Latvia, and all experienced a large-scale outward migration of young people partly as a consequence of the implementation of fiscal austerity policies. Within the Visegrád group Poland was an exception in that it did not record negative GDP growth during the 2008/09 crisis. During the COVID-19 crisis the Nordic countries were particularly successful in containing the spread of the pandemic, apart for Sweden which sought to achieve 'herd immunity' at considerable cost to its population. In terms of the number of COVID-19-related deaths the Visegrád group was the hardest hit of the three country groups, followed by the Baltic states.

All the countries in the country groups under study have been badly affected by the conflict in Ukraine, especially Poland, Hungary and Slovakia, which have a border with Ukraine. The Baltic states have also been affected by a flow of refugees from the Middle East via Belarus.

Since the collapse of the Soviet Union the world has shifted from a bipolar world (the US versus the Union of Soviet Socialist Republics –USSR) to a unipolar world (the US) and then more recently to a multipolar world (the US, China and Russia). This poses a challenge for small states/powers that they need to address. How can they best protect their interests in the balance of power competition between the great powers?

The US may not be interested or even able to play the same role in Europe as it did during the Bretton Woods Conference (formally known as the United Nations Monetary and Financial Conference) held in 1944 and after the Second World War ended in 1945. After the collapse of the Soviet Union in 1991 the US served to inspire the former Soviet republics and satellite states that made the transition to from a centrally planned economy to a market economy and democracy. Among the groups discussed in this book, this is perhaps most striking when considering the Baltic states that followed the Chicago type of free market economics rather than the Nordic economic and social policy (see Hilmarsson 2018).

After the Second World War, the US exercised a 'Europe first' foreign policy. Following the collapse of the Soviet Union the threat that Europe was perceived to face diminished but with the rise of China the importance of Europe has further diminished for the US. East Asia, because of China, and the Persian Gulf, because of oil, have become more important than Europe for the US. The old transatlantic link has become weaker, and as China continues to rise, the more the US focuses on Asia and less on Europe.

China is now often seen as being increasingly aggressive towards its neighbours in Asia. Its poor relations with the Republic of China (Taiwan) have worsened. In fact, Taiwan is often seen as the focal point where the US and China could potentially start a war with serious consequences for the Asia and the rest of the world. Countries around the South China Sea are concerned about what they consider China's aggression. China also has tensions with Japan and India. Once it has dominated Asia, China may seek to expand its influence in other regions, including Europe. We are already seeing this via the Belt and Road Initiative (BRI) and the 17+1 (now 16+1 following the departure of Lithuania) Initiative. China is not only approaching countries in Asia and Europe via the BRI but also Africa and particularly South America – the back yard of the US. While the BRI can be viewed as a Chinese effort to increase its influence in other countries and could eventually be used for military purposes, one also needs to keep in mind that China is a very large and growing export-driven economy and it needs to secure its export routes via land and sea in order to be able to function well and to meet the demands of its clients around the world.

The ongoing conflict in Ukraine and tensions with Russia continue to be of great concern. Proposals to expand both NATO and the EU to the east backfired, with consequences for Georgia and then Ukraine. This has caused tensions within the EU, the US and NATO. The fact that Europe, and one of its largest powers, Germany, in particular, depends on Russia for supplies of natural gas makes this situation complex. Heightened tensions between the US and Russia, both of which are nuclear powers, may not be in the best interests of the US when China is rising. The US may need Russia's support in the long term and US/NATO direct involvement with troops in support of Ukraine seems unlikely at present. Prior to the Russian invasion of Ukraine, there were tensions between Germany and the US owing to former's joint participation with Russia in the Nord Stream 2 pipeline project. The US cannot afford to have tense relations with both China and Russia, nor is it feasible for the US to endanger its relationship with Germany.

How can Europe move forward? The EU and the flawed euro area framework make this difficult. Of the 12 countries discussed in this volume only five have chosen to join the euro area. Economic growth within the EU and the euro area has been slow and new member states have turned to China for investment funds. The UK's decision to leave the EU (known as Brexit) is another recent challenge.[2] It was clear from the outset that the UK was a reluctant partner in the European project and was unwilling to surrender its sovereignty, including its own currency and with it its independent monetary policy. Europe faces a further challenge with the COVID-19 pandemic. Once the health problems have been resolved the debt accumulation among EU and euro area member states will get more attention and it is not clear how these problems will be resolved. The EU may need to introduce more flexible fiscal policies as the region recovers from the COVID-19 crisis and a higher government debt-to-GDP ratio.

So, how can small states and their alliances survive and prosper in a multipolar world? The most important decisions in the world are not made by small powers or alliances of small powers. The small states must co-exist with the rest of the world, but their individual situations, such as their geographic locations, all differ. For example, there is a huge difference between Iceland located in the middle of the Atlantic Ocean and Finland which has a long eastern border with Russia. Meanwhile, the Czech Republic (Czechia) is surrounded by four friendly EU member states, Germany, Poland, Slovakia and Austria, Poland shares a border with countries such as Russia, Belarus and Ukraine. The small powers discussed in this volume have formed alliances to promote their interests in other larger alliances such as the EU or NATO. But those alliances are dominated by greater powers, the EU by Germany and France, and NATO by the US. The rise of China poses a serious challenge to the countries and country groups discussed in this volume because the world is now multipolar with greater uncertainty than before. Should these countries continue to lean towards the EU and to rely on US-led NATO? History has shown that forming strong alliances with great powers can be critical for these countries. Compare, for example, the fate of the countries that were part of the USSR and the Warsaw Pact to those who allied with the US via NATO and formed what is now known as the EU. NATO was established in 1949 to counter the threat of post-war communist expansion as the Soviet Union sought to extend its influence in Europe. NATO remains the world's most powerful regional defence alliance. In addition to focusing on what NATO sees as security threats posed by Russia, China is seen as a growing problem by NATO. A recent speech by Jens Stoltenberg, secretary-general of NATO, made this very clear.[3]

What should the small states/powers discussed in the book do to promote their future economic prosperity and security in the world? Three potential scenarios are considered here: (i) the status quo scenario; (ii) the pivot to China scenario; and (iii) the pragmatic scenario.

The status quo scenario

Under the status quo scenario the small powers will continue to integrate within Europe and to rely on the continued commitment and ability of the

US to defend Europe mainly via NATO. This is how the countries under study behaved in the unipolar world lead by the US. By stationing a large military force in Europe, the US has extended its influence over large powers such as Germany and France, but at the same time these European powers are putting themselves in a position of power over lesser powers in Europe via the EU and euro area rules and institutions. An enlarged EU and NATO will put even more pressure on the US as the main security guarantor for Europe that has many formal members of NATO, as well as countries such as Finland and Sweden which work in partnership with NATO and the US and at the time of writing had applied to join NATO.

Strengths

- The countries continue to rely on partners that they already know, embrace globalization and a market economy. They share similar values, including democracy, individual liberty and human rights.
- A united Europe and deeper European integration via the EU may strengthen the European economy and result in more trade with the US. This could encourage the US to maintain strong ties with Europe via its leadership of NATO.

Weaknesses

- The EU remains divided on many issues and the level of EU integration remains diverse with some EU member states joining the euro area while others opt to stay out. Some countries choose to stay out of the EU with EFTA membership (e.g. Norway and Iceland) or bilateral agreements (e.g. Switzerland).
- The monetary union means less flexibility in economic policy at the national level. With a higher level of integration countries joining the euro area give up their autonomy for monetary policy and implement strict discipline in fiscal policy. This can result in higher unemployment and lower GDP growth. The scope for the development of a welfare state – the creation of a social Europe – is diminished. Smaller powers are forced to implement austerity policies as the Baltics did during the 2008/09 global financial crisis.
- Large countries such as Germany and France may not want continued US military dominance in Europe via NATO. Germany had close ties with Russia in the field of energy (e.g. the Nord Stream 2 pipeline project[4]) and it needs cheap gas to compete with East Asia, especially China.
- Some new EU member states (those that have joined since 2004) may want closer relations with China for much-needed infrastructure investment e.g. via the BRI.[5] This is especially true if the EU and the European Investment Bank cannot provide sufficient investment capital for these countries. Many new EU member states feel that the eastern flank

of Europe has been neglected, lacking in infrastructure links with Southern, Northern and Western Europe. In addition to the 16+1 Initiative with China this has also promoted the Three Seas Initiative supported by the US.

Opportunities

- It may be possible to continue building the European project via the EU, strengthening it, and maintaining transatlantic ties with the US.
- Further integration could further increase trade within the EU and increase internal gains from trade and economies of scale.
- It may be possible to sign a comprehensive trade deal with the US.

Threats

- The US may be forced increasingly to abandon NATO if China continues to rise economically and militarily. The US that was about 40% to 50% of the world economy as measured by GDP during the Bretton Woods Conference is now only about 20% of the world economy. The US could become overextended economically and militarily, and thus unable to support Europe. The President of France, Emmanuel Macron, has argued that NATO is 'brain-dead' and has called for the formation of a European army.[6] The US President Joe Biden has stated that NATO is still vital to maintaining American security[7] (White House 2021) His predecessor, Donald Trump, often expressed concern over the level of burden-sharing among the NATO member states and argued that US allies must do more.[8] At one point Trump claimed that NATO was obsolete.
- The EU could disintegrate further following Brexit and become weaker. Countries such as Poland and Hungary have issues with the EU over democracy and an independent judiciary and the Visegrád group has had disputes with the EU over immigration policies and quotas.
- The common currency, the euro, may collapse as countries see the benefits of increased economic sovereignty and more flexible economic policies, including independent monetary policy and less restrictive fiscal policy.

Pivot to China scenario

Given the rise of China economically and its potential to be the dominating global superpower the countries discussed in this volume should strengthen their relations with China in terms of trade and investment and rely less on EU trade and investment and less on US-backed NATO for their security. In the short-to-medium term there is a scenario for a bipolar world (the US and China) or a multipolar world (the US, China and Russia). Given the size of its population and growing wealth China could drive the US out of Asia, dominate Asia and in the longer term the world could become unipolar and dominated by China. The countries under study would need to radically rethink their relations with China economically and militarily.

Strengths

- Given the rise of China it could in the next decades become the dominating power in Asia as well as becoming increasingly powerful in Europe and other continents of the world. If the Chinese economy becomes between two and four times larger than the US economy,[9] it would be better to side with China, especially if hostility grows between the US and China.
- As China grows, Europe, including the countries under study, would benefit more from trade and investment from China.

Weaknesses

- If China stops growing economically increased dependency could result in slower growth in Europe. One needs to consider the Japanese experience with a period of high growth followed by stagnation. China is facing challenges, including an ageing population.

Opportunities

- Siding with China may bring benefits to the countries discussed in the volume through increased trade and much-needed investment in some of the countries.
- The new EU member states (those that have joined since 2004) need more investment, especially for infrastructure links, that China may be able to provide on a larger scale than the EU and the US.

Threats

- Increased trade with and investment from China means more dependency on China e.g. via growing debts with China that could undermine the sovereignty of European countries.
- China has a single-party government that does not share the democratic values of the EU and the US. Human rights, including those of various minorities living in China, may not be treated in a way acceptable for the European countries under study, but China may increasingly want to impose its values on countries that depend on it economically.
- The tensions between China and its neighbours in Asia suggest that China takes a hard line, for example with Taiwan, countries with borders on the South China Sea and even towards large states such as India and

Japan. China could also take a hard line with European states that depend on it. Chinese border and sea disputes with its Asian neighbours do not suggest that China is soft, rather that it takes a hard line and uses its strong and growing military to support it.

Pragmatic scenario

In a pragmatic scenario, countries would build stronger relations with China, as it grows economically, but would seek to avoid irritating the EU and the US taking whatever economic benefits and security they can offer. This scenario is for a multipolar world dominated by the US and China but with Russia as smaller great power. Given this level of uncertainty the European countries discussed in the volume may want to be careful in committing themselves too firmly with great powers. European relations with Russia remain problematic following the imposition of sanctions as a consequence of the military invasion of Ukraine and this may take a long time to resolve. Currently China has better relations with Russia than the US has. Given the reduced US relative power economically and militarily the countries and the EU should reduce their military dependence on the US. Furthermore, Europe may still depend on Russia for its energy requirements, particularly Germany for natural gas supplies. The old Cold War was mainly played out in Europe which viewed the USSR as a threat. The new Cold War is between the US and China, and Europe should continue its security cooperation with the US and as well as expanding its trade relations with China.

Strengths

- Great powers (such as US and China) have interests, not friends. Relying on great powers is risky. The countries under study should strengthen their national defence and encourage the EU to strengthen Europe's common defence and rely less on NATO.
- Flexible policy is important. Countries should take advantage of what great powers can offer at different times without becoming too committed to them. Security cooperation with the US can continue in tandem with good trade relations with China.
- Small powers can play those powers against each other to get the best outcome from the great powers for themselves.

Weaknesses

- The US may become irritated and increasingly want to abandon NATO and Europe, but this will weaken the US as it will have fewer allies with similar values, such as democracy, individual liberty and human rights.
- Stronger ties with China may reduce unity within Europe as countries look to China rather than the EU for solutions.

Opportunities

- Europe could build on its strength, thereby increasing its own military capabilities and become more independent from the US and China.
- European countries can benefit economically from a rising China while also benefiting from EU integration and from the US as a security guarantor.

Threats

- Relations with China may become stronger in such a way that it will increasingly interfere with Europe and the EU. The US may abandon Europe and focus more closely on China in an attempt to contain its economic supremacy and military build-up. A stronger China may result in China eventually becoming a regional hegemon in Asia and then becoming more involved in Europe and increasingly interfering in the affairs of European countries.

Security in the Baltic states, the Nordic countries and the Visegrád group: strengths and weaknesses

Tables 11.1–11.3 are not comprehensive, but provide some indications of the strengths and weaknesses of the countries and country groups discussed in the volume in terms of their security. Membership of alliances such as the EU and NATO is seen as a strength for small states/powers. Further integration, such as being a member of a currency union, in this case the euro area, can also help with security, but may not do so from an economic point of view as it limits countries' options to respond to recessions and crises. Added security with closer integration is especially important for small states such as the Baltics but matters less for larger countries such as Sweden or Poland that are not great powers but that do have a substantial military force. It is noteworthy that the only countries in the three country groups to have adopted the euro also share borders with Russia, with the exception of Slovakia which has an eastern border with Ukraine. Sharing borders with a major adversary, as Russia is viewed by NATO, is considered a weakness. Close proximity to weak states such as Ukraine and Belarus that are under threat or pressure from an adversary such as Russia is also considered a security weakness as Russia can create instability in such countries. Ukraine is under attack from Russia and Belarus can be viewed as a Russian satellite state.

Baltic states

The Baltic states have the highest level of integration with the EU of the three country groups considered and identical levels of European and NATO integration. They are members of the EU, the euro area and NATO. This is the most vulnerable group among the three in terms of security and would be hard to defend in the event of a war with Russia. For example, if Russia and Belarus were to close the Suwuałki Gap NATO troops would lose land access to the Baltic states. The Baltics appear to participate in any activity that links them to or further integrates them to the West. The NATO/US defence commitment means that countries benefit from Article 5 that guarantees that the resources of the whole alliance can be used to protect any single member nation. However, the Article 5 guarantee has not been tested in any serious way in Europe. NATO has a relatively small military presence in the Baltic states (see Table 11.1).

Table 11.1 Security in the Baltic states

Country	*Strengths*	*Weaknesses*
Estonia	• Membership of the EU, the euro area and NATO	• Long eastern border with Russia • Can be attacked by the Russian Baltic Fleet from the seas to the north and west • Large Russian minority population and tensions with Russia since the collapse of the Soviet Union and independence in 1991 • Relatively small NATO military presence
Latvia	• Membership of the EU, the euro area and NATO	• Long eastern border with Russia Eastern border with Belarus • Can be attacked by the Russian Baltic Fleet from the sea to the west • Large Russian minority population and tensions with Russia since the collapse of the Soviet Union and independence in 1991 • Relatively small NATO military presence
Lithuania	• Membership of the EU, the euro area and NATO	• Southern border with Russia (Kaliningrad). Eastern border with Belarus. Should Russia and Belarus close the Suwałki Gap NATO troops' lose land access to Lithuania • Can be attacked by the Russian Baltic Fleet from the sea to the west • Tensions with Russia since the collapse of the Soviet Union and independence in 1991 • The opening of a Taiwanese Representative Office in Lithuania has caused tensions with China • Relatively small NATO military presence

Nordic countries

The Nordic countries have a diverse approach to security, but they all participate in European integration, either as EU or EFTA/EEA member states. They are either NATO members or work in partnership with NATO. At the time of writing Finland and Sweden had applied to join NATO. The Nordic countries have a long-standing tradition of cooperation. This group is the wealthiest of the three country groups under study and the continental Nordic countries have purchased modern military equipment from the US, including a substantial air fleet. Overall, the Nordics are more confident about their defence than the other two groups and have the lowest level of integration with the EU and NATO (see Table 11.2).

Table 11.2 Security in the Nordic countries

Country	*Strengths*	*Weaknesses*
Denmark	• Membership of the EU and NATO	• The southern border with Germany has historically been difficult, but Germany and Denmark are now allies via the EU and NATO • Can be attacked by the Russian Baltic Fleet from the seas to the east, north and west
Finland	• Membership of the EU and the euro area • Has applied for NATO membership and cooperates with NATO	• Long eastern border with Russia • Can be attacked by the Russian Baltic Fleet from the seas to the south and west • Not a member of NATO • The most vulnerable country among the Nordics in the event of an attack by Russia
Iceland	• Membership of NATO • Cooperates with the EU via the EEA/EFTA Agreement • In the Atlantic Ocean far away from possible war on the European continent • No borders with great power. Has no serious disputes with great powers • Has long-standing military support from the US with a bilateral defence agreement • Location of strategic importance for both Europe and the US and thus likely to receive military support if attacked	• Has no formal military, only a coastguard that cooperates with NATO • Could be attacked from the sea as the country is an island in the Atlantic Ocean • Relies on NATO and the US for its defence • No permanent NATO military presence

Country	*Strengths*	*Weaknesses*
Norway	• Cooperates with the EU via the EEA/EFTA agreement • Membership of NATO • Finland and Sweden are buffer states in the event of an attack by Russia from the east	• Short northern border with Russia, but this border is far from the capital, Oslo, and any of the major Norwegian cities so it cannot be considered a major threat and was not considered a threat during the Soviet era/Cold War • Can be attacked by the Russian Baltic Fleet from the seas to the north, west and south
Sweden	• Membership of EU • Has applied for NATO membership • Finland is a buffer state in the event of an attack from Russia from the east • Relatively large military and cooperation with NATO	• Not a member of NATO • Can be attacked by the Russian Baltic Fleet from the seas to the east, south and west

Visegrád group

The Visegrád countries are all EU and NATO member states. Only Poland borders Russia via the exclave of Kaliningrad. Hungary, Poland and Slovakia have a border with Ukraine. This group is less vulnerable than the Baltic states. In an event of attack from Russia from the east the Baltic states, Ukraine and Belarus would serve as buffer states. Instability in the Western Balkans can be a security risk especially for Hungary. The Visegrád countries are less integrated into the EU (only Slovakia is a member of the euro area) than the Baltics but they are more integrated than the Nordic countries (see Table 11.3).

In the Introduction to this volume the following questions were asked:

- How can small European states survive and prosper within a multipolar world of great powers?
- What part should small states take in European integration? Does one size fit all?
- Do EU fiscal and monetary policies allow for Keynesian economic stimulus when needed and are the euro area convergence criteria viable as the world recovers from the COVID-19 crisis?
- Are small state alliances within the EU useful to counterbalance the influence of the larger EU member states?
- How far should EU and NATO expansion go? Should it include countries such as Ukraine?
- Can the EU rely on a US-led NATO for its security?
- How should small states/powers relate to major powers influencing Europe, particularly the US, China, and Russia?
- Do smaller states/powers need to choose a single ally among all the great powers?

Table 11.3 Security in the Visegrád countries

Country	*Strength*	*Weakness*
Czech Republic (Czechia)	• Membership of the EU and NATO • Only borders EU member states and is far away from Russia	• Located close to larger states, Germany and Poland, but both countries are now allies. Germany is an EU and NATO member state and Poland is an EU, NATO and Visegrád member state
Hungary	• Membership of the EU and NATO • Ukraine would act as a buffer state in the event of an attack by Russia	• Borders seven states including two non-EU member states • Eastern border with Ukraine • Southern border with Serbia • Instability in the Western Balkan states south of Hungary
Poland	• Membership of the EU and NATO • Is a large country by European standards and has a relatively large military • The Baltic states, Belarus and Ukraine would act as buffer states in an event of attack by Russia	• Northern border with Russia (Kaliningrad) • Eastern border with Belarus and Ukraine • Can be attacked by the Russian Baltic Fleet from the sea to the north • Has historically been vulnerable due to its proximity to two powers, Germany and Russia
Slovakia	• Membership of the EU, the euro area and NATO	• Borders five states including one non-EU member state • Eastern border with Ukraine

All these questions have been discussed in the previous chapters in this volume, but will be briefly discussed below:

All the Baltic, Nordic and Visegrád countries have taken part in European integration. They are all members of the Schengen area. Most are members of NATO, and two have applied for membership of the alliance. But does one size does fit all? We have seen that different countries take different approaches depending on their economic circumstances and security concerns. They weigh up their options and choose which level of EU integration will work in their best interest.

EU fiscal and monetary policies need to be reconsidered as the world recovers from the COVID-19 crisis and due to the Russian invasion of Ukraine. Some countries are now heavily indebted after allowing for Keynesian economic stimulus to keep their economies going. All the large euro area member states, France, Germany and Italy, have government debt ratios higher than 60% of GDP. Italy is especially vulnerable because its government debt is above 150% of GDP, but so is France (115%). Even the German debt ratio has increased to 70% of GDP. The EU and euro area fiscal rules seem obsolete.

The EU and the euro area remain vulnerable due to the conflict in Ukraine. Contingent liabilities due to Ukraine and its reconstruction pose risks to the EU. Massive destruction in the EU's back yard does not help the EU. Ukraine is now an EU candidate country and if it does eventually become a full member of the EU it will be in need of EU grants for a long time to come. Prior to the invasion Ukraine's population was larger than that of Poland and geographically the country is twice as large as Poland.

The small state alliances discussed in this volume can act as a counterbalance to the influence of the larger EU member states if the states within these alliances have a common view and can form a united front. Such alliances are less effective when countries' views and interests differ, and a common policy and agenda cannot be formed. The country groups do not agree on all issues. For example, the Nordics take a different approach on European integration and the Visegrád countries have different views on Russia.

The feasibility of EU and especially NATO expansion further to the east is questionable. Ukraine might benefit from full access to the EU common market and a partnership agreement with NATO rather than full membership of the EU and NATO which are likely to result in tensions and conflict with Russia. Ukraine's potential membership of NATO is an especially sensitive for Russia as it views NATO as a military alliance, rather than a defence alliance. It is also unlikely that either the EU or NATO will be willing to accept Ukraine as a full member in the near future.

The EU cannot rely solely on US-led NATO for its security. The US is currently engaged in a new Cold War, not only in Europe because of Russia, but also in East Asia, because of China. Security cooperation with the US can continue, but Europe should become more independent in its defence arrangements. EU countries should seek to normalize their relationships with Russia in the long term. Relying on sanctions is not likely to result in favourable results or to foster a healthy relationship with Russia. Less military dependence on the US will enable Europe to engage more freely in trade with both China and Russia in the longer term.

Small states should not individually or in groups rely on a single ally among all the great powers. Whom they partner with depends on their specific issues and interests. The EU needs to diversify its energy sector. It must increase its use of clean energy sources and expand its access to fossil fuels from a larger number of suppliers so long as these sources of energy are needed. The country and country groups should seek to cooperate with the US on security and at the same time engage in growing trade with China.

Notes

1 At present, NATO has 30 members. In 1949 there were 12 founding members of the Alliance, namely Belgium, Canada, Denmark, France, Iceland, Italy, Luxembourg, Netherlands, Norway, Portugal, the UK and the US. The other member countries are Greece and Turkey (1952), Germany (1955), Spain (1982), the Czech

Republic (Czechia), Hungary and Poland (1999), Bulgaria, Estonia, Latvia, Lithuania, Romania, Slovakia and Slovenia (2004), Albania and Croatia (2009), Montenegro (2017) and North Macedonia (2020). See www.nato.int/cps/en/natolive/topics_52044.htm.

2 In addition to challenges related to NATO and US relations, Brexit has been difficult for the EU. In 2019 the President of France, Emmanuel Macron remarked: 'Look at what is happening in the world. Things that were unthinkable five years ago – to be wearing ourselves out over Brexit, to have Europe finding it so difficult to move forward, to have an American ally turning its back on us so quickly on strategic issues – nobody would have believed this possible'. See www.theguardian.com/world/2019/nov/07/macron-warns-of-nato-brain-death-as-us-turns-its-back-on-allies.

3 According to Jens Stoltenberg, secretary-general of NATO, 'China's growing influence and international policies present challenges to Alliance security. Leaders agreed that we need to address such challenges together as an Alliance. And that we need to engage with China to defend our security interests. We are concerned by China's coercive policies which stand in contrast to the fundamental values enshrined in the Washington Treaty'. See www.nato.int/cps/fr/natolive/opinions_184959.htm?selectedLocale=fr.

4 www.bbc.com/news/world-europe-57923655.

5 www.cfr.org/blog/belt-and-road-initiative-forcing-europe-reckon-china.

6 www.economist.com/europe/2019/11/07/emmanuel-macron-warns-europe-nato-is-becoming-brain-dead.

7 www.whitehouse.gov/briefing-room/speeches-remarks/2021/06/13/remarks-by-president-biden-in-press-conference-2/.

8 www.reuters.com/article/us-usa-nato-trump-idUSKCN1RE23P; and www.nato.int/nato_static_fl2014/assets/pdf/2021/3/pdf/210316-pr-2020-30-en.pdf.

9 If China reaches the GDP per capita level of the Republic of Korea (South Korea), Hong Kong or Singapore its economy could become between two and four times the size of the US economy. China could then also dominate in military expenditure, becoming a regional hegemon in Asia and increasingly powerful in other parts of the world, including Europe.

References

Havelka, V. (2021). Visegrád Group. In Tamás Levente Molnár (Ed.), *Minilateral Cooperation in the EU: Internal Cohesion, Group Dynamics, and Voting Behaviour of Selected State Blocks*. Budapest: Institute for Foreign Affairs and Trade.

Hilmarsson, H. Þ. (2018). *The Economic Crisis and Its Aftermath in the Nordic and Baltic Countries: Do as We Say and Not as We Do*. London and New York: Routledge.

Hilmarsson, H. Þ. (2011). How Can the Baltic States as Non-DAC Donors Best Contribute to International Development Cooperation? *Baltic Journal of Economics*, 11(2), 27–40.

North Atlantic Treaty Organization (NATO) (2022). *Member Countries*. Available at: www.nato.int/cps/en/natolive/topics_52044.htm (accessed 24 August 2022).

Sadecki, A. (2018). The Visegrád Group Policy towards the EU Eastern Partnership. In Péter Stepper (Ed.), *Central Europe and the Visegrád Cooperation: Historical and Policy Perspectives*. Budapest:Antall József Knowledge Centre.

White House (2021). *Remarks by President Biden in Press Conference*. Available at: www.whitehouse.gov/briefing-room/speeches-remarks/2021/06/13/remarks-by-president-biden-in-press-conference-2/ (accessed 20 August 2022).

Index

Page numbers in italics refer to figures. Page numbers in bold refer to tables. Page numbers followed by 'n' refer to notes.